Mayhem & Men on Pause

SANDY CURTIS

ORMISTON PRESS

Published in Australia 2016 by
Ormiston Press
PO Box 8297
Bargara Queensland 4670
Australia

Copyright © Sandy Curtis 2016

All rights reserved. No part of this book may be reproduced or transmitted in any form or by any means, electronic or mechanical, including photocopying, recording or by any information storage and retrieval system, without prior permission in writing from the publisher.

National Library of Australia
cataloguing-in-publication data:
Curtis, Sandy
Murder, Mayhem & Men On Pause

Paperback ISBN 978-1-925337-06-08
E-book ISBN 978-1-925337-07-5
A823.4

The characters and events in this book are fictitious and any resemblance to real persons, living or dead, is purely coincidental.

Printed in Australia by Ingram Spark
Cover design and formatting by Two Decade Designs

Also by Sandy Curtis

Romantic Suspense Thrillers
Dance with the Devil
Black Ice
Until Death
Deadly Tide
Dangerous Deception
Fatal Flaw
Grievous Harm

Romance
No Cure For Love
A Tender Deception
The Marriage Merger

REVIEWS

The Marriage Merger
'The Marriage Merger was a fresh, unique story by Sandy Curtis. It was not the usual love story involving the arrogant jerk and humble heroine and a blackmailed marriage etc. It was a heart-warming novel about Braden and Jenna falling in love under unforeseen circumstances and being drawn to each other through the mutual love of his niece. A well-written plot by the author. Character description and dialogue was interesting. I would recommend this romance to others as it was a charming read.'
Readers Klub

Until Death
'Until Death is a fast-paced thriller, with a twist of romance. This is the fourth offering from author Sandy Curtis who manages to make each successive book a little more complex. A gripping read.'
Sally Murphy, Aussiereviews.com.au

Dangerous Deception
'Be warned: the cracking pace of this book never lets up. What was the shattering information that researcher Breeanna should have been given by the now paralysed Professor Raymond? Why is she on the run? Who is after her? Her family has secrets to hide as Rogan McKay, hunting for his missing brother, soon learns. Have chocolate on hand to keep your energy levels up as you keep the pages turning.'
Woman's Day

Dance with the Devil
'Sandy Curtis has made an amazing debut. Dance with the Devil combines action, adventure, suspense and romance in a very readable package… It's like reading a Matthew Reilly novel with romance added.'
Robinsons Book News

Black Ice

'Set on Queensland's Sunshine Coast and in Cairns, this thriller has an authentic touch with plenty of intriguing twists and turns. It's the story of an artist haunted by memory loss and the American who tracks her down to reveal the gaps. The final twist is quite unexpected.'
Kerry Heaney, 50 Something magazine

'Sandy Curtis writes with a lot of flair seamlessly combining a furious well-constructed thriller with an emotion charged love affair.'
Australian Crime Fiction Database at www.crimedownunder.com

Fatal Flaw

'All I can say is I loved this! Sandy has taken the Genre of Aussie Romantic Suspense and made it her own. Very well written, fast paced with some very interesting sex scenes, I thoroughly enjoyed it!'
Kelly McLean, Aussie Book Reviews

No Cure For Love

Love is the best thing that ever can happen to a human being. However, when love becomes an obsession it turns into hatred. Lani and Luke had been in love eleven years ago but something happened and they broke up going separate ways. Now, Luke appears again in Lani's life which terrifies her. What happened years ago? Why does Lani pulled away every time he tries to touch her? Why is she so angry with him? Well-written, quick to read, page turned story where the author doesn't reveal anything till the very end. A great read for anybody.
Marichus Real, Story Cartel

ACKNOWLEDGEMENTS

In 2004 I wrote the first few pages of a women's fiction that I showed to my then publisher. She wanted me to finish it, but somehow I couldn't. I had envisaged the story of three friends whose lives suddenly implode and they are forced to confront the loss of everything they value. It was going to be full of angst and drama, and, frankly, it depressed me to think about it.

Fast forward ten years and the long-rejected characters raised their voices in protest. They told me that I had had enough time to realise that women have the kind of enduring strength that enables them to cope with what life can throw at them. Yes, they might go down for a while, but they grit their teeth and get back up and take control of their lives.

But what they really emphasised was that women support each other. Women look out for their friends. And women often see the humour in life, especially when it comes to men and relationships.

So I started writing the story again, but this time with a different flavour. Yes, there are losses, and sorrow, but there's also happiness and laughter, and the kind of friendships that I've been incredibly lucky to have in my life.

I'm grateful for my amazing women friends who have given my life richness and joy, my wonderful husband who has shared many years of marriage and never wavered in his support, and my fabulous Ormiston Press publisher who believed in Ellie, Cass and Kandy's story. This book is for you.

About Sandy Curtis

Sandy Curtis lives on Queensland's Central Coast, not far from the beach where she loves to walk and mull over the intricate plots in her novels. Her husband says he doesn't know how she keeps it all in her head, and her friends think she must be far more devious than she appears.

Actually, after having dealt with the chaos involved in rearing three children, dogs, cats, guinea pigs, and a kookaburra (teaching it to fly was murder), creating complex characters, heart-wrenching stories and edge-of-your-seat suspense is a breeze for Sandy.

Interviewers often ask Sandy to describe her normal writing day. "Normal is when the chaos in my life subsides to frantic rather than frenzied. I once told a friend that I must have a chaos attractor glued on my forehead and she said that creativity hovers on the edge of chaos, to which I replied that I'd long ago fallen off the edge into the middle."

Her various occupations, from private secretary to assistant to a Bore Licensing Inspector, as well as hitch-hiking around New Zealand and learning to parachute, have given Sandy lots of people and research skills. It's the paperwork going feral in her office she has trouble with.

www.sandycurtis.com
www.facebook.com/SandyCurtis.Author
www.twitter.com/SandyCurtis1
www.amazon.com.au
www.goodreads.com

CHAPTER ONE

'When is a marriage not a marriage?' Ellie Cummins tried to stop the words but the wine had been flowing freely and her tongue had loosened in ratio to the glasses consumed. She watched Cass Brighton's forehead crease in concern and told herself to lighten up. This was her birthday, for heaven's sake, not a pity party. She should be grateful she was sharing it with her best friend in a great restaurant and not sitting at home alone.

'Is this a joke, Ellie?'

'When it's *my* marriage,' Ellie tried to laugh but it came out a sob and she gulped the rest of her red wine, 'then, yes, it is a joke.'

'Ellie, don't you think you've had enough?' Cass gently moved the bottle to the other side of the table, just out of Ellie's reach.

'That's just the point, Cass. I never get enough. Just because your randy husband spends half the night chasing you around the bed, don't think the rest of us are as lucky.'

Damn, there was the pity party trying to break out again. Ellie mentally smacked herself. 'You know my parents were divorced?' she asked, and watched Cass blink at the sudden change of topic, but nod anyway.

'They separated first. Then my father used to come around some nights so we could play happy families and they could talk and try to sort out their problems. Well, that was the theory. But the selfish bastard only wanted to have sex and my mother never realised she was being used. And he *always* came around on Wednesday nights.'

Cass hesitated, her plump cheeks quivering as though unsure if they should move, but then asked, 'Always? On a Wednesday night? Why?'

'Rissoles!'

'Rissoles?'

'Every Wednesday night. Without fail. My mother made them from some old family recipe, and my father loved them. So he would come around every Wednesday night.'

Cass's expression said that if this was a joke then she was waiting for the punch line.

'So Saturday morning is like rissoles!' Ellie announced triumphantly.

Now Cass raised an eyebrow.

'Sex,' Ellie sighed, and shook her head to try to clear the fuzziness in her brain. 'Saturday mornings. It's a ritual. Like rissoles on a Wednesday night. Damien wakes up with a hard on, rolls over, fiddles with my boobs for a few seconds, then tries it on. If I knock him back he's grumpy for a week, so I let him go, then he's happy until the next Saturday. He doesn't care if I get off or not, selfish prick. If I take the initiative he tells me he's too tired.' She tried to ignore the pain that spiked through her, but it tumbled out in almost-whispered words. 'And it's been too many months now since he's even bothered about Saturday mornings.'

She pulled at some hair escaping her chignon and watched the blonde strands flutter in the faint draught from the air-conditioning. 'All he thinks about is business. Thinks the sun shines out of Melba's mouth.'

Cass didn't hesitate this time. 'Melba's mouth?'

'On the hundred dollar note!' Ellie smiled. 'Cass, no wonder I like you - you're so innocent. Pollyanna and pecan pie. I bet you even wear a nightie to bed.' Ellie laughed as though it was the funniest joke she'd ever heard, but she heard the desperation in the sound and forced herself to stop.

'Do you?' She queried when she'd calmed down. 'Wear a nightie to bed, I mean?'

'Not normally. I used to wear pyjamas years ago, before I met Joe. But he slept in the raw and …' Cass smiled, then patted her almost non-existent waistline, 'now I can't stand the tight elastic.'

'I could wear a g-string, fishnet stockings and high heels to bed and Damien wouldn't notice. Maybe if I wore the business section of the Courier-Mail he'd get an erection.'

When Cass laughed, Ellie realised how serious she had sounded. Well, she *was* serious. And frustrated. Not just sexually, but in every aspect of her life. The frustration had been brewing and bubbling inside her for quite a while and she was desperately afraid that if she didn't find a solution to it soon it would erupt into something she wouldn't be able to control.

'Have you talked to Damien about how you feel?' Cass asked.

'I've tried to. But it doesn't work. He doesn't seem to think there's anything wrong with our relationship. Says he can't understand what I'm grumbling about, he works hard to provide a good home so I should be grateful. Then I feel like a bitch for complaining but frustrated that I can't make him see a marriage is more than a fancy home and a full wine fridge.'

'Have you thought about getting a job?'

Ellie laughed. 'Doing what? After we lost Paul, Damien would go ballistic if I even mentioned the idea.'

'He didn't blame -'

'No. SIDS can happen at home just as easily as at a crèche, but when I had Pru we were both pretty paranoid. I gave up work and we installed every device possible to make sure it didn't happen to her too. Then Miranda came along and by the time she went to school I was involved in the P&C committee and tuckshop and sports coaching and,' she sighed, 'every other school activity you could think of. By the time the girls went to uni and Damien had gone into his own business I'd morphed into *the corporate wife*,' she scribed inverted commas in the air and sighed at the description she found so unlike what she really felt. A corporate wife would have understood her husband forgetting her birthday. A corporate wife would have understood that even when she reminded her husband and he said he was too busy to take her out or even have a meal with her that that was okay. That's what corporate wives did. But she'd never really been a corporate wife, had she. The role had slid over her and sucked her up before she'd realised what had happened.

'How is Miranda? You had lunch with her today, didn't you?'

Ellie nodded. 'She's okay. Still job-hunting. Speaking of jobs, do you still like working at the real estate office?'

'It's all right,' Cass shrugged, 'but lately I've felt as though something... something's missing. It's a great job, and being part-time means I can still do all the gardening and sewing I like, but,' she smiled wryly, 'I'm probably just tired of waiting for those kids of mine to give me some grandkids to spoil.' She looked at her watch. 'Time to go. I have an early start in the morning.'

Ellie took deliberate steps and tried to clear her head as they walked from the restaurant. The fuzziness had eased a little, but her stomach was sloshing upwards with each step and she didn't want to repay Cass's kindness by throwing up in her car. Although friends since their younger daughters had been in high school together, it was only when Cass's sister had become ill and died a few years ago that they'd become close. Ellie knew what losing someone you loved felt like, and she'd done her best to help Cass cope with months of helping her sister through intense chemotherapy and finally coming to terms with the inevitable.

Now she watched as Cass concentrated on negotiating the traffic. Most Brisbane drivers seemed to view the speed limit as advisory rather than mandatory, and although not a risk taker by nature, Cass kept with the traffic flow.

By the time they'd reached Ellie's house in the northern suburbs, the effects of the wine had lessened and Ellie had slipped into a pensive silence. Cass parked in the driveway, leaned over and gave her shoulder a squeeze. 'Ellie, any time you need to talk, just give me a call. Doesn't matter what time it is or where I am.'

Ellie blinked away the tears that threatened and nodded. She gripped Cass's hand in gratitude, and got out of the car. 'Thanks for tonight,' she said, 'I really appreciate it.'

'That's what friends are for,' Cass smiled, waited for Ellie to close the door, and backed out of the driveway.

Ellie watched the car drive away, then turned and, like a reluctant Roman at the Colosseum, walked slowly to her front door.

It wasn't a hangover, Ellie decided next morning as she dragged herself from her bed to the ensuite. More like depression. There didn't seem to be much to get out of bed for, lately. The house was always immaculate because Damien was rarely home during the day. Her normal housework routine left nothing to do after 10am, except read, go shopping or spend more time at the two charities where she volunteered. She sometimes wondered why she couldn't get more enthused about working on the fundraising committees for those charities. She really believed in what they did, and she liked the people she worked with, but lately she went home wondering if she should be doing something else with her life as well.

An hour later the built-in vacuum system hummed quietly as she dusted the marble, steel, glass and leather that constituted the modern decor Damien insisted on and she tolerated.

'No soul,' she grumbled as she polished and primped.

She didn't hate the look, but her heart longed for the rustic elegance of white wood furniture, delicate florals and vintage fabrics. Sometimes she felt like an impostor, an old-fashioned country girl in the guise of a well-heeled corporate wife, continually worried that one day someone would find her out. And find her wanting.

The drone of the garage roller-door rising made her frown. Damien never came home from work in the mornings. She'd been asleep when he'd returned from a business meeting last night and he'd left before she'd woken this morning. Curious, she put the duster away, walked to the kitchen, and turned the electric kettle on. When Damien hadn't appeared a minute or two later, she went into the garage.

Damien was slumped over the steering wheel of the BMW, his hands cushioning his forehead. Slightly alarmed, Ellie hurried over and opened the car door.

'Damien, are you all right?'

He didn't answer, and Ellie's heartbeat accelerated. She shook his arm. 'Damien! Are you ill?'

He pushed himself back into the seat. For a man of only forty-nine he looked a lot older, his face creased and grey, eyes blood-shot and dull with fatigue. Ellie felt her stomach drop. She realised that she hadn't really looked at him in the past week, their communication concentrated into his rushed phone calls and her notes about his evening meal languishing in the oven.

He turned towards her, and the bleakness in his eyes almost made her heart stop beating. There was only one other time when she'd seen him look like that, and it chilled her to the core to remember it.

CHAPTER TWO

Cass picked her husband's work socks off the bedroom floor and tossed them into the bathroom clothes hamper as she hurried down the hallway in response to the front doorbell's chimes.

'Ellie!' she exclaimed as she pulled open the door. 'Come in.' She bit her lip. 'I hate to say it, but you look terrible.'

'You should see the other bloke,' Ellie quipped, but her voice was hollow. 'I was hoping you were home from work.'

'Just got here. Peak hour traffic was lousy. Cup of tea?' Cass led the way into her kitchen. 'Coffee? Or something stronger?'

'Better make it coffee.' Ellie slumped onto a chair and rested her elbows on the timber table, her hands cupping her chin as though she were incapable of holding her head up any longer. 'We're bankrupt,' she blurted out.

'What?' Cass whirled around so fast water splashed from the kettle she'd just filled.

'Damien. He's lost everything.'

'How?' Cass flicked on the switch, put two mugs on the bench and sat opposite Ellie.

'He borrowed against the company and invested in a big

development scheme that's turned out to be a scam. The fellow running it had an impeccable record, or so he thought. He'd checked him out and couldn't find anything to make him suspicious. He'd even made big profits for some of Damien's friends in the past. But it looks like he was just leading up to this one big killing. Once he got all the money and the project was supposed to start he skipped the country.'

'Hell!'

'Double hell. Damien even mortgaged the house.'

'Ooooh.' Cass felt the air leave her lungs. If *she* felt stunned, she could imagine how Ellie must have felt. 'When did you find out?'

'This morning. Once he knew there wasn't a hope of getting any money back, he came home to tell me. I thought he was going to have a heart attack, he looked so bad.'

Cass refrained from telling Ellie that she didn't look much better.

'He went back to the office an hour ago to see what he could salvage.'

The kettle bubbled, and Cass rose and made the coffee. She opened a packet of chocolate biscuits, emptied half onto a plate and placed it and the two mugs on the table. 'What are you going to do?'

'Get a job.'

'Doing what?'

Ellie sat up straight. A touch of defiance lit her eyes. 'I was an interior decorator before I married. Someone might take me on as an assistant.'

'Ellie, your house is proof of your talent, but you haven't

worked in nearly twenty-six years. You'll probably have to do a training course. I saw in the newspaper that TAFE have some starting next week.'

'I can use a computer. At least I'm not totally out of touch with technology.' The bravado seeped out of her like a slow leak. 'Hell, Cass. I don't know what I'm going to do. Damien's at least had the sense to transfer what little savings we have left into my personal account so we won't lose that when the company goes to the wall. And we won't be leaving a string of creditors chasing us for money, only the bank.'

'How long can you last?'

Ellie shrugged. 'A couple of months, probably three at the most.'

'Would Damien go on unemployment benefits?'

'Are you kidding? Can you see him lining up at Centrelink? He's too proud for that.'

'Pride doesn't pay the grocery bills.'

Ellie picked up a biscuit and nibbled at it. 'I'll put my name down for the dole if I have to, but that can't happen until after everything's finalised. Honestly,' she sighed, 'you'd think the stupid bugger would have had more sense.'

'With his experience, he might find it easy to get a job,' Cass tentatively offered, but agreed with Ellie's expression that said flying pigs were now in season.

'Perhaps Phillip could find something for him? Even something temporary? I know he and Kandy are away at a conference this week, but you could ask when they get back.'

Unlike Ellie who Cass had met through having children in

the same classes at high school, Kandy had whirled into their lives when Ellie was organising a charity fund-raising function and had hired Kandy's catering firm. Kandy had charged them only a nominal fee, and also came to help at the event. Her enthusiasm might not have been viewed too kindly by some of the other workers, but she inspired more donations in that one evening than the charity normally got in six months.

She was also an enigma who had puzzled Cass and Ellie for the three years they'd known her. Married to Phillip Breckham, a much older man for whom the word "ultraconservative" had obviously been coined, she was discreetly promiscuous with younger men who exuded the virility Phillip seemed to lack. Normally this would have put her on Ellie's and Cass's be-polite-to-but-don't-encourage list, but there was a child-like quality about Kandy that had sneaked under their barriers and they liked her in spite of not agreeing with her behaviour. That she never slept with married men also helped ease their minds.

'I think Damien would only accept something from Phillip as a last resort. The two don't exactly hit it off.'

'Joe couldn't take to him either. Mind you, Joe doesn't feel comfortable talking with anyone who wears a suit and a tie and drinks wine that costs more than ten dollars a bottle,' Cass smiled.

An hour and several projected scenarios later, Cass watched Ellie walk out her front gate.

For the first time since they'd bought their home, Ellie was almost afraid to walk in the door. Not because she was scared of what she might find, but because it was so ... *empty*.

Her footsteps made no noise in the carpeted hallway, in the expansive living room, in the spacious built-in wardrobe where she changed into a tracksuit to combat the chill in the crisp autumn air. It was a relief to go to the toilet and listen to her sneakers squeak on the tiles, the tinkle into the bowl and the flush as more of Brisbane's water went out to sea.

She could play a CD, have music fill up the spaces and bounce off the walls, or watch television and immerse herself in someone else's life. But she knew it wouldn't fill up the space that frightened her the most.

Because it *was* frightening, this vast emptiness inside her - like some desert where even the sound of her voice would seem out of place. At other times it scared her to think that she might allow Damien, or someone, in to disturb this hollowness she had created for herself. It *was* a hollow, she had to admit. It certainly wasn't a sanctuary.

For a brief moment she thought of phoning her brother, then realised that the time difference in Perth would mean he was still at work. And she didn't feel like telling her mother yet. After Ellie's father had died, her mother had moved into a granny flat behind her brother Peter's house, not quite in a baby-sitting position to their young teenage children, but as a backup for Peter and Marie as they both worked. Although older than Ellie by two years, Peter had married much later, and his move to Perth meant they only saw each other on infrequent visits. Ellie knew she would eventually have to tell them what had happened, but now she hesitated. It was too soon, the shock was too raw, the prospects too grim. She wanted to cry, but no tears would come. It was as though crying would be too big an effort at the moment and she had to conserve her energy for better things.

Or maybe crying would make her feel things that were best left unfelt.

She thrust the thought away and went into the kitchen. For once, Damien might actually come home for dinner on time.

Ellie watched the moonlight streaming in through the bedroom window and illuminating the lumpy shape of Damien as he huddled beneath the covers. When had that started? Damien never huddled. When they'd first slept together he'd sprawled diagonally across the bed and barely left any room for her.

And it wasn't the only thing that had changed. The trim young man she'd married now had a spare tyre that evoked four-wheel-drive rather than sports car.

She slipped from the bed and pulled on her robe. A few minutes later, cup of hot chocolate in hand, she snuggled into the comfortable sofa in the rumpus room and looked out through the sliding door to the perfectly manicured lawn and immaculate white-stone and dracaena gardens surrounding the designer swimming pool. She'd been delighted by the large backyard when they'd bought the house, but Damien's need for prestige had seen her vision of an English cottage garden and vegetables growing in fertile rows become a page from a home beautiful magazine.

Above all the questions that had run through her mind

after Damien had confessed his folly this morning, the one that most plagued her was, did she still love him? Was the pity she had felt at his haggard face and moans of self-recrimination enough? She'd been stunned, disbelieving, angry - but surely she should have felt compassion, and not the kind of pity she would feel for some charity case on television.

The thought of not loving Damien any more filled her with dread. If that was gone, then the prospect of that emptiness inside her growing until it consumed her had suddenly become very, very real.

CHAPTER THREE

Cass choked back a sigh on hearing her mother's voice on the phone. When Audra had married Gerry Collins twenty years ago, Cass had been pleased that her mother was no longer alone. Although ten years older than Audra, Gerry had been quite young in his outlook for a seventy-year-old. Unfortunately he hadn't stayed that way.

During the past year, Audra had started to become more demanding of Cass, asking her to do tasks she was perfectly capable of performing herself. In the beginning, Cass had complied because Audra always had a seemingly feasible excuse, but as the demands grew more frequent, and the age gap between Gerry and Audra became more apparent, she realised that Audra was starting to depend on her far more than was necessary.

'Gerry's constipated,' Audra said after her initial hello.

'You're kidding.'

'No.' Her mother sounded aggrieved, as though Gerry's bowel movements were on the same importance level as world peace.

'I believe you, Mum. I mean, you're kidding about phoning me to tell me that Gerry's constipated. What do you expect me to do about it?'

'Well, there's nothing you can do about it. He's very

upset. You know how he carries on. I just wanted some support.'

'Buy a girdle,' Cass mumbled.

'What did you say?'

'Shit, Mum, what do you want me to say?'

'Don't use that word. It's not nice.'

'It would be if Gerry did it.'

'Gerry doesn't swear.'

'Sounds like he's not shitting either.' Cass muttered, but she heard her mother's sharp intake of breath. Time to change tactics. 'Do you have any suppositories?'

'Yes. He uses one every morning. You know he has a sluggish bowel.'

'Are you sure he got it in right? It didn't slip out again? He mightn't have noticed.'

Cass could almost hear Audra's silent indignation. 'I don't go into the bathroom when he's doing his ablutions. That's his business.'

'Except when he's constipated.' Cass thought back to most of Gerry's dinner conversations. 'Then it's a wonder he doesn't take out a front page ad in the Courier-Mail.'

In the silence that followed, Cass resisted the urge to hang up. Her mother's constant phone calls about nothing in particular and everything in general were beginning to stretch their already tenuous relationship. There were never enough hours in Cass's day, and certainly none to waste discussing Gerry's bowel movements, or lack of them.

'I read about Ellie's husband's company in the newspaper.'

Cass smiled. Audra had obviously decided to change the

subject. 'Yes,' she said, 'it's really tough on them.'

'How could he let himself be duped like that? Poor Ellie and their daughters won't be able to hold their heads up in public.'

Air hissed through Cass's teeth. How like Audra to be concerned about what people thought rather than the personal effect on her friend. 'I'm sure they'll be fine, Mum. Ellie's a very resourceful person and Damien will soon find another job.' Before her mother could reply, she pretended there was someone at the door and said goodbye.

She hated lying to her mother, but sometimes she couldn't cope with Audra's intolerant attitude. And at the moment she was too worried about Ellie's emotional state to argue with Audra. She glanced through the lounge room curtains to the front yard. A storm a few days ago had greened the lawn a little, but the trees still dropped their leaves in an attempt to stay alive in spite of drought and water restrictions.

As though thinking about her friend had conjured her up, Cass saw Ellie walk through the front gate and up the path.

Ellie's stomach churned with trepidation and excitement as she walked up to Cass's front door. She noted how the white paint on the chamferboard walls had weathered to a tired cream but pots of lush ginger plants gave the small patio a welcoming look, and she realised how much she preferred this to the starkness of her own brick and tile entry.

It had been two weeks since Damien's company had gone into receivership. Weeks in which all of Ellie's job-seeking efforts had made her realise the huge gap her twenty-six years out of the industry had created in her knowledge and skills. Cass had persuaded her to undertake a TAFE business and computing course, but getting a job was paramount. Damien had sunk into a deep depression, and his initial attempts at finding work had dwindled to reading the positions vacant section of the newspaper when he finally climbed out of bed and toyed with the breakfast she had prepared.

Within minutes of her knocking, she was watching Cass boil the kettle and place fruit cake on the table.

'What's up, Ellie?' Cass asked. 'You've had a glint in your eyes since you walked in.'

'You know how I've applied for work with interior decorators - or interior designers as they now call themselves - and been knocked back because they reckon I don't have up-to-date qualifications and experience? Well, I've decided I should start my own business.' There, it was out, but the expression on Cass's face wasn't encouraging.

'How are you going to afford that?'

'I thought I'd go freelance. Get some business cards made up. Get samples from suppliers. Advertise that I'll come to the client.' Ellie felt her anxiety rise as Cass looked even more doubtful. 'Show them photos of my house as an example if necessary,' she added.

'Well, your home is definitely a showpiece.' Cass thought with envy of Ellie's uncluttered rooms, the paintings that matched the décor, the ornaments that added just the right touch. She looked around at her kitchen benchtops with their mismatched canisters, the growing pile of "stuff" that Joe added to after he cleared his work esky each night, the dining room already choking with bookcases that had overflowed from the lounge room. 'It's worth a try,' she added. 'And you could set up your own website. Let me know if I can help.'

'Actually,' Ellie leaned closer over her coffee, trying to appear casual, but eager for her friend's support. 'I'm hoping you'll give me some advice on the paperwork. You've always worked in administration and ... well, even when I last worked I wasn't involved in that side of things.'

'I'd be happy to help. How's the TAFE course going?'

'Like a room full of menopausal women all pretending they can remember each other's names,' she grimaced. 'Most of us are making out like we know what we're doing. I wasn't any good with that stuff even when I was at school. The only *good* thing is the teacher.'

Cass smiled. 'Good-looking, is he?'

'Gorgeous. Looks like Hugh Jackman.'

'Complete with six-pack?'

'Yep. He wears these *very* fitting polo shirts.' Ellie nearly drooled her appreciation, then she sighed. 'But with a body like that he's probably as bent as a fork in a garbage disposal.'

The teaspoon rattled against her mug as Cass stirred her coffee and laughed. 'Not all the good-looking ones are gay, Ellie. But I often wonder why magazines use male models with pecs bigger than most women's boobs. It makes me jealous.'

'It's not the pecs that get me, it's the six-pack. Most men we know have a beer gut so big they have to search for their crown jewels with a mirror on a stick. Except for your Joe, he's still okay.'

'He's starting to thicken out. Not that he'll ever match me,' Cass sighed.

'You're not too bad for someone who's had four kids.' Ellie was quiet for a minute, then mused, 'I guess there's an advantage to staying with a man who can remember what your breasts were like before they drooped - he can close his eyes and rely on memory rather than imagination.'

Cass realised that Ellie had switched thought tracks. She frowned. 'You're not thinking of leaving Damien, are you?'

'At the moment it's only a thought.' Ellie tried to sound flippant, but knew she wasn't fooling Cass. 'When he can be bothered speaking to me he just grunts or else he yells at me that if he wasn't trying so hard to make money for us he wouldn't have got into this mess.'

'He's just feeling guilty. And you said he's depressed.'

All the unhappiness Ellie had been bottling up for the last few years rose to the surface. It should have been like a volcano, erupting and spewing out all the need and loneliness and longing and doubts, but it simply spilled over in fat tears that trickled slowly down her cheeks to plop on Cass's table like the first drops of summer rain before a storm.

'Oh, hon,' Cass reached across and covered Ellie's slim hand with her broad one. 'It's that bad, is it?'

Ellie could only nod, afraid that if she spoke the words lying in the aching pit of her heart she'd never be able to stop.

'Perhaps you could do with some time out.' Cass wanted

to go around and hug her friend, but she sensed that wasn't what Ellie needed at the moment. Like when you were trying hard to be strong after the death of a loved one and people offered sympathy - it just made you want to cry all the more. She walked to the bathroom, grabbed a box of tissues and handed it to Ellie. 'Why don't you spend a few days with Pru in Sydney?'

'Pru adores Damien,' Ellie muttered and blew her nose. 'She won't understand. She'll think I'm abandoning him when he needs me. She's as work-focused as Damien.'

'I guess she's taking the business going to the wall pretty hard too.'

'When she flew up last weekend Damien hardly spoke to her. He tried to put on a brave face but then he just went silent. She doesn't know how to get through to him any more than I do.'

'What about Miranda?'

Ellie tried to laugh, but it came out like a choking sound. 'At least being broke has one advantage. We won't get so many phone calls from Miranda asking for money to finance her latest invention to save the environment.'

'So what's she doing when she's not job hunting?'

'She's still volunteering with the food handout van. Compared to the poverty she sees every day, Damien's problems don't amount to much.' She saw the surprise on Cass's face and hastened to explain. 'She's sympathetic, and she feels sorry for us, but it's not like we're starving.' She sighed. 'Not yet, anyway.'

At Cass's raised eyebrows, Ellie hastened to explain. 'Damien knows we don't have much money left to live on but when he goes out to try to schmooze his business friends into giving him a job he spends up big trying to impress them that he's okay. Our credit card will soon max out.'

'What are you going to do? Apart from set up your own business.'

'That's just it, isn't it. I'll need money to get business cards made up, money to advertise. I had a job interview yesterday at that new furniture store and they seemed pleased with me. Said they'd let me know by Friday if I got the job. Selling furniture isn't quite what I'd planned but it might provide me with some contacts when I start my own business.'

As Cass watched Ellie dab away the last of her tears, she mentally crossed her fingers that her friend would land the job. Taking some of the financial pressure off might help the problems she was having with Damien. But her gut seemed to emphasise the *might*.

CHAPTER FOUR

The eye-catching business card she'd envisaged was finally taking shape under Ellie's pencil when the phone rang. She waited for Damien to answer it, but after the fourth ring she walked into his office.

He was sitting in his leather chair and staring at the instrument as though it was about to bring him more bad news. Ellie reached across his desk and picked up the receiver. A couple of minutes and a short conversation later she replaced it and smiled at Damien. 'I have a job.'

His dark eyes flickered brief interest, but he stayed silent, a brown-haired man slouching rumples in a brown tracksuit.

'Aren't you going to ask me where?'

'Where?'

Ellie bristled at the reluctant obedience in his tone, but she was determined not to let him take the edge off the pleasure she felt. Getting a job after twenty-six years without one was quite an accomplishment, and she was going to savour the satisfaction while she could. 'At the new Fabulous Furniture Store. Most of their stock is mass market but they do have an exclusive range. Richard, the manager, said he wants to build up that facet of the business and once I've learned the ropes and if they're happy with me, I'll be in charge of that section.'

'Good for you.'

It took restraint, but Ellie managed not to react to the hint of sarcasm in his words. 'I start tomorrow.' She almost added, *if you're interested.*

Damien simply nodded.

Ellie hesitated. She felt sorry for him, but she was angry, too. He'd known for some time that his business was going to go broke, and that his efforts to find financial backup to prevent that had failed, but he hadn't told her. Hadn't even given her a hint that their lives were going to change so drastically. She almost felt that he'd cheated her, deprived her of the closeness they were supposed to share as a married couple. She didn't *want* to talk about it, but right now, with the small fire of confidence the phone call had given her, she *needed* to talk about it.

'Damien, what's happened to us?'

He blinked, surprise lighting his features for a brief second, then the closed expression she'd become used to seeing returned.

'What do you mean?'

'We don't talk any more. You don't tell me about ... *anything.*'

'I tell you when there's something you need to know.'

Ellie flinched at his belligerent tone, but restrained her instinctively angry reaction and said calmly, 'No. You tell me only when I *have* to know. When you can't keep it from me any more because it will soon be public knowledge.' He turned his head away from her and studied the Picasso-like print with its sharp angles and vivid colours that Miranda had given him during her "Art" phase at university.

Just as dispassionately, Ellie studied him. Saw the way his dark hair that once curled so thick and luxuriant had thinned with age; the sharply outlined jaw now softened with extra flesh; eyes that once flashed with laughter and enthusiasm now resentful and stubborn. 'Damien, we're like two strangers sharing a house. We're polite, considerate, but we don't know each other anymore. I don't think we've had a meaningful conversation since Paul died.'

'What does Paul's death have to do with anything? I didn't blame you, and you didn't blame me. We had counselling, we worked our way through it.'

'We went through the motions, Damien, not the *e-motions*.' It was all becoming clear to her now. 'We were so careful not to blame each other, not to hurt each other, that we forgot how to talk to each other on any level other than superficial.' She reached out a hand, saw her fingers shaking with her desperate need to reach him, to re-connect ... to re-connect with something inside herself. With what, she wasn't sure.

She knew if he took her hand, if he pulled her to him and held her the way he used to hold her, the way she needed to be held now, that it would be all right, that they'd make it through somehow.

But he didn't.

He didn't meet her gaze.

Or take her hand.

Or touch her.

He looked at the paperwork on his desk as though it would absolve him of the responsibility of having to make things right in their world.

Ellie waited.

She wanted to be able to say something that would make it all right again. Like it was when the girls were small. She wanted to be able to tell him, this man who was her husband, with whom she'd shared most of her life, that she loved him.

But she couldn't.

Because it would be a lie.

It was one thing she'd thought she'd never have to worry about again, Ellie realised when she dressed for her first day at work the next morning. The "first day" nerves - the anxiety that she wouldn't measure up, that her fellow employees wouldn't like her, that -

She gave herself a mental shake. Sensible but smart straight navy skirt, white blouse with just enough frill to be feminine without losing its business-like crispness, hair pinned up and makeup subtle but defining. The mirror confirmed the outer facade would pass assessment. The scared inner core would have to remain hidden.

Shoes had been a problem. None in her wardrobe lent themselves to standing for longer than a couple of hours, but a quick phone call to Kandy had resulted in a pair of conservative navy courts that had been worn enough to keep blisters at bay. Although the same clothes and shoe size as Ellie, Kandy was shorter, her slimness had a shape that women envied and men admired, and she was as dark as Ellie was fair.

Ellie sometimes wondered what it was about Kandy that

made it so easy to like her when some aspects of her life were totally opposite to the values Ellie always considered important.

Kind of like with your kids, she sighed as she thought of Pru and Miranda. She might not always be happy with the way they were living their lives, but she loved them and, luckily, liked them as well. Most of the time.

Miranda might appear to be the one who didn't have her life together, but she was more comfortable in her own skin than Pru. If Pru was any more up-tight she'd snap in a strong breeze. She didn't so much have a stick up her ample arse as a telegraph pole. Pru's physical features were all from Damien, but Ellie caught a glimpse of her eldest daughter in the tight press of her own lips as she looked in the mirror again. She carefully blotted her lipstick with a tissue and applied another coat of *Delightful Coral*. Recognising the gesture for the procrastination it was, she grabbed her handbag and hurried from the bedroom.

'All the information you'll need is in these folders.'

Ellie watched as Richard Brown took out folders containing information sheets and catalogues from the various furniture manufacturers and placed them on the counter. Tall, thin of body and face and nose, his forehead was so high his dandruff must have learned how to abseil. She interlaced her fingers to stop herself brushing away the white specks on his dark shirt.

'But if a customer has a query and you can't find the answer in these, either see me or Janine, and if we're not here, phone the supplier or manufacturer direct. Don't worry, it won't take you long to learn everything' The smile he beamed at her was genuine, and a few of the knots in her stomach unwound. 'The photos of your home you sent with your application indicate you seem to have a natural flair for co-ordination,' he continued, 'so let me know if you have any suggestions on setting up the various displays.'

It was an open invitation but Ellie hesitated, afraid to be seen as pushy, especially on her first day. But she indicated the rows of shelving that contained cushions, curtains, table runners, vases, artificial flowers and other decorations. 'Would you mind if I used some of the stock and made a few changes?'

'Go ahead,' Richard said, and turned to answer the phone as it began to ring.

Ellie walked towards the soft furnishings that beckoned like lustrous jewels, a tiny glow of excitement growing in her chest.

The euphoria of Richard's praise stayed with Ellie as she drove home. She hung her keys on the hallway hook and smiled at Damien as he slumped in the lounge, glass in hand, swirling the ice through the bourbon.

'Richard loved the changes I made to the displays. He said I'm going to be a real asset to the company. That I must have been a great interior designer.'

'Throwing a few flowers in a vase doesn't make you a bloody interior designer,' Damien snarled. 'If you'd done more than draped yourself around the house looking decorative and going out playing at charity queen and gone back to work years ago and earned some money we wouldn't have ended up in this mess.'

Ellie's jaw dropped at his words. Something inside her shrivelled and died, and anger grew in its place. 'You're the one who was sucked in, Damien. That's why we ended up in this mess. Your greed was greater than your common sense.'

He banged the glass onto the coffee table, splashing its contents. Bourbon trickled down the chrome table leg and soaked into the white rug beneath.

Before he could say anything, Ellie shook her head at him, trying to stop the bitter words that had festered inside her for weeks, but failing. 'You didn't even have the guts to tell me until the day before it would become public knowledge.'

The anger on his face almost made her cringe, but he pushed past her, snatched the car keys from the hook and stormed into the garage. She heard the roller door rise, the car start and drive away.

She was trembling so much it took her several minutes to realise that he'd taken her car. His wasn't there. She was so used to him not being home that that fact hadn't registered when she'd driven in. Now she remembered they didn't own the cars, they were leased. And there was probably no more money to make the payments. Her world began crumbling. And the words that had haunted her for months began again. The afraid words, the words that couldn't be said, the words that weren't said because they were the truth but they would hurt too much and things would change and never be the same again.

The *I don't love you anymore* words; the *There's nothing*

left between us, Damien words; the *It's over* words. The words that had lived in her mind but she hadn't had the courage to admit the truth of, let alone utter. Now she was forced to acknowledge her life had been confined to the world she had created in his emotional absence, and she'd been afraid to leave the imaginary security it represented.

She stared out across the manicured lawn and felt as though each perfect blade of grass was laid like a fence post to trap her. Trap her in a prison she was struggling to escape from but didn't know how to put the key in the lock. Or even where the lock was.

But she knew the key was within her grasp. Knew only she could use it.

The sound of the doorbell ringing zapped through her like an electric charge. She waited a moment for her heartbeat to slow, pulled her features into an expression she hoped approached normal, and went to the door.

'Surprise! We've come to help you celebrate your first day on the job.'

Ellie stared. Cass and Kandy, hands full of Chinese takeaway containers and bottles of wine, grinned at her. Seconds passed. Their grins faded. Ellie realised she hadn't moved, hadn't allowed her mind to register there was someone - *two* someones - who cared about her and wanted the best for her. With a cry of joy and gratitude she threw her arms around them, squashing plastic and getting jabbed in the breast by a wine cork.

'Well, that's a lot better,' Kandy joked. 'I thought for a minute there we'd come to the wrong house. Is Damien home?'

Ellie disentangled herself and shook her head. Before, she'd wanted to cry. Now, she needed to vent, to rip away her facade of a happy marriage and face reality. Words spewed out like lava as she ushered Cass and Kandy into the rumpus room and took her best wine glasses from the bar cupboard. The flow of words didn't stop until she'd gathered plates and cutlery and placed them on the coffee table next to where her friends were sitting.

Kandy took the lids off the containers and poured wine into the glasses. She handed a glass to Ellie. 'So what are you going to do about it?'

Honesty time. 'I don't know.'

'What do you want to do?' Cass, this time, brown eyes intent, sending hugging vibes.

'I don't know. I really don't.'

'It's the old freeze, fight or flight syndrome,' Kandy sipped thoughtfully, staring at the wine as though it were transmitting some kind of wisdom. 'You've been frozen for long enough. You either fight if you think there's anything left worth fighting for, or flee.'

'It's not that simple. How can I leave Damien now? He's lost everything, how can I be that cruel?'

Cass helped herself to a portion of sweet and sour pork. 'And people like my mother will automatically assume you've left him because he's broke,' she sighed. 'But you have to do what's best for you, Ellie.'

'Whatever that is.' She was silent for a moment, even the aroma of beef and black bean not distracting her from her thoughts. 'I thought it was hard going through all this sort of angst when I was a teenager, but it's no easier now.'

'Yeah,' Kandy sighed, 'getting older doesn't make it any easier.'

Deciding she needed to lighten the atmosphere, Ellie dug her in the ribs. 'Older?' she cried. 'You're just a young pup.'

Kandy laughed. 'I'm old enough to remember the Alvin Purple movie. Hell, that gave me a laugh. There's nothing funnier than a man flashing a little penis to try to catch a woman's interest. Reminded me of the boy next door when I was eight years old. He showed me his behind the chook house and his Dad's old white duck had a go at it. Every time I hear the expression "little pecker" I remember his little pink dick with the duck attached.'

'Was he badly hurt?'

'Poor little bugger couldn't sit down for a day. His mother gave him a belting for being so rude.'

She smiled at the memory, then continued. 'You know, I've never been able to figure out why a man thinks if he stands there and wiggles his willie that women will salivate. Perhaps it's the modern equivalent of the Neanderthal swinging his club.'

'As long as he doesn't do it while he's wearing socks,' Cass laughed. 'A naked man wearing socks has no credibility whatsoever.'

'Bit like those women wearing only high heels and a neck choker in blue movies.' Kandy smirked. 'I tried it once. Ripped a hole in the sheet and damn near punctured the waterbed.'

'What did Phillip think about that?'

'Phillip?' Kandy's laughter echoed in the large room. 'If

I wore anything smaller than a full-length nightie to bed he'd have a heart attack. My skiing instructor, on the other hand,' she winked, 'had a far more adventurous streak.'

'Kandy, I've never asked this before, and you can tell me to mind my own business if you like, but ... ' Ellie hesitated for a moment, 'why do you ... cheat on Phillip?'

In the three years she'd known her, Ellie had never seen Kandy's good humour flag, but now she toyed with the short curls behind her ear and rubbed the wine glass against her bottom lip as though unsure she should let the words out. 'I married Phillip because I loved him, and also for security. Not the financial kind,' she hurriedly added as she realised how her words could be interpreted. 'Phillip was such a gentleman. He never pressured me for sex. Refused nicely when I offered it. He courted me,' she smiled as though the memory came from a place she'd long forgotten, 'made me feel worthwhile, as though I mattered, I wasn't just a good lay.'

Kandy stared at a spot somewhere behind Ellie's head as silence ate into the room. Ellie glanced across at Cass, and saw her looking at Kandy with a compassion that made her feel ashamed for having asked.

'Trouble is,' Kandy continued softly, 'Phillip *is* a gentleman. A gentleman with a very low libido. He's not in the least bit worried if we never make love.' As though realising her words were falling into a pool of sympathetic silence, Kandy tipped her glass and gulped its contents. 'Back to my original question.' She said and turned to Ellie. 'What are you going to do?'

'I don't know.' It was the truth as much as a way to avoid

answering, but Ellie realised she could no longer pretend her marriage was happy and stable. Trouble was, she simply didn't know what she wanted to do about it. *Leaving from* something was different from *going to* something else. She'd spent so many years in inertia she wasn't sure she could get herself out. Getting a job had given her a certain amount of courage, but leaving Damien under the current circumstances was a cruelty she couldn't bring herself to do to him.

'Well, let's just celebrate you joining the ranks of the employed,' Cass said and raised her glass.

As the cheerful clink of three glasses sang in the room, Ellie felt a reassurance that almost settled the disquiet in her chest.

It was only later that night that she wondered about Kandy's description of her relationship with her husband. If Phillip was such a prude, surely he wouldn't tolerate Kandy's infidelity? Or maybe he simply didn't believe she was cheating on him. Some people were very good at ignoring the obvious. Then she thought of her relationship with Damien and realised that, perhaps like she had done, Phillip was *choosing* to ignore the obvious.

CHAPTER FIVE

When Ellie awoke next morning, Damien's side of the bed was empty. Empty and obviously hadn't been slept in. Fear clutching her stomach, she ran to the phone and dialled his mobile number. Relief surged through her as he answered.

'Where are you?' she asked.

'At Jim's. I stayed here last night. I wasn't game to drive. I was over the limit.'

Jim Ethan. Her mind skittered, putting a face to the name. Early forties, driven, always alert for a quick way to make money. Not someone she'd ever felt comfortable with but tolerated because he'd been important to Damien. Or Damien's business. 'I was worried. You didn't come home.' She didn't say that she'd been concerned that he might do something more foolish than driving dangerously. Once, she'd never considered he might harm himself, but she didn't know him well enough any more to dismiss the possibility. At least he still had friends who would let him stay the night, unlike those who had disappeared as fast as the man who had ripped him off.

'Sorry. I had some things to do. We need to talk. I'll be home about lunch time.'

'I'll be at work.'

There was a slight pause, then, 'Yes. You will, won't

you.' There was no derision in the words, just a tired sadness. Then he ended the call.

Ellie was grateful the day turned out to be a busy one, with interested customers and new furniture needing to be assembled and paperwork to be processed. But all the activity didn't stop the worms of worry burrowing into her stomach. By the time Cass had picked her up from the store and dropped her home, the prospect of *really* talking with Damien had taken on nightmarish proportions.

'Don't let him bully you,' Cass said as Ellie got out of the car, and the choice of words struck Ellie.

'Do you think Damien bullies me?'

Cass's expression said diplomacy was no longer necessary. 'He's been more subtle in the past, but lately he's started to sound like your father.'

The observation hit Ellie like a fist to the chest. Until his death two years ago, her father had successfully undermined her self-confidence with his constant putdowns on everything from her "lack of artistic talent" to her poor parenting skills where Miranda was concerned. She sometimes wondered how her mother had ever got the guts to divorce her father. Even after his second affair she had taken him back, and after the divorce he had remained a dominating factor in all their lives.

With more clarity than she wanted to admit to, she realised she must have inherited more than her mother's physique and colouring. Stuff cracking the DNA code, she thought, scientists need to identify the submissive gene some women were born with and blast the damn thing out of existence.

She gave Cass a thumbs-up that looked more determined than she felt, and walked into the house. To her surprise, the aroma of potato bake wafted from the kitchen. It dragged her back to memories of long-ago barbecues before Damien's culinary tastes became as exotic as his choice of business colleagues and friends.

Damien stood at the sink, apron over his Van Heusen shirt and City Club trousers, marinading two fillet steaks. Deja vu washed over Ellie, but the pang of love that used to hit her when she saw him taking over the stainless steel and tiled sterility that masqueraded as a family kitchen didn't follow. No emotion did, not anger or pleasure or even mild irritation that he looked so at ease when it had been years since he'd done more than drop bread into the toaster.

'How was work?' he asked, and she blinked in surprise. Yesterday she would have delighted in telling him, today it felt like something that was none of his business. 'Busy,' she said. She wanted to kick off her shoes and ease her aching calf muscles, but the extra height, small though it was, allowed her the illusion of being in control of herself and the trepidation at what was to come.

'Why don't you go and change into something ...' Damien hesitated, and she saw his realisation that adding 'more comfortable' could be interpreted as meaning more than the innocuous suggestion he'd intended. 'The steaks shouldn't take long to cook.'

Ellie nodded. Her shoulders tensed further as she walked to their bedroom. She put her handbag and keys on the chest of drawers, slipped out of her shoes, and resisted the urge to fall onto the bed and crawl beneath the covers and not emerge until she felt up to coping with whatever Damien had to say. Which was probably never, she sighed.

Ten minutes and a hot shower to get the kinks from her shoulders later, she donned a deep blue velour tracksuit, rejected the need to boost her confidence by wearing matching high-heeled sandals and settled for comfortable slip-ons. Damien had set the table and was turning the steaks when she walked back into the kitchen. Ellie poured red wine into the two glasses on the table. The cosy domesticity should have been a welcome relief from the tension of the past few weeks, but the uneasiness in the room was almost palpable. Damien wanted to talk. Much as she'd thought that was what she wanted, Ellie realised that it had been so long since they'd talked on an intimate level that the thought of doing so was terrifying.

Damien took the potato bake from the oven, and with a smile that didn't match the wariness in his eyes, placed it on a trivet on the table. When he took a bowl of tossed salad from the fridge, memories flashed through Ellie's mind - Sunday lunches on the patio, barbecue sizzling, children playing, satiated with good food, wine and love. But it was like watching flickering images on an old newsreel - disjointed and distant, another time, another life. Her chest squeezed so tight she felt she couldn't breathe. Now that she had finally admitted to herself that there was nothing left between them, that she no longer loved him, surely Damien wasn't trying to re-kindle what they'd once shared?

'Sit down. I'll get the steaks,' he said, and she obediently sat, reluctant to be part of what was beginning to feel like a farce but needing to play it out to the end.

As they ate, Damien told her how swiftly their finances had been eroding, though he took no blame for his spending of the past few weeks and Ellie kept silent rather than point this out. She still knew him well enough to know he was leading up to something, and it was probably something she didn't want to hear.

When he'd chewed the last morsel of his food, he leaned back in his chair and drank the last of his wine. 'Jim had a proposition for me.'

Ellie looked at him, waiting, fork poised, not sure if she could continue to eat while he revealed what it was that had brought about his change in attitude. 'He needs someone to run his Sydney office and he's offered me the job. He's also offered to buy our house. At a very good price.'

He let the words hang in the air, his eyes searching Ellie's face for her reaction, though she was sure he had already decided what he was going to do. Selling the house wasn't a problem - she'd known that would happen if their money problems weren't resolved, or if she left him. She waited for him to say that he wanted her to go with him to Sydney, but he continued, 'You were right, Ellie, when you said we don't talk, really talk, any more. We haven't for years. I guess we both buried our heads in the sand. Maybe we needed this crisis to make us see that it just isn't working anymore.'

Ellie's grip on her fork tightened as her world tilted. They were *her* words, but they were coming out of Damien's mouth. He looked like he was waiting for her input, but she found she couldn't speak. She lowered the fork and looked at him, mouth still slightly open, mind absorbing the ramifications of what he was saying.

Damien cleared his throat and continued. 'Sometimes relationships simply run their course. We've really not had much in common for a long time. The girls are grown up, it won't affect them now if we go our own ways.'

It dawned on Ellie that there was something about his words that sounded rehearsed, as though they'd been phrased to be as emotionless as possible. As though by using her own words back at her she would be made to see the logic in what he was saying. She found her voice. 'And what do you ... propose ... we do now?'

Relief lowered Damien's shoulders and he slumped briefly in the chair before leaning forward, eyes bright, his features animated in a way she hadn't seen in a long time. 'What Jim's offering for the house will pay off the mortgage and leave enough to buy you a little car so you can get to work. I can't afford to renew the lease on the one you have now.'

'And where will I live?'

'With Miranda. After all, it's my father's house she's living in. The rent she pays barely covers the rates and some maintenance.'

The air rushed from Ellie's lungs. Miranda. In Damien's father's house. With all her drop-in friends from the soup kitchen and kooky schemes and housekeeping that resembled Frank Spencer having a good day. And Damien's father, Bert, escaping from the Alzheimers section of the nursing home whenever he got the chance and coming back to claim the house he'd never wanted to leave that beckoned him with fragmented memories of the wife he'd loved till the day she died. At least Bert hadn't let love slip from his life, she thought bitterly. And living with Miranda was preferable to living with Pru and her equally up-tight husband Rodney. Or going with Damien.

She marvelled at the control in her voice as she asked, 'When will all this happen?'

'As soon as possible. Jim's manager is leaving next week, so I'll have to look for somewhere to live down there, and ...' As though realising Ellie wasn't sharing his enthusiasm, he faltered, then reached over and covered her hand where it lay on the table. 'I knew you'd be sensible about this. You've always done what's best.'

Ellie snatched her hand away as though she'd been burned. She didn't feel sensible. She felt shocked, numb, as though her mind couldn't take in what her ears had heard. 'I'm going out.' The words fell from her lips as though spoken by someone else, but Damien nodded and waved a dismissive hand at the plates. 'I'll clean up.'

Clean up. Clean up! The words echoed in Ellie's mind as she picked up her handbag and keys and drove to Cass's house. Of course he would clean up. Clean up the mess he'd made of their marriage by sweeping it away and moving. Moving away. To Sydney. Moving on. Past her. Like she was a mistake he'd just figured out a way to rectify without it showing up in the accounts or unbalancing the ledger.

All right, she'd been on the verge of leaving him, but at least she would have done it with a bit more compassion than *he'd* shown. When had he become so clinical? So capable of ... of ... cutting her out of his life like a surgeon removing a tumour?

Her disbelief and anger grew on the short drive to Cass's house.

'It was so bloody civilised! I couldn't believe it. He'd worked everything out, even to where I should live once he was free of me.' Ellie paced Cass's kitchen floor, short thumping steps because there was not enough room to stride like she felt like doing. 'He's probably over there right now, packing his things, packing *my* things ...' She stopped and looked at Cass. 'For heavens sake, Cass, *say* something.'

'Coffee or tea or something stronger?'

Ellie opened her mouth to ask, 'What?' but saw Cass's knowing expression and laughed instead. 'I should be grateful, shouldn't I. My decision has been made for me.' She plonked onto a chair. 'Guess I'm just pissed off that the decision wasn't mine to make in the end. And the way Damien was so calculating about it. And living with Miranda ...'

'You could always stay here for a while,' Cass offered.

'Thanks, but I want to keep you as a friend, Cass. I know Joe's a laid-back bloke, and he's like you, he has a heart of gold, but you don't need a third party underfoot. I can't afford to rent anywhere on my own so I'll just have to learn to live with Miranda.'

When she drove back home, Ellie saw that Damien had moved his belongings into the spare bedroom. She didn't know whether to be grateful for his diplomacy or upset that he appeared to be in a hurry to end what little remained of their marriage.

As she eyed the two-bedroom weatherboard house Damien's father, Bert, had built for his bride after World War II, Ellie's misgivings grew. She'd phoned Miranda and asked if it was all right to call around after she finished work, and Miranda had invited her to stay for dinner. Ellie had stressed that she needed to talk with her alone, and she could imagine Miranda shrugging as she said, 'That's fine.'

Cottage would have been a better description of the house, Ellie thought as she pushed open the rusty gate and walked the cracked concrete path to the front door. Miranda kept the lawn mowed and the garden weeded, and had planted some camellias that were now covered in pink and white blooms. The fading afternoon light was kind to the paintwork, disguising the slow disintegration into peeling patches and fine powder. Ellie had wanted Damien to repaint it when Miranda had moved in, but he refused, saying that as soon as his father was no longer alive he would sell the house for removal and build units on the land. It was one thing in his favour, she thought. With his enduring power of attorney he could have done that as soon as his father had entered the nursing home, but occasionally he drove the old man back for a visit, keeping alive his dream that his beloved wife Eugenia was still waiting for him.

Ellie stepped onto the tiny porch and raised her hand to knock.

'Hi, Mum,' Miranda opened the door, blonde hair caught up in a ponytail, jeans, tee-shirt and hand towel flung over one shoulder. She gave Ellie a quick smile and ushered her into the lounge room. Miranda hadn't changed anything much in the house, just replaced some of her grandparents' paintings with woven wall hangings in purples and pinks and dream-catchers that twirled lazily in the dim light.

Miranda flicked a switch, and as light flooded the room Ellie wished she hadn't. The floral tapestry lounge suite had faded to a dull motley of maroons and blues, and a purple throw hid the threadbare spots. It reminded Ellie of a kids' birthday party after a food fight. Miranda had obviously tried to tidy up - there were spaces on the coffee table between the piles of The Big Issue magazine and books about people who had given their lives to helping others. Bert's old television still sat in its cabinet in the corner, the remote a paperweight on newspaper cuttings next to it.

'I'll get you a drink.' Miranda drifted towards the kitchen. 'White wine?'

'Yes, please.' Ellie sat on the lounge, pleased no puffs of dust emitted from the sinking foam.

Miranda returned with a bottle and two glasses, plopped sideways onto the other end of the lounge and tucked a foot under one knee. 'So tell me,' she said as she poured the wine and gave Ellie a glass, 'what's so important you couldn't tell me over the phone?'

After a very long sip of wine, Ellie gave an abbreviated version of what had occurred the previous evening.

And watched her daughter's eyes widen in shock.

CHAPTER SIX

'You're joking! You're going to live *here*?' Miranda pushed a long strand of blonde hair from her eyes and looked at her mother.

Ellie raised a surprised eyebrow. 'I know it's not a big house, darling, but I don't have much choice. Besides,' she frowned, 'I thought you'd be more upset about your father and I breaking up.'

A flick of her hand indicated the extent of Miranda's anguish on that score. 'I've been expecting it for years. Honestly, Mum, I don't know how you put up with him for this long. You played doormat and he wiped his feet on you.'

If Ellie's jaw wasn't falling before, it did now. 'I wasn't a doormat. I was a wife, a ... a ...'

'Doormat. A very lovable doormat,' Miranda hastened to assure her. 'Mum, I know it's going to be a hard time for you, but it's the best thing that could have happened, honestly. You and Dad have been like puppets acting out a play for years, the more you acquiesce to what he wants the bossier he gets. Marriages are supposed to be partnerships, not dictatorships. Yeah,' Miranda held up her hand as Ellie tried to protest, 'I know Dad doesn't yell at you, he's more subtle than that, but he always gets his own way. Because you let him.'

'You've never mentioned any of this before.'

'Who am I to talk? I can't even keep a boyfriend.'

'Mirie, I'm sorry, I've been so wrapped up in my own problems I haven't even asked how you are.'

'Well, if I didn't go on the food run and see how badly off other people are, I'd probably be depressed. But at least I have a roof over my head and can afford to buy food, and even cheap wine,' she looked hopefully at Ellie, 'which I hope isn't too bad?' Her face lightened at Ellie's wink of assurance. 'Then not being able to get a job isn't getting me down too much.'

'Have you thought about going back to uni? You could complete your arts degree.'

'Mum, in this economic climate, arts graduates are waiting tables. That's if they can beat the engineering graduates to the jobs. Anyway,' she slid off the lounge and stood up, 'I'd better check on dinner. Don't want my famous chicken casserole to burn. It'd be a waste of some very cheap off-cuts.'

Half an hour later Ellie pushed her plate away with a satisfied smile. 'You're a good cook,' she told Miranda and watched the pleasure on her daughter's face at the compliment. She waited a moment then asked, 'Miranda, how *do* you feel about me moving in with you? You've had your own space for a few years now, and it's not going to be easy to share it. Particularly with your mother.'

'Well, most twenty-three-year-olds would freak out at the thought, but you and I have always got along okay. And it's not like you have a choice. If you stayed with Pru it wouldn't be any different to living with Dad.' Miranda chuckled and Ellie realised she'd glimpsed the hastily-concealed shudder that had run down her back at the thought. Just telling Pru about the break-up over the phone had been bad enough. Pru, as always, had taken Damien's side, telling Ellie that she should have been more understanding of the pressures he was under.

'Plus you now have a job,' Miranda continued. 'Did I tell you that I'm proud of you for doing that, Mum?'

The lump that formed in Ellie's throat made speech impossible, but a small flame of hope for the future kindled inside her.

The weeks that followed became a mad scramble of packing and moving and cleaning out the spare bedroom in Bert's house that Miranda had turned into an office of sorts. Miranda's computer desk now resided in a corner of her not-very-large bedroom, and Ellie's guilt at disturbing her daughter's life was only alleviated by Miranda's cheerful acceptance of the circumstances and her assertion that at least Ellie was better at housekeeping than she was.

To Ellie's surprise, her mother and brother had taken the news about the breakup with almost philosophical acceptance, and she'd been forced to consider that the sorry state of her marriage must have been only too obvious.

Between work and packing, she hadn't seen much of Damien, and she suspected his late nights going over his new job details with Jim were more to keep out of her way than business-related. She kept telling herself that it was a good thing, but a terrible ache had replaced the uncertainty she'd felt over the past couple of years and she felt less like she was going forward into a new life than running away from the old one. If it hadn't been for Cass and Kandy and their never-ceasing encouragement, not to mention their skills at packing boxes and forcing her to make decisions about keeping sentimental items, Ellie doubted she would have coped with it all. Particularly when it came to packing family photos. What do you do with reminders of a once-happy marriage, she'd asked, and watched as Cass packed them all into a box and sealed and labelled it "Family photos - to be opened in the future when Ellie feels it's the right time".

Richard, her boss, had been sympathetic, but she hadn't accepted his offer to take time off without pay. Her share of the tiny profit from the house sale had bought her a second-hand Magna that at least had hope of not falling apart if it hit a bump, which was more than could be said of Miranda's ancient Cortina, but there wasn't much left after that.

Damien flew to Sydney four days before the removalists took their furniture into storage. Ellie had dreaded this final parting, this death of a marriage with no last rites or decent burial. She didn't know what she expected - tears, recriminations, whatever - but it was as casual and emotionless as Damien's declaration that he agreed with her that they didn't talk any more and should "go their own ways".

He gave her a quick hug and promised to keep in touch. For some obscure reason that she couldn't justify, Ellie felt compelled to watch him leave. He walked to Jim Ethan's car with a spring in his step that she hadn't seen in a long time. He got in the car and she started to close the front door. As the car sped off he glanced back, and she caught a glimpse of his face before she closed the door.

She thought she saw an expression of deep sorrow on his features.

But perhaps it was just a shadow from an overhanging tree branch.

Or wishful thinking.

At the same moment as Ellie stood, hand on the door knob, emotions swirling with the reality that she was truly on her own, a young woman who had spent her life feeling isolated from those who should have cared for her stuffed her meagre possessions into a battered backpack and scurried from the squat she shared with four other people.

Cherilyn Manning had once looked up the meaning of her name on the internet and had been struck by the irony of it. "Beloved" had never applied to her.

Blood from her split lip had congealed on her chin and she scratched at it gently, careful not to pull too much and draw the skin tighter across her bruised cheek. She was grateful the mole close to her eye had missed the ferocity of the attack. If it got knocked it was hard to stop the bleeding and took ages to heal.

Jackson would probably look for her for a while, but he'd soon find another girl to share his bed in exchange for the drugs he could provide. Leaving wasn't easy, this squat at least had running water, but even a cardboard box under a bridge was preferable to the beating she'd suffered last night.

Ellie was sure Miranda's toaster had been designed by the Air Force. Every time it ejected the toast you had to send out a rescue team to find it. And it also had the inconsistency of a politician - one morning the bread was barely singed, the next it was charcoaled. She reached behind the offending appliance for the blackened bread and winced as her arm brushed the metal top. She threw the toast into the bin, grateful the smoke alarm hadn't gone off, and resolved she would go to the storage unit after work and get her own toaster. She hadn't wanted to offend Miranda by bringing her own kitchen appliances, but she couldn't afford to waste time every morning by having to battle a toaster with a personality crisis.

Coffee would have to do this morning or she was going to be late. She gulped down the now lukewarm liquid, rushed to the bathroom, cleaned her teeth, applied makeup, and ran to her bedroom and dressed. Her hair resisted her efforts to wind it into its usual French roll and she cursed the delay.

'Why don't you get your hair cut?' Miranda stood in the doorway, arms hugging her blue satin pyjamas, more asleep than awake. 'You'd look a lot younger. Might even score yourself a toyboy.' She laughed at her own joke and Ellie heard the slop-slop of her Ugg boots as she walked to the bathroom.

With an exasperated sigh, Ellie grabbed two hair clips and caught the recalcitrant strands so they formed wings on either side of her head. The effect wasn't bad, but not as practical as she liked. If she leaned over, her hair would fall forward and get in the way.

By the time she arrived at work, Miranda's suggestion sounded more and more like a good idea. Her life had changed drastically, might as well go the whole way.

'Mum! You look fantastic.'

Ellie smiled at Miranda's words and pulled at the wisps of hair around her ear. 'You really think so?'

'Absolutely.' Miranda abandoned the vegetables she'd been chopping and walked over to where Ellie hesitated in the kitchen doorway. She walked around Ellie, nodding approvingly. 'I love the way the hairdresser's feathered it around your face, and you'll only need a little mousse to keep a bit of bounce in the top. Sits well at the back too, curves into your neck. You should have had it cut years ago.' She went back to the sink. 'Should have done a lot of things years ago.'

Ellie wondered if Miranda was right. Perhaps if she'd been more assertive, done more with her life than just drift after the girls had left home, she'd still be living in her own home ... and still be married. The ache in her chest deepened.

She walked to her bedroom. It didn't matter now. She couldn't go back and undo the past. She shook her head, and laughed at the lightness of her hair. In some crazy way it had been cathartic watching the long blonde strands fall to the floor in the salon. A bit like the twenty kilometre bicycle ride she'd done at sixteen after her first boyfriend had dumped her. She'd thought she'd been in love with him, but aching muscles and a sudden summer storm had dispelled that notion in a couple of hours.

Perhaps that's what she needed now - some intense physical activity to take her mind off the ache that hadn't disappeared with Damien's departure. The tiredness that came with working full-time didn't make for good sleep, maybe a session at the gym or a long walk would do the trick. The other form of exercise she was missing teased her with possibilities - and problems. The thought of dating at her age was daunting. It had been years since she'd met a man who even vaguely attracted her. Perhaps she'd become too fussy? None of Damien's colleagues had raised her interest level to the point where she'd even contemplated seeing them in a sexual light.

Maybe ... She tried to block the thought, but it kept creeping back like an itch that no amount of scratching would relieve.

Maybe she needed Kandy's advice.

CHAPTER SEVEN

Cass poured the chocolate cake mix into the floured tin and sighed. It was always so tempting when she cooked for Joe. His metabolism disposed of calories as fast as he consumed them, but if she indulged in only a fraction of what he could get away with her clothes quickly appeared to shrink.

Joe's work truck growled up the driveway as she put the tin in the oven and set the timer. Before she could put the bowl, beaters and spatula in the sink she heard his esky clump on the laundry tiles, footsteps echo on the polished timber floor, and then his arms went around her from behind and he kissed the side of her neck.

Warmth that had nothing to do with the oven heat in the room spread through her. She turned in his arms and offered him the spatula. His eyes twinkled, and he bent his head and licked the cake mix from the tip. That did it for Cass. Always had, she thought. That sexy gleam and the slow smile. She moved the spatula away, dumped it and the bowl on the bench and kissed him.

'We have,' she looked at the oven clock a moment later, 'twenty minutes.'

He smiled again. 'I'll be waiting.'

'I'll just take the phone off the hook.' With Audra's timing, Cass was sure she'd phone before they'd made it to two-play, let alone foreplay.

By the time she got to the bedroom, the curtains were drawn, the bedspread flung back, Joe had had a quick shower and was naked. Naked, and more than ready.

Cass stripped and slid across the cool sheets. Seconds later she was giving mental thanks for oestrogen cream as Joe began a rhythm that curled her mouth in an appreciative smile. 'If you hadn't been so eager,' she purred and arched into him, 'I could have covered it in cake mix.'

She watched the way his eyes gleamed at the thought, then added mischievously, 'But that doesn't mean I would have licked it off.'

His rhythm faltered as he laughed, and Cass felt answering laughter well up. Well up and spill over, like a schoolgirl caught in a fit of the giggles. The more she giggled, the more Joe laughed. And the more he laughed, the harder it was for him to keep his erection.

'You're shrinking,' Cass gulped as she tried to suppress her mirth. But it didn't matter, because it was wonderful to laugh with him, to love him, to feel his arms wrap around her as they clung together on the bed. And when their laughter had died and the loving continued, she was glad she'd had the fore-thought to turn the oven temperature lower.

Later, as Joe sat in the kitchen with a mug of coffee and slice of cake and Cass peeled vegetables for their evening meal, Cass's thoughts turned to Ellie. Although Ellie's relationship with Damien had long ago become almost non-existent, they had a shared history and ties that would forever connect them, and she worried that Ellie had taken the break-up too well.

'Bruce had a chat with me today,' Joe's words interrupted her musing. 'Seems he wants to start another project.'

Cass had met Joe's boss a few times. A builder who specialised in renovations, particularly unit buildings, he was a block of a man whose squarish shape was accentuated by his peg-like teeth and the severe crewcut of his prematurely greying hair. Joe had started working for him as a contract carpenter twelve years before and had taken on the foreman's role on some of the projects. 'And?' she prompted Joe as he took another bite of cake.

'He's bought a three-storey block of flats in New Farm.' Joe paused slightly. 'They're pretty old - red brick, stairs only, no lift. He wants to *bring them back to their former glory*.' He made a face that only lacked eye-rolling to complete his disbelief in the project.

'What's wrong with that?' Cass asked. 'There's a real movement now for old things and times when life was slower and people weren't so stressed.'

'You know how he usually just spruces the flats up, throws in a new kitchen and bathroom and sells the whole building to an investor? Well, this time he wants to go the whole hog - sell them fully furnished so buyers know they're getting something authentic. Have them fitted out with classy interiors and furnishings that the poshies would have had in those days.'

Cass finished peeling a carrot and raised an eyebrow. 'That will cost him a lot more.'

'Yeah. That's the problem. He doesn't want to go overboard hiring some expensive interior designer and then find he's spent more on the whole project than what he can sell it for.'

Bells started ringing in Cass's mind. 'And so -'

'So I told him about Ellie. Bruce won't pay a lot but it would be something for her to start her business with - sort of an example of what she can do.'

'She could take before and after photos, and show those to prospective clients.' Cass felt her enthusiasm rising. 'And build her own website and use them on that.' She broke a piece off Joe's slice of cake, popped it into her mouth and let the warm chocolate flavour satisfy her craving taste buds. 'I'll phone her tonight and let her know.'

Ellie put down the phone and rose from the chair she'd swear had been stuffed with horsehair from the stallions that had taken Ben Hur's chariot to victory over Marsala. She rubbed her aching bottom. Tomorrow she'd get her cordless phone from storage so she wouldn't be pinned into the living room corner when she had to be on the phone. Hadn't Bert heard of telephone extension cords? Or Miranda? Then she thought of how few times she'd seen her daughter on the phone, either landline or mobile, and felt guilty - why didn't Miranda have friends calling her and chatting for hours like they used to? More guilt stabbed through her. The disconnectedness that had seeped into her marriage like a third party had obviously infiltrated Miranda's life. Or maybe it was her fault that she hadn't had a deeply personal conversation with either of her daughters for years.

She knocked on Miranda's bedroom door, waited for the faint "Come in" and entered. Miranda was lying on her bed, supported by large purple pillows, reading a magazine.

'Can we talk?' Ellie wanted to share her excitement at Cass's news, but needed to connect with Miranda more. Miranda nodded, and drew up her legs so Ellie could sit on the bed. Ellie sat, hesitated, than swung her legs around and sat cross-legged, her jeans stretching tight over her knees.

'What's up, Mum?' Miranda put the magazine on the pile on the bedside table.

Ellie noted with surprise that it was *The New Scientist*. 'I didn't know you were interested in science.'

'Always have been.'

'Then why didn't you do it at uni? I know your marks weren't the highest but you could have gone for one of the easier degrees.'

Miranda shrugged. 'Pru was always the bright one. And Grandpa always told me I was hopeless.'

'When did he say that?' Ellie couldn't keep the shock out of her voice. Her father had always been hypercritical of her when she was growing up, but she hadn't realised he had done the same thing to Miranda.

'When Pru and I would go over and stay with him and Gran.' Miranda hugged a pillow to her chest.

'Oh, Mirie, I'm so sorry.' Ellie wanted to reach out and crush Miranda to her and take away the pain those words would have caused.

'It's all right. It's past history. The old bugger's dead now. And Gran seemed a lot happier when she visited last year.'

'Yes, she is a lot happier,' Ellie agreed, taken aback by the bitterness in Miranda's tone when calling her grandfather an "old bugger". 'Mirie, I wish you would have told me what he was saying to you. It wasn't fair, and it certainly isn't true.'

'But I *am* hopeless, Mum. I had three years working in a department store and was the only long-term employee who was made redundant in their last slash of employees. And the only work I've had since then has been casual and it's been four months since I've had any of that.' She pushed her chin into the pillow as though trying to stop the flow of words. 'I keep doing those stupid courses that train you for jobs that don't exist because no-one's hiring anyone, I've put my CV in at so many businesses they're sick of the sight of me, and I *still* can't get a job.'

'It must have ... upset you ... when I got a job.'

'No. I told you, I'm proud of you for that.' A tear trickled slowly down her cheek and she dashed it away with the back of her hand. 'Sorry. It's not you. It's just that sometimes being unemployed really gets me down.'

Ellie sat, feeling helpless, knowing nothing she could do could make Miranda feel better about her situation. Or herself. And feeling terrible that she now had the prospect of more work when Miranda had none.

'What did you want to talk about?' Miranda asked.

As Ellie told her the scant details she'd got from Cass, an idea grew.

'Mum, that's a great opportunity.' Miranda's face lit with excitement. 'Are you going to do it?'

'To be honest, I'm scared stiff I'll stuff up. No,' she said as Miranda started to protest, 'I know you think I can do it, but it's been a long time since I've done this sort of thing, and there are nine units to refurbish. I can't afford to give up my job. If this work for Bruce turns out okay then I might consider going full-time as an interior designer, but it will take more money than I have at the moment. But I was thinking,' she leaned forward, 'how would you like to help? I couldn't pay you until I got paid, but it would be something you could put on your CV.'

Miranda looked dubious. 'I don't have any qualifications in interior design. And I don't have any talent.'

'But you can use a computer and a phone and find out which suppliers have the wallpapers and furniture I'll need and get prices for me. It will be impossible for me to do that during business hours.' Ellie saw the moment Miranda started to believe it was possible and said, 'Cass said she can help with the bookkeeping, but I really can't do it without you, hon. Please say you'll help.'

'Okay. If you think I can.'

'Great.' Ellie held out her hand. 'Shake, partner.' As Miranda's fingers touched hers, Ellie realised that it had been a long time since she'd touched her daughter apart from perfunctory cheek kisses at birthdays and Christmas. She thought of Cass and Joe and the way they interacted with their four children, who, although adults now, still hugged when greeting each other. Okay, so she and Damien weren't "huggy" people, but she wondered if their lack of physical contact was a result of their emotional lack, or the other way around. Not that it mattered anymore with Damien, but she didn't want to lose her daughters in the same way. She gave Miranda's hand a gentle squeeze. 'I love you, you know.'

'You too.' Miranda's words came out as though she was surprised at saying them, but then she leaned forward and gave Ellie a quick hug.

Blinking back sudden tears, Ellie returned the embrace, then rose and walked to the door. 'Would you like a hot chocolate?'

Miranda nodded. 'Please. And thanks, Mum ... for believing in me.'

'I always have, Mirie. I just neglected to tell you.'

The next day at work Ellie's mind buzzed with the possibilities Bruce's job could open up for her, and the terrifying prospect that she mightn't be up to the task. At least she didn't have to outlay any money to purchase samples of materials or trade books or all the other trappings of business. It had been a long time since she'd had to budget, but her limited income now made that essential. It reminded her of the early days of her marriage and the memories brought a surge of loss so fierce she had to fight back tears.

In her lunch break she wrote down what she would need to do for the units: research room decor, wallpapers and paint colours that matched the era when the building was built; source appropriate furniture; look at methods of incorporating modern appliances like dishwashers so they weren't obvious or look out of place. Her already shaky confidence began to slide even further. So much to do and she barely had enough time after work to fit in what little else she had to do. Thank heavens Miranda had agreed to help.

She was so engrossed in her thoughts that when her mobile rang she jumped like a startled rabbit. A male with a nasal twang identified himself as Bruce Moloney, Joe's boss. 'You'd better have a look at the job first,' he told her, 'and see if you're up to it.'

Up to it? Tiny hackles of anger rose on Ellie's neck. It was the sort of thing her father would say, and from what Cass had said, Bruce was only in his forties. 'That would be a good idea, Bruce,' she told him. 'I don't know what condition the rooms are in. It might not be possible to re-create that authentic early 1920s style without going over your budget.'

'Glad we understand each other, love. I can't afford to go overboard on this project. How about you come over to the place tomorrow afternoon and I'll show you around.'

Ellie grimaced. By the time she finished work it would be at least six o'clock before she could get there. She told Bruce this, and heard his sigh of frustration. Tomorrow was Friday, and she knew from Cass that Bruce went to the pub for a counter meal on Friday nights. But he gave her the address and said he would meet her there.

As Ellie drove home that evening, she wondered if a nine-unit refurbishment was too big a job to take on as her first foray back into the world of interior design. But in her current situation, it was probably the only opportunity she would get. Starting a new career had seemed like a good idea when she'd first mentioned it to Cass, but now her years out of the workforce felt like a wasteland she wasn't sure she had the ability to cross.

Cherilyn couldn't remember the last time her parents had spoken to her with any trace of affection in their voices. Perhaps they never had. Married through necessity - oh, they were fond of reminding her that her conception had been the cause - they were so busy bemoaning their lot in life and dragging up the son and daughter that had quickly followed her birth that Cherilyn had often felt they wouldn't notice if she wasn't there. To prove it, she'd packed her bags when her mother was out and went to stay with a young man she'd met in a nightclub. Two days later her mother had phoned her mobile, called her ungrateful in words that had splintered Cherilyn's heart, and told her she'd better not come back because she wouldn't be welcome.

She pulled her jacket close against her thin chest and tugged the hood further over her forehead. The nights were getting too cold to be outside. She'd have to find some place to doss down soon. The coffee had warmed her, and she looked at the foam cup as though it might magically refill itself. She hated being dependent on the food van, but was grateful for what they provided. Not just the food, but the way the volunteers talked to her like she was worth something. Like she mattered. It was an illusion, she knew that, but it was the only one she had left. She stuffed the remainder of the sandwiches into her backpack. They'd do for breakfast.

New Farm Park was well lit, but huge Moreton Bay Fig trees danced shadows on the ground and shrubs created dark caves of rustling leaves that offered shelter on a rainless night ... or a hiding place where someone could lie in wait. She fingered her bruised cheek and shivered. When Jackson had started using Ice his violent outbursts had increased, and she wouldn't feel safe until she'd found somewhere she could hide from him. Even then she knew the fear would not go away.

Not until he was dead.

Or in jail.

Her breathing stopped as a low voice asked, 'Wotcha doin', Cherilyn?'

CHAPTER EIGHT

Cherilyn spun around, heels rising as though to flee.

'Mouse.' Air rushed from her lungs on the word as a skinny young man moved from behind one of the trees. Her body relaxed in relief.

'Do you -' he caught sight of her face. 'What happened to your face? Did Jackson do that? He likes to hit girls.'

Panic reared, tightening her throat. 'Please, Mouse, don't tell him you saw me. Please.' She gripped her backpack, unsure if she should trust him. Mouse was a loner, someone she knew little about, but they'd exchanged names last year after they had, quite literally, bumped into each other at the food van here. She hadn't told him about Jackson, but some months later had seen him buying off Jackson. She didn't let on she knew him, and he hadn't acknowledged her. Word on the street was that he was a retard, but in subsequent meetings at the food van she'd gained the impression that he was just a bit slow.

'I won't. Don't like him anyway,' he shrugged. 'You need somewhere to stay?'

She shook her head. She couldn't take the risk he would tell Jackson. 'I'm okay.'

'Sure you are.' He didn't try to hide his disbelief. 'There's a block of units a few streets north of here. They're working on 'em in the day but no-one's there at night. Go around the back yard - a window doesn't lock properly.' He shrugged again. 'Just gotta get outta there real early. Before they start work.' He took out a small pouch and gestured to a part of the park where the lights didn't reach. 'Wanna share?'

The compulsion to feel the mind-numbing bliss he offered was almost too much to resist, but she couldn't take the risk. She couldn't think properly when she was stoned, and that would make her even more vulnerable. 'Another time.' She slung her pack onto her shoulders and hurried away.

Friday dawned with grey skies that turned to drizzling rain by lunch time and a steady downpour by mid-afternoon that brought with it a coldness that seemed to creep into Ellie's bones. It didn't surprise her when Bruce Moloney phoned and told her he wouldn't be able to show her around the units that afternoon.

'Why don't I drop the keys into you on my way home,' he suggested, 'and you go have a look at the place on the weekend?'

Ellie watched the people outside the store trying to avoid the large puddles that had formed in the car park. 'That sounds like a good idea, Bruce.' A hot shower and a hot drink sounded more enticing than wet feet and tramping around an old building that would be as empty as she'd felt these past few months.

That morning she'd told Richard about the project and had been pleasantly surprised by his enthusiasm, and touched by his offer to let her contact his suppliers in her search for furniture and furnishings. She hoped he was only offering because it would be a sensible business suggestion, but lately she'd wondered if there wasn't a little more to his friendliness than good personnel management skills.

Twenty minutes later, and ignoring the signs that said no parking, Bruce drove his ute as close as possible to the front door and clomped into the store. Ellie recognised him instantly from Cass's description and hurried over and introduced herself. He handed her a keyring containing several keys and explained what doors they opened. 'Just be careful,' he told her, 'my men have already started pulling out the kitchen and bathroom fittings on the top floor so there's a bit of mess around. If you decide to take on the job you'll have to get a blue card. I can't have you on site without one. But I can arrange that.' He handed her a business card, 'Call me when you've had a look.' And turned to leave.

'Wait.' She stepped around so he had to talk to her. 'Do you have a copy of the original plans?'

'No, they were destroyed in the '74 flood. The council lost a lot of records then. But the unit layouts are the same on each floor so you won't have to look at the whole nine.'

'Don't you want to be there when I look at the place? So I can ask questions? Or make suggestions?' Ellie felt she was floundering. She had no idea of his budget or time frame.

He raised one bristled eyebrow. 'You're the interior designer. Give me a quote on a full fit-out for the biggest unit and we'll go from there. Besides, footy's on this weekend.' He grinned in anticipation and stomped out.

'Cass, I don't think I can do this.' Ellie paced the lounge room floor that evening, cordless phone to her ear, mind seething with self-doubt. Miranda had gone to help on the food van again, and Ellie hoped she was keeping warm. The rain had ceased, but the chill had intensified, and grey and dismal skies had turned crisp in their blackness.

'Of course you can, Ellie.'

Cass sounded so sure Ellie stopped pacing. 'Bruce didn't sound like he had much confidence in me.'

'Bruce sounds like that all the time. Don't worry, you'll be fine. Would you like me to come with you tomorrow?'

'Would you? I hate to be a nuisance, but ...'

Cass's chuckle sounded in Ellie's ear. 'You're not a nuisance. It will be interesting to see what Bruce has got himself into. How does nine o'clock sound?'

'Wonderful. I'll pick you up. Thanks, Cass.'

When had she become such a wuss? Ellie looked at the phone as she placed it back in the holder. Her self-esteem and self-confidence had been on the wane for years, but Damien's cold-blooded attitude to the demise of their marriage had her wondering if she'd been more to blame than he was. Had she not been the wife he needed? Or wanted? Had she become so boring that he had lost interest in her? She groaned. She'd never really considered herself assertive, but perhaps she'd become an emotional coward. If Damien's business crisis hadn't happened, would she have ever had the courage to confront him about the state of their marriage?

Confront. That was the important word. She simply wasn't a confrontational sort of person. But if she didn't learn to become more assertive soon she was going to lose this opportunity to prove herself. She was about to grab a pen and write a few more ideas on her list but stopped. She might not have come kicking and screaming to the computer age, but she'd been reluctant to drag herself too far into its unfathomable depths. Now she regretted her lack of enthusiasm. Miranda had sourced several programs for her that would make working out measurements and placing furniture so much easier. She just wished she understood how to use them.

With a determination she forced herself to feel, she walked to the computer desk.

'Thank God the sun's shining. Still cold though.' Ellie parked outside a three-storey red-brick building in New Farm. A huge Poinciana tree bowed leafless but graceful limbs over the road and footpath. The rain of the day before had refreshed everything. Even the adjoining houses, wide-verandahed timber Queenslanders, remnants of a more genteel era, appeared to sparkle in the sun. Paintwork looked bright, roofs clean. Even the gardens, some lovingly tended, others left to run a little wild, seemed almost Spring-like with their glossy leaves and winter blooms.

Ellie surveyed the low brick fence and tiny front yard of Bruce's property. A large skip bin overflowing with discarded timber and plumbing fixtures sat between the fence and the building. Lasiandra shrubs formed purple sentinels either side of the front door, and she wondered if

Bruce would allow them to stay. She hoped so. Colour was important, particularly for creating good first impressions. She would tell him to keep the garden as old-fashioned as possible. Then she thought of his less-than-subtle personality. No, she would *advise* him.

She noted the driveway going down the side of the yard and wondered if there was parking behind the building or if Bruce planned to provide some.

'He's going to have to spruce up the outside,' Cass pulled her red tartan coat closer together as they walked into the yard. 'The windows could all do with re-puttying and painting,' she pointed to the mullioned windows, their mottled glass gleaming dully in the sunshine, 'and so do the glass panels either side of the door, and the door needs replacing.'

Putting her briefcase containing her camera, pads, pens and tape measure at her sneakered feet, Ellie searched her handbag for the keys Bruce had given her. She selected the longest. The key went smoothly into the lock, then needed a little jiggling before it turned. She pushed the door open and braced herself for the theatrical creak she expected from its weathered appearance, but it simply whispered over the coarse woven mat inside.

The foyer walls had yellowed with age, and the carpet runner covering the timber staircase leading to the upper floors had worn almost to the threads. Ellie walked over and inspected the curved hand-rail and carved railings. Good timber, it would be easily restored.

She wasn't too sure about the foyer floor tiles. Although none were broken, dirt seemed to have permanently stained their muted cream colour. Probably be better to replace them than try to bring them back to their former glory.

The staircase took up a lot of the rectangular-shaped foyer, with one doorway in front of it, straight to Ellie's right, a brass number One screwed into it. On the long wall to her left were two doorways, then another directly opposite the front door. All darkly varnished. All doors closed.

'The unit doors shouldn't be locked,' Cass commented. 'Joe said they've been working their way through from the top, taking out the bathroom and kitchen fittings. They haven't reached the bottom floor yet.'

'Good. I'd like to see what's been done with them. Most of these old buildings were only renovated when things started to fall apart. If we're lucky we might find some original pieces.' It was a slight hope, Ellie knew, but she was anxious to find something that might give her an idea of how the units were originally furnished. She turned to her right. 'We'll start with unit One.'

Twenty-five minutes later she was still measuring and taking notes, muttering her disappointment at finding the unit had been decorated in the "bare basics" el-cheapo style so reminiscent of flats of the 1970s. Black and white floor tiles, tight-looped multi-coloured carpet that hid stains well, plain beige bathroom wall tiles, kitchen cupboards in beige laminex. Curtains so old she thought they'd crumble if she touched them.

As she worked, the fear that had niggled at the perimeter of her subconscious disappeared, to be replaced by a burgeoning excitement. In her mind she could see the changes that needed to be made to bring a mid-1920s ambiance to the unit. An era when the horror of the First World War and the devastating Spanish Flu had begun to ease from memories and the Great Depression had yet to occur.

Last night she'd spent hours researching the furniture and furnishings of the era and had been excited to discover that a furniture craftsman named Edmund Rosenstengel had set up a workshop and showroom in an old New Farm picture theatre in 1922. She'd found photos of his work and had fallen in love with its intricately carved elegance, his use of Queensland timbers such as oak, silver ash and maple, his styles incorporating aspects of French and English traditional furniture.

She looked around the living room, imagined the carved Broadwood piano, the finely-curved chairs and carved-leg table, the tall china cabinet with its slender, haughty elegance, the ... They'd have to be reproductions, of course. She couldn't see Bruce forking out the kind of dollars needed for originals.

She didn't notice that Cass had wandered from the room, didn't hear her friend's shoes clack across the foyer tiles, didn't hear the soft creak as the door to unit three opened to Cass's firm push.

Her notepad dropped from her hand at the scream that echoed from wall to wall in the empty building.

CHAPTER NINE

'Cass! Cass! What's happened?' Ellie raced into the foyer and saw Cass backing out of the third doorway, her face white, hand over her mouth as though trying to prevent another scream breaking through. She turned to Ellie and Ellie's heart raced faster at the shock and horror in her eyes. She squeezed Cass's arm in brief comfort and walked, reluctantly, into the unit.

The multi-hued carpet would never hide the stain beneath the head of the young woman who lay, body twisted, head tilted at an awkward angle, long brown hair fanned like a halo. A deep gash split her forehead and one eyebrow and parted the skin over her smashed cheekbone. Blood, now dark and dried, had flowed across the nose and cheek, leaving the lips untouched. Chafed and swollen lips that, except for an almost-healed scar, were alabaster in death.

Fighting the inertia of shock, Ellie fumbled in her bag for her mobile. For a second she couldn't remember what buttons to press to unlock it, then habit kicked in and she was soon dialling the triple zero emergency number and asking for the police.

The connection was made, and her words were like autumn leaves in a storm, scattering everywhere, until she forced herself to take a deep breath, close her eyes, and concentrate on giving coherent information. At the end of the call she opened her eyes. She didn't want to look at the body. She wanted to run from the room, the building, to some place safe where death didn't take children from their parents. The young woman looked about Pru's and Miranda's age, and the fear rose in Ellie that she could lose them as swiftly as she had lost her son all those years ago. That same fear she'd fought so hard to control so she wouldn't smother her daughters in protectiveness and stop them from living life to its fullest.

The sound of Cass's quiet sobbing broke through the fear's paralysing grip and she moved leaden feet, one by one, until she stood close enough to Cass to hug, but her arms refused to reach out. 'I've called the police.'

Cass balled up the tissue she was using to wipe her eyes and pushed it into her pocket. 'Can we wait outside?'

'In the sunshine.' Ellie thought her voice sounded different - like she didn't own it.

'Sunshine would be good,' Cass agreed, and they hurried through the front door and stood on the path. For a minute they stood silent, then Cass started talking, asking questions that had no answers. 'Who is she?' 'How did she get in?' 'Who would have done that to her?' And Ellie stayed silent, not because she knew Cass had to talk to come to terms with what she'd seen, but because she felt as though she'd used all her words in talking to the police. She felt as though there wasn't a word left in her. So she stood, nodding her head to agree with Cass how terrible it was while inside her the emptiness, the aching, grew bigger.

When a police car pulled up and two officers got out,

Cass almost ran to greet them, but Ellie's feet refused to move. Police had come after Paul had died. Routine, they'd said, and they'd been kind, but Ellie had never fully lost the sense of bad news that seeing their blue uniforms imparted to her.

'Ellie Cummins?' the taller of the two asked, and Ellie nodded. She tried to find the words to introduce Cass, but they wouldn't leave her throat.

'I'm Senior Constable Chris Ryan and this is Constable Allan Pierce,' he tilted his head to the younger man standing beside and slightly behind him. He looked at Cass, but before he could ask she told him her name and how she'd found the girl and how horrible it was. 'Could you show me where you found her?' he asked, and Cass flinched as though he'd threatened to hit her.

'I'll show you,' Ellie said. She didn't want Cass to have to go into that room again. It was her fault that Cass was here; if she hadn't been such a wuss and asked Cass to come with her, Cass would be at home with her usual rituals of Saturday mornings instead of dealing with this trauma.

Ellie led the police officer into the house. She hesitated outside the third doorway, then stood aside. Chris Ryan walked into the room and wrote swiftly in a notebook as he surveyed the scene. Ellie followed his gaze. The body still lay like a broken doll, and although she tried not to look at it, her eyes were drawn to the face, to the hint of beauty that might have been there once. The deeply shadowed eyes and pimpled skin told of the young woman's lifestyle as much as the drug paraphernalia she now noticed strewn nearby. A scruffy backpack lay a few feet away, its contents scattered around as though they'd been tipped out and searched through; a small pink teddy bear looked up at her with dull eyes and cotton-thread mouth.

Humming started in Ellie's head. It was progressing to buzzing when she heard the officer's voice, sounding so far away, ask, 'Are you all right?'

The faint 'No' that formed in her mouth didn't come out, but he cupped her elbow and led her from the room and gently sat her on the stairs just as dizziness swept through her and her legs turned to rubber. Before she could think, her head was pushed between her knees and a firm arm went around her shoulders and stopped her from falling towards the floor. With relief, she felt the buzzing gradually abate and realised she needed to draw more air into her lungs.

'I don't normally faint,' she explained, and as she gradually pulled upright she realised Chris Ryan was sitting beside her. He held her just a fraction longer then moved his arm away.

'I fainted at my first autopsy.'

Ellie looked at him. He'd pushed his cap back to reveal unruly black hair sprinkled with grey. His eyes were a Paul Newman shade of blue, and they twinkled as he added, 'I found out later the coroner deliberately showed the worst parts to the new recruits. Apparently he liked hearing the thud as they hit the floor.'

'Obviously had a macabre sense of humour,' Ellie responded, and saw the twinkle deepen. 'Oh, in his profession ...' she mumbled as her choice of words registered in her slowly-clearing brain.

Before she could say any more, he pulled his lanky frame from the stairs and walked to greet more police officers. Suddenly it seemed like the place was swirling with blue uniforms. Before Ellie could work out their various ranks, two men in suits came through the front door. Chris Ryan spoke with them for a minute, then indicated the third doorway. The two men walked towards it, one nodded at Ellie and said, 'Be with you soon, Mrs Cummins,' as they passed.

Ellie thought about standing up but decided not to trust her legs just yet. She looked at Chris Ryan. 'You'd better brush your pants. The stairs weren't clean.'

He twisted around in a vain attempt to see his backside, then chuckled softly and swatted the dust from his dark pants. The movement was so natural and the sound so genuine she found herself smiling at him as though they'd shared a mutual secret. Then she wondered if that was his way of distracting her from the memory of their grim discovery and her smile faded.

A moment later the two suited men returned, one of them putting away his mobile and telling the other that the forensic girls had been delayed but were now on their way. The older of the two, a craggy-faced, pot-bellied man in his fifties, introduced himself as Senior Detective Wayne Warren from the local CIB, and the other man as Detective Mick Jones. He asked Ellie questions and Mick Jones wrote her replies in his notebook.

After she'd explained why she and Cass were in the building and what they'd seen, and given him Bruce Moloney's contact details, he told her she was free to leave.

'But you and Mrs Brighton will have to come into the station in the next seventy-two hours to make a statement.' He handed her his card. 'In the meantime, if you think of anything that might help us, please let me know. Would you like us to call someone to come and get you and Mrs Brighton, Mrs Cummins? Or are you okay to drive?'

'I'll be all right, detective.' Ellie got to her feet. She still felt a bit shaky but the fresh air outside would help. 'My bags are in the front unit. Is it okay if I get them?'

'Senior Constable Ryan will get them for you.'

Chris Ryan got her bags and escorted her to the front door. 'You'd better tell your husband about this as soon as you can,' he told her. 'You don't want him hearing about it on the news and thinking you might be the victim.'

Ellie smiled wanly. 'My husband and I are separated, Senior Constable Ryan. He lives in Sydney now. He doesn't know I was here today and I doubt it would worry him overly if he did.'

His face wore an expression of sympathy but she thought she saw a spark of something in those brilliant blue eyes that she could easily misconstrue as interest. 'So is there someone who can be there for you? Sometimes things like this can lead to delayed reactions.'

'I'm living with my youngest daughter.' Ellie thought of Miranda and her compassionate nature and relief flowed through her. She'd get far more sympathy from Miranda in a minute than Pru would give in a lifetime. Pru would just scold her for everything from taking on the work to not having the builder there to ensure her safety.

The officer who'd come with Chris Ryan was cordoning

off the building with crime scene tape. As he finished, a television van pulled up in front of the house, followed by a stationwagon with a newspaper logo on the side. A cameraman spilled from the passenger seat of the stationwagon and began clicking madly. Quickly angling them away from the camera, Chris Ryan hurried Ellie and Cass into Ellie's Magna.

By the time she had driven a couple of blocks, Ellie could almost imagine that the previous forty-five minutes had been a bad dream. But she closed her eyes for a second when they stopped at traffic lights and the girl's bloodied face swam into her mind. After that she focused so intently on the traffic as she drove back to Cass's house that she doubted she'd blinked the entire way.

Although she didn't want to stop at Cass's for coffee and discuss the horror they'd witnessed, Ellie knew she couldn't leave her friend alone if Joe had gone out. To her relief Joe was pruning shrubs in the garden and she said goodbye to Cass with a promise that she would go straight home and rest.

'Will you be all right?' Cass worried at her as she went to close the car door.

Ellie nodded. 'Miranda makes a great coffee. I'll probably have a full pot. Or maybe a bottle of ...' she was about to say red but the image of blood changed her mind. 'Maybe hot chocolate with lots of sugar,' she amended.

An hour later she realised just how good a listener her daughter had become. Miranda asked only a few questions and Ellie surprised herself by blurting out what had happened. After a while she fell silent, aware that Miranda's questions had been couched in terms that drew out information without appearing to be probing. 'Where did you learn that technique?' she asked and put her mug on the coffee table as she snuggled into the purple doona Miranda had placed around her on the lounge.

'What technique?' Miranda blinked at her over the top of her mug.

'Your questions. They ... let me tell you everything without feeling pressured. I was sure I wouldn't be able to talk about it.'

Miranda smiled. 'I saw the way the clients would talk to Ben - he's the guy who runs the food van. He wouldn't let us call them druggies or deros or anything like that. We had to treat the clients with respect and not pry into their lives. Just accept them. But I noticed that Ben would ask questions like *How did you feel about that?* or maybe just make statements like *That must have upset you* and even the most stubborn person would gradually open up to him. Then I read some books on active listening and saw the value in it.'

'You're quite amazing, Mirie.' Ellie found it difficult to accept that she had been oblivious to the layers that made up the unique human being Miranda had become. And with that realisation came shame she had let that happen. Skidding along the surface, she thought. Always being afraid to dig too deep into emotions. 'Thank you,' she said.

'For what?' Miranda seemed genuinely puzzled.

Ellie smiled. 'For being you.'

CHAPTER TEN

Dead!

The stupid bitch was dead.

Geoffrey Lenard stared at the television screen and cursed until his mouth became as dry as the bottle of cheap scotch he'd finished before collapsing on the futon that doubled as his bed in his tiny bedsit. But even in sleep he couldn't escape the memory of his bag of tools crunching into the woman's face, her cry of pain, the blood bright red in the glow of his torch beam, her bag spinning away from his boot and spilling its contents across the floor.

If he hadn't quite literally tripped over her as he made his way back to the window, he would never have reacted like that. It was the shock that made him lash out, striking her as she'd tried to rise. He kept telling himself that, but he wondered if it were true. He'd never killed anyone before. But *his* life was on the line. And he had so little time left. If he didn't find it soon ...

The newsreader droned on, her voice scraping at the ache in his head. He flicked the television off.

Silence.

There was no silence in jail. Even in the dead of night. There were always sounds to remind you that you weren't alone. You couldn't relax and let your guard down.

He couldn't go back there again. He almost shuddered at

the thought. Murder would mean a long stretch, and he'd barely survived his last short dip in that pool of human excrement. And he was getting too old to cope with the young toughs whose heads were screwed by drugs.

No, he would have to keep searching. But he'd have to wait a few days in case the cops were still around. And it would be harder now, they'd be sure to fix the window latch.

He had no choice.

He hoped no-one would get in his way, but if they did ...

He wondered if killing was easier the second time.

CHAPTER ELEVEN

The nightmares came again that night. Only this time Ellie's dreams swapped the lifeless bundle of a baby boy with the bloodied body of a young woman. A woman who had the face of Miranda, then Pru, then the girl on the floor of unit Three. By the time Ellie woke up on Sunday morning she felt as though she'd only slept for two hours all night. The bathroom mirror confirmed her suspicions. A long hot shower eased some of the creases around her eyes but the dark shadows beneath them needed more help than steam could give.

Cass had phoned last night to make sure Ellie was all right, and Ellie had reassured her she was fine. But as she'd slipped into bed, she had envied Cass the comfort and reassurance she knew her friend would get from Joe. And she wondered if Damien would have broken from his habitual indifference to soothe the fear and ease the ache in her heart if they'd still been together.

Now, as she finished showering and dressed in an old tracksuit that had been downgraded from fashion to house-and-yard-only status, she decided she would phone him this morning and tell him what had happened. He'd promised to keep in touch with her but so far hadn't done so.

She phoned him after breakfast, but as he was expressing

sympathy that sounded more polite than concerned, she heard a woman's voice in the background, and she didn't sound like she was discussing business. Well, only the kind of business that sprang to mind on a Sunday morning after a *very* good Saturday night.

'I see you've moved on,' Ellie said, trying to make her tone as cool as possible and not allow the little quiver of her lips to get worse.

Damien started to mutter an excuse, but Ellie found she didn't want to know. 'I hope you have a good life, Damien,' she said and hung up. In the past few weeks she'd believed she'd come to terms with the breakdown of her marriage, but now doubts flooded back. She'd thought they were both to blame for the disintegration of their relationship, but had Damien been seeing someone else all along? She told herself it didn't matter now, she was moving on, making a new life for herself. But she couldn't stop the terrible sense of betrayal that made her want to throw things at the wall or phone Damien back and scream at him that she hoped his dick dropped off or he caught something hugely embarrassing from the woman who didn't even have the diplomacy to shut up when her lover's wife was on the phone.

She looked up to find Miranda standing in the lounge room doorway, jeans tucked into her ugg boots, and pink jumper stretching halfway to her knees.

'It's really final then,' Miranda said. 'Between you and Dad I mean.'

Ellie took a deep breath and slowly released it. 'Yes. It certainly looks that way.'

'It's sad. I kind of hoped you two could get back together, now that you've become' she smiled apologetically, 'a bit more assertive, but I guess some things just aren't meant to be.'

'No, maybe they're not,' Ellie agreed, then stood up. 'But if I'm going to make a go of this interior design business then I'd better get stuck into it.' She looked around the room. 'Would you mind if we get rid of some of this furniture and put in a desk I can use to work from? There's no room in my bedroom.'

'Do what you want,' Miranda smiled. 'But when Grandad Bert visits next you'll have to explain why things have been changed.'

'Oh.' With a sinking heart Ellie remembered the temper tantrum Bert had thrown when Damien had brought him to visit and he'd seen Miranda's clothing on the washing line. Unable to make him understand that his beloved wife Eugenia didn't live there anymore, Damien had had to tell him that Miranda had come to visit for a few weeks before he would stop pulling out pegs and throwing her jeans and shirts in the rubbish bin. He wouldn't touch her underwear - Ellie doubted that he even knew what the thongs and brightly-coloured bras were. Eugenia had believed white was the only colour underwear should come in.

'I'll just have to handle that when the time comes,' Ellie said. 'In the meantime I'll use the kitchen table.'

'Don't forget to phone Pru and tell her what happened.' Miranda's *rather you than me* expression made Ellie's heart sink. Telling Pru about discovering a body would be difficult enough, she wasn't going to risk the righteous indignation that Ellie knew would be her elder daughter's response to the revelation about the other woman in Damien's life. Not that Ellie anticipated Pru being shocked at her father's actions. On the contrary. Ellie wouldn't be surprised if she complained it was due to Ellie's lack of support that Damien had been forced to find solace elsewhere. With a sigh of gratitude, she acknowledged Miranda's sympathetic grin.

Ellie wasn't the only one dreading making a phone call to a family member. Cass had picked up the phone twice last night and once this morning to phone her mother, but, at the thought of Audra's "I told you so" attitude, had quickly returned the handset to its cradle.

She gazed at the newspaper photo again. If it wasn't for the quick thinking of that Senior Constable, hers and Ellie's faces would have been clearly visible. As it was they were half-silhouettes she hoped were sufficiently indistinct as to be unrecognisable.

That hope was shattered when the phone rang and she saw Audra's number on the Caller ID panel. Cass looked at her watch. Audra and Gerry stuck to a routine that was more regular than Gerry's bowel movements, and right now they would be eating breakfast and reading the morning paper. She picked up the phone. 'Hello, Mum.'

'Is that you in that photo in the paper? What were you thinking of, going to that derelict place? And was it Ellie who was with you?'

Best to get it over with, Cass sighed. 'Yes, Mum. Joe's boss wanted Ellie to look at the units he'd bought and advise him how he could refurbish them in 1920s style and I said I'd go with her.'

'I told Gerry that was you in that tartan coat. I remember when you bought it. They haven't made anything like that in years.' Audra's voice faded, and Cass said nothing to fill in the silence that ensued. Then Audra spoke again. 'Are you all right? It must have been a terrible shock for you, finding that poor girl like that.'

It was almost as big a shock to hear the sympathy in Audra's voice. For an absurd moment Cass felt like crying. 'Yes, it was horrible. But I'm okay.'

'Well, I always did say you were made of sterner stuff than your brother. Heaven knows how he'd cope if he came across something like that. Probably lock himself in his ivory tower and throw away the key.'

Cass knew that Audra would never forgive her bookish brother Leon for refusing to go into the family shoe store after he left school. He had fled to the cerebral joy of university and never ventured back. Their father had died of a heart attack, brought about, Audra insisted, by the stress of running the business on his own when he should have had the support of his only son. She seemed oblivious to the fact that Cass had worked there, often putting in longer hours than her father, and never asking for overtime.

She wasn't sure if she was made of "sterner stuff", but Cass wasn't going to knock back Audra's unexpected support. Especially as it happened so rarely.

By three o'clock that afternoon Ellie had worked out a preliminary design for unit One. It was frustrating not having all the measurements for the unit. Cass discovering that poor girl's body had interrupted that, and now the building would be cordoned off as a crime scene for who knows how long. Her chest constricted at the memory of the girl's inert form. She pushed the image from her mind and concentrated on viewing the websites on furniture and furnishings Miranda had found for her on the internet. She'd seen several wallpapers she thought were promising and sent off emails requesting availability and prices. The second design she had in mind required knocking down walls to increase the size of the bathroom and add a small en suite to the master bedroom as well as create an office nook that could be easily disguised with folding doors or a feature curtain. She wasn't sure how much renovation Bruce was prepared to do - money seemed to be a big worry for him, and in the current economic climate she couldn't blame him for wanting to keep costs to a minimum. As it was he was taking a risk with such an innovative project.

She pushed the drawing board aside and stood up to stretch her back. In the past five minutes her thoughts had become more centred on a steaming cup of tea and a chocolate biscuit than claw-foot bathtubs. As she walked over to the kitchen bench to put the kettle on, a knock sounded on the front door.

'I'll get it,' Miranda called.

Ellie smiled. She'd noticed the dreamy look that had crossed Miranda's face when she'd spoken about Ben, the man who organised the food van, and she'd wondered if there could be more to it than wishful thinking.

When Miranda appeared in the kitchen doorway a

moment later, Ellie was surprised to see the enquiring look on her face. 'There's a man here to see you. Says he's a police officer. But he's not in uniform.'

'It's probably that CIB detective,' Ellie said and walked into the lounge room. And stopped in surprise. It wasn't Wayne Warren with his lined face and sloping stomach, but Senior Constable Chris Ryan, checked shirt and jeans covering his lanky body. Ellie blinked. Riding boots. He was wearing riding boots. All he needed was an Akubra and she could imagine him rounding up cattle or herding sheep.

He saw her staring and grinned. 'Sorry for the informality. A mate of mine owns a property up Samford way and we go riding sometimes. He has some great horses.' He paused a moment, then as Ellie made no response, continued. 'I was a bit concerned about you. You didn't look too good yesterday.'

Ellie had trouble finding her tongue. Yesterday she'd noticed little about him except his striking blue eyes but now she noticed the pleasing symmetry of his bone structure and the way it made his facial features, which were nothing extraordinary on their own, quite attractive. 'Would you like to sit down?' she finally managed. 'I was just going to make some tea ... or coffee if you'd rather?'

'Thanks. I could do with a coffee. I had a beer with my mate but when you're driving ...' he let the sentence hang and sat on the lounge.

'I'll make the coffee and bring it out,' Miranda called from the kitchen, and Ellie didn't know whether to be grateful she didn't have to leave Constable Ryan alone to gaze at the conglomeration of furniture and furnishings that laughed at her story about being an interior designer, or worried that being alone with him when he was obviously off duty was putting their relationship on another level.

Relationship? Where had that word come from? All they'd shared yesterday was a distracting smile and she'd assumed it had been his way of taking her mind from the horror of what she'd just seen.

She settled herself at the other end of the lounge, annoyed that the other lounge chair was tucked into a corner and supporting a pile of Miranda's books. With them both on the lounge they had to angle their bodies towards each other in order to make eye contact. Which brought their knees perilously close together. 'It was kind of you to think about me.' The words sounded inane, but she was having trouble thinking of anything brilliant to say.

'I know you didn't know the ... victim,' he began, pacing his words as though making sure they were the right ones, 'but even so, it's not something you get over in a hurry.'

'No,' she agreed, 'I guess not.' She felt awkward, aware that his coming to see her was completely unofficial. 'Thank you for being concerned, but you didn't have to worry.'

'When I was riding I remembered what you said about your husband probably not worrying about you. But I see,' he smiled as Miranda brought in a tray with mugs, coffee, milk, sugar and a plate of chocolate biscuits and put it on the coffee table, 'you're being well looked after.'

Ellie hurriedly made introductions.

'I'll get the kettle as soon as it's boiled,' Miranda said. 'Have they identified the woman yet, Constable Ryan?' she asked.

'Please, I'm off duty, call me Chris. And yes, her belongings were in the room and her bag contained ID. The details will be on the news tonight so it won't matter if I tell you now. Her name was Cherilyn Manning. She was twenty-three and -'

'Shit!' Miranda's face paled. 'Cherilyn!'

'You knew her?' Chris asked, his body tensing to an alertness that told Ellie the police officer part of him wasn't far beneath the surface.

'You remember Cherilyn, Mum?' Miranda plonked down onto the floor as though her legs were suddenly unable to hold her up.

There was something about the name that seemed familiar to Ellie, but no details, no face - certainly not the one on the dead body, came to mind. 'Was she at school with you?'

'No, but she was on my netball team when I was still in high school. Remember, the plump one with the mole on her cheekbone that wouldn't stop bleeding when the ball hit it that time?'

'But that ...' Ellie found it hard to reconcile the memory of that girl with the lank-haired, skinny young woman on the floor of unit three.

'Remember how we gave her a lift home that Saturday afternoon because the game was cancelled when the storm hit and she would have had to wait for an hour in the rain for a bus?' Miranda pressed on, as though by making Ellie remember she was able to share her disbelief and maybe her fear that murder could strike someone she knew. Or had known.

'I remember the girl,' Ellie shook her head, 'but I would never have known it was her. In the unit, I mean.'

'We don't have any leads on who killed her,' Chris directed their thoughts back to the present, 'so if there's anything you could tell me,' he looked at Miranda, 'that might give us some insight into her life, it might help.'

Miranda opened her mouth but the whistle of the kettle stopped whatever she was about to say. She pulled herself to her feet. 'I'll get the hot water.'

When she returned she filled the mugs, handed them to Ellie and Chris and picked up her own. 'I don't think I can help you, Chris,' she said. 'I was seventeen when I last played netball with Cherilyn. If you don't mind I'm almost finished a book I was reading and I'd like to get back to it. Nice meeting you.'

'Sure. Thanks for the coffee.'

As Miranda walked away, Ellie had the uneasy suspicion that her daughter was hiding something. She looked at Chris. If he had sensed anything it wasn't showing on his face.

'Have you been able to work on any designs for the units?' he asked, and Ellie was grateful the subject of Cherilyn Manning had been abandoned. She told him what she'd been able to do so far, and as he asked questions about the project - questions that showed he was truly interested and not simply being polite - she felt her enthusiasm growing. It had been such a long time since a man had shown any interest in her capabilities that she found herself almost glowing in the unexpected attention. Then, to her horror, she actually was glowing.

Heat rose in her like a tidal wave, washing sweat from every pore. She nearly gasped with surprise. In the past couple of months she'd had the occasional hot flush, but they'd been mild. Especially compared with this one.

'Are you okay?' Chris asked.

Ellie took a tissue from her pocket and dabbed at her face. 'I'm just warm. These old houses hold the heat in the afternoon,' she lied, and the lie compounded her embarrassment. 'I'll just let some air in.' She jumped up and went to the front door. As she opened it, she saw Cass and Kandy walking up the path.

CHAPTER TWELVE

'Ellie, we've been so worried about you,' Kandy called and hurried ahead of Cass. She took the two steps to the front porch in a leap and hugged Ellie. 'It must have been horrible. You -' She stopped as she looked into the lounge room. Her arms dropped to her sides. 'Sorry. I didn't realise you had a visitor.' She looked back towards the street as though confirming something to herself.

'My Rodeo is parked a little further up the street. I missed the house number,' Chris said as he stood up, and Ellie felt a stab of disappointment at the smile he gave Kandy. She quickly tamped down the surge of jealousy that shot through her, surprised at the unfamiliar emotion.

Surprise was also written all over Cass's face, but she quickly concealed it. 'Hello, Constable,' she said. 'I didn't recognise you at first. Have you found out who killed that poor girl?'

'Not yet, Mrs Brighton.' He looked at Ellie. 'I'd better get going. It's my turn to cook tonight and I haven't taken anything out of the freezer yet.'

Ellie's mood dropped even lower as Kandy practically purred, 'Your wife is lucky to have a husband who doesn't mind cooking.'

Chris looked at her as he replied, 'My wife died ten years

ago,' then his gaze returned to Ellie. 'My son and I have been looking after each other since. He's more adventurous in the kitchen than I am, but he tolerates my lack of imagination.' He walked towards the door, and Ellie saw the amusement in his eyes at the way Kandy scrutinized him as though he were a suspect in a line-up. Or a slave on the block. Or, and Ellie fought to control the thought, a potential bed-mate.

'Come on,' Cass ushered Kandy towards the kitchen, 'we'll make a cuppa while Ellie sees the constable out.'

'Ladies,' Chris nodded to them. Ellie walked him to the door. 'Thanks for the coffee,' he said as he stopped on the top step. 'I'd like to repay the favour. Would you go out with me some time? Perhaps to the movies?'

The refusal that sprang instantly to Ellie's tongue refused to shape into words. In all the years of being married to Damien she'd never strayed. Never even seriously been tempted by a sexy grin or a nicely toned body. There were barriers in her mind with "Married" written all over them. But the conversation with Damien that morning, or rather the conversation the woman in the room with him was trying to have, had chipped away at those blocks as surely as Michelangelo's chisel had carved out the statue of David. 'I'd like that,' she said.

'I'll call you.' The warmth in his eyes stayed with her even after he'd walked to his vehicle.

Kandy pounced as soon as she walked back into the lounge. 'Ellie, you'd better not tell me that gorgeous man had come to see you simply to tell you they hadn't caught the killer yet. He could have done that over the phone.

Besides, he's not on the homicide squad, Cass said he's a uniform cop. Not that he was in uniform.' Her appreciation of that fact showed on her face. 'So? Why was he here?'

'He came to see if I was all right after yesterday.' Ooops, there was that heat starting again. Ellie dug in her pocket for a tissue and dabbed at the sweat that beaded on her forehead and neck.

The smile on Kandy's face widened. Ellie gave up and flung herself down on the lounge. 'All right! He's asked me out. To the movies. Some time.'

'Praise the Lord!' Kandy waggled her hands in the air. 'I was beginning to think he must have been blind and stupid.'

'He'd have to be to be interested in me,' Ellie muttered, and saw Cass shaking her head at her.

'Don't put yourself down, Ellie,' Cass said. 'You're a very attractive woman.'

'I'm forty-eight-years-old, in a tracksuit that should have been sent to the ragbag but is so comfortable I can't make myself do so. I look like I haven't slept in a week. And I'm menopausal.'

'It's about time you started,' Cass said. 'I've been on the downhill slide for years. But I am a bit older than you.'

'I need a red wine,' Ellie groaned. 'Just when I thought I was carrying on an interesting conversation, I started sweating like I'd run a marathon and flushed so badly I was grateful the horrible curtains in here make the room dull.'

'It's not fair,' Kandy commiserated. 'Men go through male menopause and get a red sports car and a buxom blonde but it's the opposite for women. Have you ever noticed,' she twirled a shapely jeans-encased leg in the air, 'that if your best feature is being x-rayed, the radiologist looks like John Candy, but the gynaecologist who's examining your forty-four-year-old vagina that resembles an eroded creek bed obviously moonlights as Hunk of the Month?'

'And the red wine that makes you forget that you can't remember what you did in the previous twenty-four hours leads to big hot flushes that remind you you're still menopausal,' Cass muttered, seemingly unperturbed by her convoluted logic.

'It's been months since I've had a period, so that's a bonus,' Ellie smiled, then her hand flew to her mouth. 'Shit! I hadn't plucked those chin hairs!'

'But your copper still asked you to go out with him,' Kandy pointed out. 'So spill, Ellie. What's his name? And how long was he here and when are you going out? And did you notice what a nice firm butt he's got? Those jeans fit *very* well.'

'You lot are worse than teenagers!' Miranda said from the doorway.

'Teenagers have more to ogle,' Kandy informed her, probably with more meaning than necessary. 'When you get to our age you have to take what you can get.'

'Are you going out with him, Mum?' Miranda's question hung in the air with all the intent of a pointed gun. Cass and Kandy concentrated on drinking their coffee.

Ellie's teeth caught at her bottom lip. All the implications of going out with Chris Ryan hit her. It wasn't just seeing a movie with an attractive man, it was a date, a foray back into the world of possibly finding a mate, of building a relationship. Or, her rational mind interjected, it could be just a fun evening with a nice man and nothing more. 'Yes,' her rational mind said, and her hopeful one crossed its fingers behind her back.

Miranda shrugged. 'He seems okay.'

'It's only the movies.'

'Whatever.' It was a reply typical of when Miranda had been a teenager and thought pretending complete indifference to the subject would say more than any statement she could make. Ellie wanted to ask what was bothering her but decided to wait until they were alone.

The opportunity to talk came later that day when Ellie was cooking omelettes for their dinner and Miranda wandered into the kitchen for a drink.

Ellie poured the whipped eggs into a pan. 'Mirie, do you have a problem with me going out with Chris Ryan?'

'No way.' Miranda's response was genuine. 'Go for it, Mum, you deserve some happiness.'

Ellie changed tack. 'I had the feeling you knew a bit more about Cherilyn Manning than you told Chris,' she said as Miranda poured lime mineral water into a glass.

'Why would you think that?' Miranda put the bottle back in the fridge and picked up the glass.

'I could tell by the look on your face. You've never been very good at hiding things, Mirie.' *Even if I haven't always been good at seeing them, and for that I'm sorry.*

'I couldn't tell him, Mum. If the cops come snooping around the food van asking questions Ben will lose all the trust the clients have in him.'

Ellie sprinkled ham and cheese onto one half of the omelette and folded it over. 'Did Cherilyn come to the van?'

Miranda nodded. 'She came about six months ago. I didn't recognise her at first, and when I did and tried to talk to her she didn't want to know me. I think ...' Miranda's top teeth worried at her bottom lip in a gesture Ellie realised was so like her own, 'I think she didn't want me to see how she'd changed. Maybe she thought I would judge her. But I wouldn't do that. Ben says any one of us could have ended up on the streets if our lives had been different.' She looked up at Ellie. 'Do you remember what Cherilyn's house looked like, when we gave her a lift that afternoon?'

The rain had been pouring down for a while by the time they'd reached Cherilyn's house and Ellie had only gained a vague impression of an overgrown front yard and old car bodies surrounded by weeds in the back yard. 'It was pretty messy.'

'Cherilyn hated living there. She said all her mother cared about was going to the pub and playing the pokies. I know most teenagers complain that their parents don't understand them, but basically they know their parents love them. From what Cherilyn said I think hers hated her.'

'Do you think she was abused?'

'I don't think so. But she had a pretty poor opinion of herself and that seemed to come from what her parents said to her.'

Ellie thought of the thinness of Cherilyn's body that her jacket and jeans couldn't disguise and the pathetic bundle of belongings and her heart ached with sadness. To die such a terrible death was bad enough but to have lived without being loved was cruel. 'I hope they catch whoever killed her.'

'They probably won't. They'll make a few enquiries but no-one will talk to them and they'll put it down to a drug deal gone wrong and move on to a more important case.'

For one vividly clear moment, Ellie remembered the meagre contents of Cherilyn's backpack: underwear, jeans and a couple of tee-shirts, a notebook, some crumpled envelopes and photos, a toiletry plastic bag. And a small pink teddy bear. Ellie felt herself crumpling at the thought that the bear was the only remnant of a childhood that had not given Cherilyn the love all children deserve.

'Mum? Are you all right?'

Ellie blinked. Miranda was shaking her arm. 'You went all funny,' she said and gently pushed her onto a chair. 'Sit down. I'll finish the omelettes.'

In that subtle role reversal, Ellie discovered she was no longer *the mother*. Somehow over the past couple of weeks, and without her really noticing it, she had become a housemate and, she hoped now, a friend. And there was a certain amount of freedom in the realisation. Sometimes being a mother could be a burden - you were always supposed to know what to do, what was the correct decision to make. As a friend she could offer her opinion and not, supposedly, be offended if it wasn't held in high regard.

'When did you last see Cherilyn?' she asked.

Miranda flipped the omelette onto a plate, turned the electricity a little lower and poured more beaten eggs into the frypan. 'Two nights before you and Cass found her. It had been ages since I'd last seen her. And before you ask, no, she didn't say anything that could give any idea of who killed her. She -'

When Miranda didn't continue, Ellie prompted her, 'She what?'

'When we were packing up the van to leave, I saw Cherilyn talking to one of the other clients who come to the van. They were a bit far away, but I'm sure I recognised him.'

'What did they do?'

'Just talk, as far as I could see. Then Cherilyn left.'

'Well, it's a start. At least that's one name we can give to the police.'

Miranda looked at Ellie as though she'd grown another head. 'No, we can't! Didn't you hear what I said before? We can't have the cops sticking their noses into our clients - they'd never trust us again. They'll think we'll tell the cops.'

'But we just can't -'

'I want Cherilyn's killer caught too. But you'll just have to trust me on this, Mum. If I can find out anything that will help I'll let you know and you can tell the cops.'

Ellie wanted to protest. Up until now she hadn't been overly worried about Miranda helping on the food van, but Cherilyn's murder had reminded her that some of the clients Miranda spoke about so protectively were drug addicts and dealers who could get desperate enough to eliminate anyone who interfered in their lives. She looked at the calendar on the wall. 'You're rostered on tomorrow night, aren't you?'

'Yes. And it's usually a night when Mou -' she glanced quickly at Ellie then concentrated on flipping the omelette.

'When I can get a chance to talk with the clients.'

With one particular *client*, Ellie thought, but she kept that observation to herself.

Two hours later Ellie phoned Kandy and asked for her help.

'You want to do *what*?' Kandy asked.

'I want to follow the food van Miranda volunteers with and make sure she doesn't get into trouble when she questions the clients.'

'Clients!' Kandy snorted. 'How very PC. So where do Cass and I come in?'

'Not Cass.' Ellie shook her head vigorously. 'She got such a shock when she found Cherilyn's body, I don't want to put her in a situation like that again. She doesn't need the trauma.'

'But I do?'

Hell! Ellie couldn't believe she'd been so thoughtless to imply Kandy's feelings meant less than Cass's. Then she heard a low rumble of laughter and realised Kandy had been teasing her.

'So when do I pick you up?' Kandy asked.

'No, I'd better pick you up. One look at your Porsche and we'd be mugged the moment we opened the door.'

By Monday evening Ellie had almost changed her mind about "Operation Mou", as she'd begun to call her plan. But when she arrived home in the cold and the dark the anxiety about Miranda that had bothered her all day increased. She ate a toasted sandwich, gulped down a coffee, and changed into boots, jeans, sweater and a dark coat. She was just pulling on a black wool beanie that she'd bought in her lunch break when there was a knock at the front door and she rushed to open it.

Kandy stood there. And so did Cass. Both dressed in dark pants and jackets.

'Before you get mad,' Kandy said and stepped into the lounge room, 'I figured it was only fair that Cass had the chance to decide for herself if she wanted to be part of your cloak and dagger scheme.'

'And I do,' Cass said, following her and giving Ellie a quick hug. 'I know you were only trying to protect me Ellie, but I'm tougher than I thought I was. And I couldn't live with myself if something happened to Miranda.'

A wobble started in Ellie's jaw but she clenched it instead.

'Get your bag, honey bee,' Kandy said, 'and let's get moving. I've got coffee and muffins,' she indicated the large bag she was carrying, 'and binoculars. I know private eyes carry empty bottles to pee in when they can't stop watching the subject, but there's no way I'm trying that in your little car. I'd probably end up with the gear stick up my arse. Besides, I figure with three of us there, nicking off to a loo for a few minutes won't be a problem.'

For one mad moment, Ellie was sure she could feel the swish of capes and the zing of rapiers meeting in a mad Musketeer chorus. Then sanity returned and she hurried to get her car keys.

CHAPTER THIRTEEN

The Magna slid quietly to a stop beneath an overhanging Camphor Laurel tree in New Farm Park and Ellie switched off the headlights. The food van was parked three hundred metres away, under a street light, easily seen from most parts of the park.

'I can see Miranda,' Kandy said from the back seat, binoculars to her eyes. 'The back door of the van is up and she's there with a big box. I can't see what's in it. Wait, she's just handed a packet to a scruffy-looking kid, so they must be the sandwiches and cake. And there's a nice-looking young man at the side of the van who's giving out Styrofoam cups, so that must be Ben the coffee boy.'

Ellie looked through her binoculars. So that was Ben. Good-looking in a straw-haired, country-boy sort of way. She wondered how he felt about Miranda.

She'd expected to see only street kids coming to the van, but as the minutes dragged on people of all ages and some she came to think of as the stereotypical homeless, drifted towards the van, took what was offered, and moved on. Some, like wraiths, seemed to be swallowed up by the darker areas of the park. Others, like the old woman pushing a supermarket trolley half-filled with blankets and cardboard boxes, stayed chatting to Miranda and Ben for a considerable length of time. What surprised Ellie was the quiet dignity of most of them.

After thirty minutes of conversation and speculation, Ellie, Cass and Kandy gradually drifted into silence. The reality of being a watcher set in, along with a numb bum, aching back and the urge to sleep that boredom brought. The warmth from the car heater had dissipated, but their thick jackets staved off the chill that crept in.

Just as Ellie thought she'd have to ask Kandy for a coffee to keep her eyelids from drooping closed, she saw Miranda and Ben close up the van and drive off. 'Come on,' she said and started the car, 'we have to follow them to the next location.'

'I thought you said you'd asked Miranda where they park the van?' Cass asked.

'I did. But when I looked up some of the streets I realised they were so long I should have asked her for the nearest cross street. If I drive past the van I risk her recognising my car.' She swung out into the road and followed at what she hoped was a reasonable distance.

A few minutes later the van pulled up in an ill-lit street in an industrial area. Ellie quickly switched off the Magna's headlights and parked.

'Why would they come here?' Cass looked at the wire fences surrounding huge steel-walled warehouses, older brick buildings that bordered the footpath, wholesale shops and takeaways that screamed functional rather than fashionable.

'For the ones who aren't game to come into the park,' Kandy said softly.

If she hadn't been using binoculars, Ellie wouldn't have seen the faces shadowed by hoods and scarves on the shapes that emerged from the darkness and shuffled in spasmodic bursts to the van. Wouldn't have seen the despair, the hopelessness, the dull resignation, the intelligence lost to drugs or mental retardation. Or the flicker of gratitude for the caring expressed in food and drink.

She watched the way Miranda interacted with the "clients", the genuine compassion her daughter obviously felt for these people who had become the forgotten part of society, and realised how superficial her own giving to the community had been.

After speaking with one particular client, a woman dressed in an ankle-length skirt and old sheepskin jacket several sizes too big for her small frame, Miranda nodded to Ben, grabbed something from the front seat of the van, then followed the woman up the street. The woman stopped in front of an alleyway, pointed somewhere into its dark cavity, then hurried away. Ellie watched Miranda hesitate, then walk into that darkness.

'Where the hell is she going?' Ellie growled. She waited, eyes straining, the seconds ticking by. It was probably only a minute, maybe two, but it felt like a lifetime, and Miranda didn't reappear. 'That does it.' Ellie put down the binoculars, picked up a torch, and opened the car door. 'I'm going after her.'

'I'm going with you,' Cass opened her door.

'We're all mad,' Kandy muttered, and got out. 'You two follow. I'll drive closer and keep the car running in case we need to make a quick getaway.'

They'd worn sneakers, but their footsteps sounded loud in the still, crisp night air. The pavement was bitumen, broken and uneven in places, and they stumbled in their haste, grabbing each other for support. At an old brick building that formed one corner of the entrance to the alleyway, they stopped. Ellie looked around the corner. Dark though the street had been, the alleyway was darker. She took two paces forward, closed her eyes for a moment to let them adjust to the greater darkness, then opened them. Rubbish bins, industrial size. Boxes - some cardboard, some timber. Garbage lay in windswept piles against doorways and obstacles. The smell of rot hung in the air - timber rot, food rot, and, Ellie was sure, body rot. And the acridity of stale urine.

Cass stayed behind her, closer than a shadow. Ellie was tempted to switch on her torch, but didn't want to betray their presence.

They moved cautiously, slowly, trying to see where Miranda had gone. Cockroaches scurried in the garbage, making it seem alive. Ellie hoped it was cockroaches. Better them than rats. She remembered rats from her childhood - the derelict house across the road that swarmed with them, the way they boldly ran across in the night and invaded her home in their search for food. The council rat-catchers with their fox terriers that ferreted out the rats and bit their necks and killed them. Blood dripping. Limp furry bodies. Nightmares. She shuddered.

Halfway down the alleyway her trepidation turned to gut-shrivelling fear. Miranda had disappeared.

'Are you scared?' Cass whispered, so close the back of

Ellie's neck prickled.

'No,' Ellie hissed. 'I'm pissing my pants because I like the warmth.'

The words were barely said when she felt sorry for their harshness. She turned to apologise, and found her mouth wouldn't work.

Nothing would work - her mouth, her legs, her arm that should have been lifting up to point out to Cass the dark shape coming down the alleyway after them.

CHAPTER FOURTEEN

Cass had heard that fear could be paralysing, but it wasn't until she turned around to see what Ellie was staring at that she knew it was true. Her tongue stuck to the bottom of her mouth.

A man, tall, broad across the shoulders, face in shadow from the faint glimmer of a light further up the road behind him.

Something cudgel-shaped in his right hand.

He walked towards them.

His arm came up and light seared across their eyes. Instinctively they raised their arms in front of their faces.

'Who are you?' the man called out. 'What are you doing?'

Kandy's voice echoed down the alleyway. 'Ellie? Cass? Are you all right?'

'Mum?' Miranda's voice joined in from the other end.

Ellie spun around. Miranda was jogging down the alleyway towards them, torch flickering across the garbage in her way. Relief rushed through Ellie, making her knees weak. If Cass hadn't grabbed her elbow she was sure she would have slid to the ground. When Miranda reached them, Ellie wanted to hug her, but the expression on Miranda's face indicated that wasn't a good idea.

'*What* are you doing here, Mum?' Miranda looked around. 'What's going on?'

Before Ellie could answer, Ben intervened. 'I saw two people follow you in here and got worried. I didn't know one of them was your mother. When I saw the car pull up outside I thought you might need some help so I came over. But I think we should go back to the van now, grab a coffee, and talk there.'

'Did you lock the van?' Miranda asked as they walked.

'Yes. But I wouldn't trust it to stay in one piece if we're away from it for too long.'

Ellie thought about her car and how desperate she would be without it and increased her pace. She didn't relish telling Miranda why she'd followed her. Even as a child Miranda had been independent and Ellie wondered if she would understand how worried she'd been.

Five minutes, a hot coffee and a reluctant explanation later, Ellie discovered Ben was on her side.

'Your mother had every right to be concerned, Miranda,' he said. 'If I'd known why you were trying to contact Mouse I'd have gone with you.'

'Would you?' The surprise on Miranda's face was almost surpassed by pleasure. Ellie noticed that Ben seemed oblivious to this, but forgave him this lack as the veiled threat of lynching in Miranda's eyes lessened as she said, 'Sorry, Mum. I thought if Mouse would tell me what Cherilyn did after she spoke to him I could pass that to the police and they wouldn't come and harass the van clients.'

'But this ... Mouse ... could have been the killer,' Ellie protested. 'And you could have put yourself in danger by trying to find him.'

'I don't think Mouse is capable of violence,' Ben said. 'He's not like a lot of street kids. He's naive in a lot of ways. He loves animals, shares his sandwiches with stray cats and dogs.'

'I watch television crime shows,' Kandy mused. 'He probably lures them into the bushes and kills them.'

'I would never do that.'

The five of them spun around, searching for who had spoken. The words had been soft, as though the speaker had said them to himself. Miranda walked around to the street side of the van. 'Hello, Mouse. Did Nipsy tell you I needed to talk to you?'

Like a wave on the sand the others followed her. Mouse took a step back, worry compressing his eyebrows, and looked to Miranda for reassurance. His eyes were hazy, his clothing permeated with the unmistakable muskiness of marijuana. 'She said it was about Cherilyn. It's my fault, you know. I shouldn't have told her to go there. I never told Jackson, but he must have found out.'

'What did you tell her, Mouse?'

'To go to the building. I thought she could sleep there at night and be safe. The latch on a window at the back didn't work.'

'Who's Jackson?' Ben asked.

'Cherilyn's boyfriend. But he bashed her.'

'Did you see her again after you talked to her in the park?' Miranda this time. Mouse looked at her as though not comprehending. 'I saw you talking to Cherilyn two nights before she was killed.'

'No. Didn't see her after that. I told her I wouldn't tell Jackson I'd seen her.'

'What's Jackson's other name? Do you know where he stays?'

'Dunno. You just gotta ask around and you get to find him.'

'Is anybody saying who might have killed her?'

Mouse shook his head. 'Can I have some sandwiches? I got nothing since breakfast.'

'Sure, mate.' Ben opened the van's back door and pulled a couple of packets out of a box. 'Here's some for lunch tomorrow too.'

'Thanks, Miranda.' Mouse ignored Ben and smiled at Miranda. He clutched the packets to his chest and wandered off as silently as he'd arrived. They watched him drift into the alley and get swallowed by the darkness.

Ellie shivered, acutely aware of how alien she felt. This was her city, she lived here, had raised two children here, but right now she felt as though she didn't know it at all. 'I guess we have a possibility at least.' She turned to Miranda and Ben. 'Do you know this Jackson?'

Miranda shook her head. Ben thought a moment then said, 'I haven't heard anyone mention him, but I can ask around.'

'Mum, you're not going to tell that policeman about Mouse, are you?'

Ellie hesitated. Mouse was their only connection to Cherilyn before her murder. But she understood Miranda's dilemma. They both wanted the killer caught but the trust Ben had worked so hard to achieve with his clients could be shattered by a heavy-handed police investigation. 'I'll give Jackson's name to the detective investigating the case. I won't tell him how I got it.'

'Thank you, Ellie,' Ben said. 'Now we'd better get moving. We have one more stop to make.'

'And *we*,' Kandy pulled her jacket closer around her chest, 'need a drink. Preferably somewhere warm.'

The answering machine was beeping when they returned to Miranda's house. Funny, Ellie thought, even after all the weeks she'd lived there she still felt like a visitor, as though she had no right to call it *her* house.

Cass and Kandy decided to go straight back to their homes, so Ellie poured a glass of wine, grabbed pen and paper and listened to the messages. And cursed herself for the flutter of reaction when she heard Chris's deep voice asking if she was still willing to go to the movies with him. She scribbled down the number he'd left and checked her watch - ten fifteen. Too late to return his call. She'd phone him tomorrow.

The second message was from Bruce Moloney, wanting to know if she was still going to do the interior design on the units. He grumbled about the unit being a crime scene and not having access to it. Some of the brashness had gone from his voice, and Ellie wondered if he was worried that Cherilyn's murder in his block of units would lead to them being harder to sell. She also noted that he hadn't expressed any concern for her wellbeing, but from what Cass had told her about the man, people skills were not his forte.

Two glasses of wine later, she slipped into bed. Miranda

still hadn't come home, but she wasn't game to phone and ask where she was. Once in a night was probably all she was allowed on Miranda's interfering-mother scale. Maybe even once a week was stretching it.

Ellie's dreams that night weren't quite nightmares, but dark alleyways figured prominently and Miranda's face became jumbled with Cherilyn's and she woke several times with her heart beating so fast she was gasping in panic. She wondered if Cherilyn's murder had become so personal to her because of the association with Miranda, or if everyone who saw a dead body reacted this way.

After breakfast she phoned Chris and discussed movie choices and times. Then she phoned Detective Warren and told him about Cherilyn's boyfriend Jackson. When he questioned her as to how she'd come by the information, she was glad she wasn't talking to him in person. She'd never learned how to lie effectively, and even evasion made her fumble her words. Now she had the added complication of a hot flush suffusing her body. She mumbled something about not being able to reveal her source, hung up, and ran to the bathroom.

'If that's what the flames of hell feel like,' she mumbled at her mirror image as she doused her face with cold water, 'then I'd better start praying for the redemption of my immortal soul.'

She made a mental note to make a doctor's appointment. HRT loomed on her horizon like an oasis.

Luckily Ellie's hormones behaved themselves when she and Cass went to the police station on her Tuesday lunch break to make their statements, but that was probably because Detective Warren wasn't there and she didn't have to lie to him.

As she gave her statement to a young policeman, she couldn't help glancing at every blue uniform she saw, and mentally berating herself for acting like a gauche teenager. Chris Ryan had asked her to the movies - it was no big deal. It was a casual date, nothing more. And if her knees went weak at the memory of how good his butt looked in jeans and the warmth in his eyes as he'd told her he would look forward to their date, well, it was probably because she was starved of male attention and it really didn't mean anything.

But she knew she was no better at lying to herself than she was to other people.

By the time Wednesday evening came around she was more nervous than on her first date with Damien. Ah, the brashness of youth, she thought. Back then she hadn't had to stay home on a Saturday night unless she was sick. The trail of young men to her parents' door didn't seem to cease. Nor did her father's criticism of each and every one of them.

Now she wondered if that was why she'd married Damien. He was the only boyfriend who'd achieved her father's stamp of approval, and life was so much easier when her father approved of things. Like it was when Damien approved of things.

'Mum, it's a suburban cinema, not opening night at the Opera House,' Miranda told her when she asked her advice on yet another outfit. 'Just wear your black pants and that nice green shirt that matches your eyes. And take a jacket. The air-con in that theatre hovers around freezing. And it will be cold when you come out.'

'Yes, Mother,' Ellie quipped and smiled at Miranda's raised eyebrow and quirk of her lips. It wasn't easy, this balancing act of feeling like a mother but acting like a friend. She'd thought she'd cut the apron strings years ago, but was discovering that time didn't lessen biological instincts. Unlike some other species, she decided, the need to protect your offspring didn't cease when they left the family nest. But her chick was grown, and sometimes now Ellie felt like a cuckoo in the nest.

She glanced at her watch, realised how much time she'd wasted, and quickly dressed in what Miranda had suggested. She gathered her jacket and bag just as a knock sounded on the door.

If she'd been appreciative of Chris's jeans-clad butt it was nothing compared to the mouth-watering sensation that gripped her as she took in the dark grey pants, pale blue shirt and steel-grey leather jacket he wore tonight. She knew he wasn't drop-dead gorgeous, but something about him called to every feminine instinct she owned that said sex with this man would not be boring.

As if sensing her reaction, the gleam in his eyes deepened. She knew the tingling that started running down her breasts had nothing to do with menopause. Especially when it went further.

It was his eyes, she decided. That brilliant shade of blue that had an almost laser-like quality to it. And there was just the right length between nose and lips. She'd noticed that on

Viggo Mortensen when she'd watched the *Lord of the Rings* movies. His nose wasn't short or long, but just right. Symmetry. Balance. Like when furniture fitted in a room exactly how it should.

She took his outstretched hand and walked with him to his vehicle.

When the movie finished, Chris took Ellie to a small restaurant that specialised in exotic desserts. A blueberry Danish swirled with chocolate and plumped with the lightest custard cream Ellie had ever tasted complemented a rich Moroccan coffee and left her feeling delightfully decadent. Lately, food had become a necessity rather than a pleasure, but she wondered if tonight her taste buds had been sensitised by the enjoyment she found in Chris's company.

After the trauma of the past few days, she was grateful the movie she'd selected was a romantic comedy. There was something cleansing about a good laugh. And now she was discovering how enjoyable it was to have a conversation with a man who was genuinely interested in her. Well, that's what it felt like, and she wasn't willing to believe otherwise.

It was only on the drive home that he asked the question that put a dampener on her mood. 'How did you get that information about Jackson?'

It was as effective as the cold water she'd splashed on her face when she'd evaded the same question from Detective Warren. 'I can't tell you. It would be betraying my source.'

To her surprise, he burst into laughter. Laughter that

rumbled deep in his chest and split his face into a grin that negated her decision to be aloof and offended. 'I'm not asking you to dob anyone in, Ellie, I'm simply concerned that you could be getting involved in something dangerous.'

'Something you think I wouldn't be able to handle?' Damn, but she wished he would stop smiling - it made it difficult not to relent and tell him everything. Then another thought struck her. 'How did you know about me contacting Detective Warren? You're not in Homicide.'

'Wayne and I go back a long way.'

'Were you ...' she searched for the right terminology, 'uniform cops together?'

'No.'

He wasn't smiling now, and Ellie could see he appeared to be concentrating on the traffic harder than before. The silence became a little awkward, and she didn't know how to break it. Silences with Damien used to mean he was ignoring her, but Chris wasn't doing that. If the tension on his face was anything to go by, he was more than aware of her.

'I used to be in Homicide.'

'But you're ...'

'A uniform cop? I am now.'

'But you weren't always.' Ellie felt the eggshells under her shoes and decided to tread very carefully.

Again another silence, then Chris relaxed with a sighed, 'No,' and glanced at her with a half-smile that held more apology than amusement. 'I was a detective once.'

More sure of her footing now, Ellie was about to ask what had happened, but she saw they were almost at

Miranda's house.

Chris walked her to the porch. Miranda had left the outside light on, but its glow had been softened by years of dust and cast a weak glow over them. 'Would you like to come in for coffee?' Ellie asked.

'I'd like to, but I have an early shift in the morning and unfortunately I still have to iron that uniform.' The last two words weren't emphasised, but that twinkle was back in his eyes, and something delightful tingled through Ellie and softened her mouth in a way that made her think of kissing and cuddling and ... She gave herself a mental shake. Hot sex was definitely where her thoughts were heading, and she'd only known the man a few days!

'Thank you for tonight,' she breathed. 'I really enjoyed it.'

'We could do it again.' The twinkle was still there but the slight uncertainty in his voice told Ellie he wasn't as sure of himself as he acted.

'I'd like that.' Now it was her turn to be unsure. What was the protocol on a first date these days? Should she expect him to kiss her? Should she kiss him? Should she offer him her hand? Hell, at her age she could do what she bloody-well liked! And she wanted to kiss him. Just to see what it would be like.

So she did. She leaned towards him, rising on her toes to meet his height as he bent his head to hers.

It was a gentle kiss, a tentative kiss.

But there was chemistry.

Definitely chemistry.

Enough to make her want more.

Enough to scare her into stepping back to try to control her breathing and slow her heart to a more normal rhythm.

Now Chris looked even less confident than he had before. The twinkle in his eyes had gone, and Ellie saw her own desire mirrored there.

She realised that, in all their conversations, she had never told him that this was the first time she'd gone on a date in almost thirty years. Or that it had only been months since Damien had left her. And she was feeling vulnerable in a way she'd never thought she would.

'Perhaps next time we could go out to dinner?' he suggested.

'You have my number,' she smiled.

She watched him walk back to his vehicle - a tall man with an assured set to his shoulders and a measured stride - and delicious anticipation warred with the butterflies of caution in her chest.

On Friday night Chris called around on his way home from his shift. Ellie opened the door to him, and had to admit the saying about a man in uniform had a lot of truth to it. Especially when his blue shirt made his eyes appear even more brilliant. The foreboding feeling that police uniforms used to evoke in her was quickly being replaced by something the exact opposite - but equally disturbing.

As she stood aside to let him walk in, her welcoming smile faded. 'I hope this isn't official. You don't have bad news, do you?'

'No. Not bad, but it is about Cherilyn Manning. Is Miranda home?'

'She's out with the food van. I'm sure she'd go every night but apparently Ben only rosters the helpers on a couple of nights a week,' Ellie said as she sat on the lounge.

Chris took off his police cap and sat beside her, and she was acutely aware of the warmth, the presence of him. 'What do you know about Ben?' he asked.

'He's very involved with his church, he started the food van up with donations from the congregation and he gets various businesses to donate the food he hands out.'

'How long has Miranda been volunteering with him?'

'About a year. Why? Is there something wrong?'

'Quite the opposite. He obviously does something right when he can find out more than we were able to.'

Ellie shifted nervously. 'Are you talking about me telling Detective Warren about Jackson?'

The smile that creased his face was a tired one. 'We know where that information would have had to come from, Ellie. And we found Jackson. He wasn't too hard to track down. He was arrested for dealing drugs the same night Cherilyn was murdered, and from Cherilyn's time of death Jackson would have already been in custody so he's off the hook on that score.'

'Oh.' Disappointment washed through Ellie. She'd been so sure ... It was so logical ... 'So we're back to square one. Are there any other leads?'

'No.'

There was something final in the way he said the word. 'But Detective Warren is going to keep looking, isn't he?' Ellie tried to curb the impatience in her tone.

'Of course. But you have to realise that we don't have

any evidence, or any clues as to why she was killed. We can speculate that it was a drug deal gone wrong, or two addicts who argued. There was no money in Cherilyn's bag, just some coins in her jeans pocket, but that doesn't mean robbery wasn't the motive. We have no matches for any of the fingerprints we found, but the killer could have been wearing gloves. The back window had been tampered with so it could be accessed from the outside but there wasn't any evidence that the place had been used by squatters.'

'So what happens now?'

Chris twisted his cap in circles. 'Homicide will keep looking. But it might take a while. Unless the killer talks to someone or if a friend or relative becomes suspicious and tells us then we really have nothing to go on.' He slanted her a meaningful look. 'Unless Miranda has more information she wishes to share?'

Like dominoes falling in a pre-arranged sequence, things slotted into Ellie's mind. 'You knew, didn't you?' she accused. 'That first time you came here. After you told us Cherilyn's name. You knew Miranda wasn't telling you everything.' Disappointment swamped her. 'Did you only ask me out so you could use me to find out?'

'If you remember,' he spoke quietly, but each word was spaced to make sure she paid attention, 'I came to see you on my own time. Something I really shouldn't have done until this case was finished. I risked compromising possible future testimony.'

'So why did you?'

'Sometimes,' he stopped twisting his cap and looked intently at her, 'if you don't do what you feel you should straight away, you regret it.'

Ellie had the feeling he wasn't just talking about asking her to the movies. 'Did you tell Detective Warren you asked me out?'

'I ... um ... did happen to mention that if I called on you unofficially I might glean some more information.' He smiled wryly. 'I just forgot to add that I'd already done so.'

If the effect of that smile was anything to go by, Ellie should have thrown him out and locked the door. The shiver of excitement travelling down her back and the tingling in areas that hadn't tingled in a long time told her further contact with him could be dangerous. She almost salivated at the thought. All the years of Damien's neglect had left her aching ... and probably more vulnerable than she wanted to admit.

If she hadn't grown so far away from their relationship, Damien's eagerness to end their marriage would have devastated her. But it had still left her with doubts as to her attractiveness and worth. Her hollowness no longer had the same magnetic pull it previously had, but right now it beckoned with flashing neon "safety" signs. She'd been more than adventurous kissing Chris the other night, and pleased with herself that she'd done so, but she was starting to develop feelings for him. Real feelings, and that was scary.

'I'd planned on asking you to dinner tomorrow night,' Chris continued, 'but a couple of the blokes are down with the flu so I have to work. How about Sunday night?'

The neon sign flashed and died like a shooting star. 'I'd love to,' Ellie breathed.

'Pick you up at six?' As his smile deepened, Ellie would have agreed to 5am and breakfast in the rain. She nodded.

He stood up and she slowly rose and followed him to the door. He hesitated on the doorstep and she wondered if he wanted to kiss her. She knew she'd initiated it last time, but then it had been after a date, and felt ... right. But now it could be construed as a girlfriend/boyfriend thing and she wasn't sure she wanted to imply that. Yet.

She stepped back, said, 'See you tomorrow night,' and watched him walk to his vehicle. For a second she almost called him back, eager to again experience the thrill that first kiss had sparked in her, but she was afraid she might enjoy it too much. Or discover the chemistry had been a fleeting thing and kissing him again would be disappointing.

Then her mind switched tracks and she remembered he dealt with death in his job, and that scared her even more. For a moment she allowed the image of Cherilyn's battered body to surface, then fought it back. What had happened to the seventeen-year-old Cherilyn that had led her to end up dying such a lonely and terrible death six years later? The thought lingered long after she'd spent several hours working on her plans for the units before going to bed.

'I'm going to see Cherilyn's parents,' Ellie told Cass on the phone the next morning.

'Why?' Cass's tone was as much disbelief and caution as enquiry.

'Well, if Pru or Miranda had been killed, I think I'd like it if somebody apart from family and friends cared enough to let me know they remembered her and were thinking about her. I might take them some flowers.'

'From what Miranda said about Cherilyn feeling that her parents hated her, it might not be a good idea. They might resent a stranger turning up on their doorstep. Grief can be a funny thing, Ellie.'

Ellie knew that only too well, and she was sure that's why Cass was trying to warn her. Just as her own grief had stopped her from seeing what was happening to her marriage years ago, the Mannings might not see her as someone offering sympathy, but as a stranger intruding on their lives. The thought was daunting, but she felt she had to do it.

'Would you like me to go with you?' Cass asked.

'Thanks for the offer but no, I'll go alone. I only work one Saturday in three and today's one of my free days.'

'Then I'll meet you afterwards. For moral support. I'll bring Kandy if she's free.' Cass named a coffee shop and a time and wished Ellie good luck.

As soon as Ellie returned the headset to its holder, the phone rang. A rather cranky-sounding Bruce Moloney wanted to know why she hadn't contacted him with her designs.

'I haven't done all the costings for wallpaper and furnishings yet, and I can't do those until I take the last couple of measurements in unit one, so I can't give you a quote,' she explained.

'Don't worry about that yet. I've had my boys working on another job but it's nearly finished and I can't keep them hanging around while I wait for you to waffle over some pretty designs. Just show me how you think the renos should go so I can tell them what to rip out and what to leave. The cops have removed the crime scene tape from the building, so you can do the rest of your measurements. But unit three is still off limits.'

'I could come around to the units this afternoon,' Ellie offered, trying to keep her tone light. Cass had warned her Bruce could be blunt, but she wasn't in the mood to pander to his blatant chauvinism.

'Yeah ... Okay. That'll still give me time to get to the footy. I'll see you there at two.'

As she gathered her drawings together a little later, Ellie wondered how Bruce would react to some of her suggestions. She believed what she'd designed was not only feasible, but made the best possible use of the unit layout without resorting to too much structural change. But she worried that Bruce didn't have the imagination to see it that way.

CHAPTER FIFTEEN

When she parked outside Cherilyn's parents' house later that morning, Ellie was grateful her car definitely didn't fit into the "new" category. All the houses in the street were pre-World War Two vintage, but most were presentable, though some a little tired looking. The Manning residence, however, shrieked neglect louder than a heavy metal band. If the rust on the car bodies in the side yard was anything to go by, they were the same ones Ellie had seen six years ago when she'd given Cherilyn a ride home.

As she picked up the flowers from the passenger seat, she again debated if she was doing the right thing in coming to offer Cherilyn's parents her condolences. She didn't know them, she barely even remembered Cherilyn, but she knew, if Pru or Miranda had been murdered, she would want to know that whoever had found them had cared about them.

Weeds and grass flecked dew on her pants as she walked to the front door. A broken timber chair lay in the yard as though it had been thrown from one of the windows. Stubbies overflowed from a beer carton on the first step to the porch. A carton on the second step bulged with empty spirits bottles. The top step was clear, but the floor of the porch had become the receptacle for old newspapers and empty beer and cola cans. Something rustled in the cans and

Ellie shuddered.

A moment after she knocked on the door it was flung open. A blonde in her forties, lycra top and bike pants clinging to her thin body, moved her cigarette to one side of her mouth and narrowed her eyes. 'Yair?'

'Mrs Gloria Manning?'

'Who wants to know?'

'My name's Ellie Cummins. My daughter Miranda played netball with Cherilyn. I ... My friend and I were at the block of units and found Cherilyn after ...' She held out the flowers.

Gloria Manning assessed Ellie a moment longer, then took the flowers and moved back and gestured for Ellie to follow her. 'Come in. Might as well sit down as stand there giving the neighbours something to gawk at.'

As she walked into a lounge room that resembled an op shop after a delivery from their collection bins, Ellie's heart sank. Trying to dress casually but not wanting to appear disrespectful to Cherilyn's family, she'd worn navy slacks and a matching jacket, but in this room she felt as though ragged jeans and a sweatshirt would have been more appropriate.

'Want a drink?' Gloria asked as she tossed the flowers onto a wall unit. She clicked the television remote and the sounds of an energetic game show ceased. At Ellie's shake of her head, Gloria shrugged her shoulders and picked up a stubby. She sat down on a single lounge chair and thumbed towards a spot on the lounge that was free of clothing. Ellie made her way to it and perched on the edge.

'Mrs Manning, I want you to know how very sorry I am

about Cherilyn. I only knew her through netball when she was on the same team as my daughter, but she was a very nice girl. I can't imagine how you must feel. You must miss her terribly.'

'She was an ungrateful bitch. I sacrificed my life for her.' Gloria drew deeply on her cigarette. 'I only married Zeb because I was pregnant. Me mum wouldn't let me have an abortion and me dad told Zeb he'd rip his nuts out if he didn't marry me.'

Ellie almost winced. Gloria Manning seemed totally unconcerned about her daughter's murder. 'It must be hard for you,' she ventured, 'not being able to have a funeral for Cherilyn until the police ...' she hesitated. Saying 'release the body' seemed so cold, so ... CSI-like. She knew how devastated she would be in Gloria's situation.

'Don't know how we're going to afford it anyway.' Gloria flicked ash into a saucer. 'We ain't got no money.' She looked at Ellie, at her fashionable shoes, her designer-label clothes, eyes calculating. 'You wouldn't like to help out, would ya?'

'I would if I could, Mrs Manning. Believe me, I would. Unfortunately, I've recently ... My circumstances have changed recently and I don't have access to any ready money. But I'll see what I can do to help you out.' The woman's total lack of emotion was abhorrent to Ellie. Even if she and Cherilyn were estranged, surely Gloria could at least feel some human decency and grieve for her daughter.

'Anything would help,' Gloria looked slyly at Ellie. 'We got two other kids - can't take the food out of their mouths just to bury Cherilyn.'

Just then one of the 'kids' sauntered into the room, munching on a piece of chicken that had obviously come from the red cardboard "bucket" held in the crook of his other arm. 'Mum, we've run out of Coke,' he whined.

On a good hair day the teenager would have passed as a young version of Ozzy Osbourne having a bad hair day. Ellie tried not to look at the piece of chicken skin that had caught at the edge of his mouth. She stood up, arranged her face in a bright smile as she mumbled, 'I have to go, Mrs Manning. I hope everything works out for you,' and hurried to the door.

She heard Gloria Manning's 'See ya,' as she avoided the cartons on the steps, then the woman's voice rose as she cursed her son for everything from drinking the last of the soft drink to being born.

As Ellie drove away, she gripped the steering wheel tightly to stop her hands from shaking. A terrible anger seethed inside her. No wonder Miranda had thought Cherilyn wasn't happy at home. The poor girl hadn't had much of a chance in life, and now, in death, she appeared to be forgotten by the very people who should have cared about her.

If she hadn't agreed to meet Cass and Kandy at a nearby coffee shop, Ellie was sure she would have gone home and done a great deal of damage to a bottle of red wine or put a token ice cube in a couple of bourbon and drys and finished them before the ice had a chance to melt. She couldn't remember feeling so angry. She wanted to go back to Gloria Manning and slam her against a wall or shake her until the fillings fell out of her teeth. Maybe then the stupid woman would realise just how precious life was and cry for the life her daughter would never have.

The anger still seethed in her when she parked the car and walked to the coffee shop. Cass and Kandy were waiting outside, but Kandy raised one eyebrow as Ellie approached and said, 'I don't think coffee is what you're in need of, Ellie,' and, tucking a hand around Ellie's and Cass's elbows, propelled them to an adjacent hotel.

Clean, and relatively quiet for late Saturday afternoon, the lounge bar swirled with the sounds of nearby poker machines and a television giving racing results, and the smells of beer and spirits and aromas of deep-fried chips and battered food and sizzling steak and women's perfume and men's aftershave that couldn't disguise some patrons' body odour.

Like soldiers returning from battle, the women fronted the bar, bought their drinks, and settled into the curved leather seating around a corner table.

'I gather it didn't go well,' Cass ventured.

Ellie took a long swig of her bourbon and dry and crunched on the ice. 'No wonder Cherilyn hated her home life. If I'd had a mother like that I would have hated it too.'

'What was she like?' Cass asked.

'Brassy blonde, fake tan and so thin that if she had a twin you could rub the two of them together to start a fire,' Ellie exploded. 'And her pants were so tight you'd see if she did pelvic floor exercises.'

Kandy smothered a laugh and Cass slanted her a patient look. 'You know what I mean, Ellie. Was she coping all right?'

'She was coping just fine. Couldn't give a damn about Cherilyn. All she wanted to do was get money out of me. Supposedly for Cherilyn's funeral, but I doubt that's what it would get spent on. Probably more booze.' She described the abundance of empty bottles and Gloria Manning's attitude towards her daughter.

Kandy's expression grew pensive. 'Sounds like Cherilyn didn't have much of a chance in life.' She plucked invisible specks from her pants. 'Poor kid should at least have a decent burial.' She took a cheque book from her handbag, wrote quickly, ripped out a cheque and handed it to Ellie. 'Seven thousand should cover it. But don't give it to the mother. Pay it straight to the funeral parlour.'

Ellie looked at her in amazement. 'Kandy ... That's a lot of money.'

'We have more money than we need. We're always giving to charity.'

Although Kandy tried to look indifferent, Ellie wasn't convinced this was just another charitable donation. 'Why Cherilyn?'

Tears formed at the corners of Kandy's eyes. 'Because it could have been me lying in that morgue with my head bashed in. It nearly was.' There was a touch of defiance in the look she gave Ellie. 'You've never met my parents and you never will. I told you once I don't have anything to do with them. Well, it's because my mother is an A-grade bitch and my father was an abusive prick who drank himself to death years ago. If the drug scene had been as bad when I was a kid as it is now I might not have been able to drag myself out of it.'

'Shit,' Ellie whispered and slumped against the backrest. Her mind fumbled to find sympathetic, supportive words, but before they could reach her tongue, Cass asked, 'Do you want to tell us about it?'

To their surprise, Kandy smiled. A little sheepishly at first, then with genuine amusement. 'I think I just précised it all. I ran away from home when I was fifteen, got into bad company, but escaped after a couple of years. Got a job as a waitress in a cafe, worked my way up to manager, and I do mean *worked*,' she winked, 'and ended up running my own catering business. Which is how I met Phillip. He was holding a business function, hired me to do the catering, and somehow we clicked. Attraction of opposites, you could call it.'

Opposites was right, Ellie thought. Although Phillip seemed genuinely fond of Kandy, there was something about him that made Ellie think he viewed Kandy as a trophy wife rather than the other half of a love match. Something in the relationship didn't gel, but she couldn't pinpoint what it was.

She looked from Kandy to Cass and wondered, for what was probably the umpteenth time, how the three of them had become such firm friends. Their husbands shared no common interests, and on the few occasions they'd been forced to socialise with each other, hadn't even come close to forming a friendship. It seemed the attraction of opposites law had only worked on their wives.

The block of units looked no more sinister than it had on the day Ellie and Cass had discovered Cherilyn's body, but

Ellie couldn't suppress the shiver that ran down her back as she stepped inside. The Poinciana tree on the footpath no longer seemed graceful, its bare branches now resembling skeletal fingers reaching for the sky.

Although Bruce's ute was parked outside, he wasn't waiting for her in the foyer. The doors to all the units were closed, and police tape still covered the doorway of unit three.

'Hello?' Ellie's call echoed in the emptiness.

'Up here.' Bruce's head popped over the landing rail on the third floor then disappeared.

Ellie started to climb the stairs, careful not to catch her heels on some of the more worn areas of the carpet runner. By the time she'd reached the third floor, she'd taken off her jacket and gained a new appreciation for the stamina people must have needed before lifts became routine in multi-storey buildings.

The door to the unit, in the same corner as unit three below but with a brass number nine attached, was ajar. She walked over and looked inside.

'Vandals!' Bruce exploded as he kicked a piece of plaster across the room. 'Fu-' he broke off as he caught sight of Ellie. 'Bloody vandals! Look what they've done!' He waved a piece of timber in the air. 'It'll be impossible to match this quality. I was going to get it polished and not worry about carpet, but that won't happen now.'

Ellie stared at the holes that had been punched in the walls, the timber flooring prised up in seemingly random places, graffiti in bright red from room to room as though the writer had needed to vent his anger in words as well as actions. 'How did they get in?'

'Back door. Ground floor. It's an old lock, didn't need much to break it. Damn! I can't afford to get security patrolling the place. Insurance will cover the damage but too many claims will up the premium.'

'What about security lights? Could you install some?' She stepped into the room to get a better look at the damage.

'Not now. When we started the job the sparky - the electrician - disconnected the electricity and set up a power socket for the tradies to use. I'm replacing the wiring - it's old and we need more power points and other things. In case you need to know,' he gestured to what had obviously once been a kitchen but was now a bare area with cut-off and capped pipes coming from the floor and walls, 'the plumbing's also disconnected on this floor and the one below. But there's still water to the ground floor if you need a toilet.'

Ellie touched the red lettering on the wall and looked at her fingers. 'It's chalk.'

'Yeah.' Bruce picked up a half-stick from behind a piece of plaster. 'One of the chippies must have left it behind. They use it to mark things that need to be done.'

'Have you called the police?'

Bruce snorted. 'What for? If they can't find who killed that girl I don't like their chances of finding whoever did this.

She handed him her folder. 'I only have designs based on the front unit downstairs, and as I said they're not complete because I didn't get all the living room measurements. And I didn't get a chance to look at the other units.'

'Have a look around now. They're pretty similar in set-up. If I like what you've done already we can work out the individual differences.'

As she walked from room to room, Ellie saw the destruction wasn't confined to the kitchen and living areas. The bedrooms and bathroom had been dealt with just as severely. She gazed at the holes, her mind not quite in sync with what she was seeing. Something about them bothered her, but she couldn't figure out what.

When she looked out the windows she saw why it would have been possible for the intruder or intruders to have created so much damage without being heard by the neighbours. The adjoining houses might have been high-set Queenslanders, but they were still way below the third floor of the unit block, and large trees and high shrubs not only gave each yard some privacy but acted as sound barriers. Even the back yard of the unit block was heavily vegetated. A commercial skip bin similar to the one at the front of the building stood near the fence, and she thought how it would have provided excellent cover for Cherilyn and whoever had killed her while they broke in.

Gloria Manning's callous disregard for her daughter's fate still rankled with Ellie, and she switched her thoughts back to Bruce's job before the anger could swamp her again.

In spite of the damage to the walls and floor, the unit had a light and airy feel, and it was a quality she hoped could be retained in the renovation. Sunlight streamed in through the living room windows, and when she opened them she could imagine the smells of early summer floating in, fragrant jasmines and gardenias, grasses beginning to seed, the not-too-distant tang of river water. She imagined the room as she knew it should be - light furnishings, Madras lace that was all flowers and feathers, polished brass pendant lights with petite frost glass -

'What do you reckon?' Bruce tapped her folder. 'Think you can come up with something like what you've designed for unit one?'

'This unit has a different aspect. It needs a different feel.' Ellie couldn't contain her enthusiasm for the ideas flowing through her. 'Just think of the appeal, Bruce, with each unit offering something different, having a different *theme* if you like. Light and whimsy for young romantic couples, cosy and comfortable for older buyers, practical and serviceable for the career-minded, a fabulous kitchen for the closet chefs. We could make this work. It would be different to everything else on the market.'

The interest in Bruce's eyes was almost as intense as his scepticism. 'I don't own the bloody bank, woman. How much would it all cost?'

Ellie's neck tingled. *Woman!* She gritted her teeth, and counted to - She didn't make it to ten before grinding out, 'My name is Ellie, Bruce, not *woman*. And if we're going to work together on this I would appreciate it if you tried to remember my name.' Her heart pounded as shock registered on his face. Oh, hell, she'd done it now. She'd pissed him off and he'd probably tell her to take a hike and she had nothing signed to recompense her for the work she'd done so far.

Then he laughed. 'Sure, love. Ellie. No problems. Now

tell me how I can afford this.'

Ellie hid the faint tremor in her fingers and allowed her knees to relax. Ground rule number one set out. 'Perhaps we can go down to unit one where there's a bench and I can spread out the designs. And I can do some sketches to give you an idea of how some of the themes will work.'

'Sounds good.' He gestured for her to lead the way. As they walked down the stairs he said, 'Joe mentioned you and your old man have split up. You interested in going to the football tonight?'

The thought of going out with him was about as appealing as following Miranda into that dark alleyway, but she hoped the brilliant smile she flashed him guaranteed her refusal didn't offend.

It was only when she was driving home that she realised she'd forgotten to take the rest of the unit one living room measurements.

Perhaps it was exhaustion from such a frustrating day, or maybe the half bottle of red wine she polished off when working on more designs at home that evening, but Ellie drifted into a dreamless sleep as soon as she lay down.

So it was like dragging herself from a deep, dark pit when she became aware something was scratching on the pillow next to her head.

Groggily she reached towards it.

And screamed.

CHAPTER SIXTEEN

Heart pounding madly, Ellie leaped from the bed and switched on the light, a tiny segment of her brain registering gratitude that she'd taken to wearing pyjamas since moving in with Miranda.

'Mum!' Miranda appeared beside her, eyes blinking in the brightness. 'What's wrong?'

'Rat!' The word strangled in Ellie's throat. 'There was a rat. On the bed.' She sagged against the doorway.

'Rat? There's no ...' Miranda walked over to the bed and pulled up the covers Ellie had thrown back. A tiny bundle of fur uncurled itself and let out a pitiful meow. Miranda picked it up, cradled it against her chest and made soft sounds of reassurance.

Ellie's relief wasn't enough to stop the bite in her voice as she pulled herself from the door jamb and said, 'I think you'd better tell me where *that* came from.'

Miranda's back straightened and there was a mutinous gleam in her eyes as she cuddled the kitten and said, 'She's a gift. And she's staying.'

Cass was worried.

She knew Ellie dealt with emotional issues differently, but she'd been so calm, too calm, when they'd discovered

Cherilyn's body. She'd handled it too well, Cass thought. But her reaction to Gloria Manning had been right off the wall. Cass had never seen her so angry, even when Damien had announced he was leaving. Then, she'd been rip-roaring mad, but the vibes she'd emitted when she'd told of Cherilyn's mother's attitude had been so intense in their fury they were several degrees below freezing.

The wind whipped the sheet she was pegging onto the line, flicking it up and over so it wrapped around the other washing. Muttering dire warnings to the god of windy weather, she unwound it and punched on another peg.

'Cass,' Joe called from inside the house, 'Ellie's on the phone.' As she reached the laundry door he opened it and handed her the cordless phone.

'We have a new addition to the family,' Ellie told her, but before Cass could register her astonishment, Ellie recounted the tale of her midnight intruder.

'I'm guessing Miranda brought it home.' Cass abandoned any hope of pegging out washing with only one free hand. She smiled as Joe walked to the line and finished the job for her.

'Who else? It has to be the ugliest feline alive,' Ellie muttered. 'Miranda said it's a Burmese-Siamese cross but I reckon it's crossed with whatever walked over the roof at night. It's got tortoiseshell colouring, big blue eyes and enormous ears that are speckled like a hyena.'

Cass wondered if the kitten was really as ugly as her imagination conjured up. 'Sounds an odd-looking cat.'

'Actually it's kind of cute. But fleas! We washed it and so many fleas drowned it was like an insect Titanic. We have to be careful not to step on it. The darn thing's so tiny if you tucked it under your armpit you'd think you hadn't shaved for a week.'

Cass chuckled. In spite of Ellie's projected lack of enthusiasm for the kitten, Cass knew she'd soon be treating it like a member of the family. Ellie had been terribly upset when their dog had died several years ago and although she'd said she didn't want another pet, Cass suspected it was more because of Damien's complaining he didn't want another animal digging up the garden and shitting on the lawn. 'Where did she get it?'

'Mouse gave it to her.'

'Mouse!'

'Last night. At the food van. Asked Miranda to look after it because it was the runt of the litter and he was worried the other cats might pick on it and hurt it.'

Warning bells tinkled in Cass's mind. 'You don't think Mouse ...'

'Has a crush on Miranda?' Ellie's worry vibrated over the phone. 'I don't know. Miranda's always had a soft spot for the under-dog, Mouse might think there's more there than kindness.'

Cass thought about that possibility as she and Ellie continued talking. After a few minutes Ellie asked, 'Guess what Mouse had named the kitten?'

'Should I be concerned?'

'Probably. It's indicative of my life at the moment.' Ellie paused, and Cass could hear a faint purring as the kitten must have climbed onto Ellie's shoulder. 'He called it Mayhem.'

Cass hoped the kitten wouldn't live up to its name. 'How's the situation with Miranda?'

'Let's put it this way - if I was a cake, she'd be the frosting.'

'That bad, huh?'

'Oh, not really,' Ellie sighed. 'It's me, really. I feel like I have to re-establish myself all over again with her. Living with her has made me realise I never really knew her before.' The purring became more pronounced and Cass knew Ellie was already a goner. The kitten obviously had her exactly where it wanted. 'I think she thinks I don't trust her to make the right decisions for herself. Maybe having Mayhem will show her that it's not easy to stop wanting to protect your children.'

Cass laughed. That sounded like the old furphy that giving your children a pet taught them responsibility. She'd lost count of the number of pets she'd looked after over the years as each once-conscientious child grew into a "I'm too busy to look after it" teenager. Or left home. She felt a slight sorrow at the thought of how far away her kids lived now. Two married, two not. But they were happy, and for that she was grateful.

As Ellie kept speaking, Cass grew apprehensive. Finally she said, 'Ellie, you're rambling. What is it you really want to tell me?'

Silence. For a second.

'The units were broken into again. One on the top floor was trashed.'

'What's Bruce doing about it?'

'Putting a new lock on the back door.'

'And that's it?'

'Yes.'

'Has he told the police?'

'No. He reckons it's just vandalism and they won't be bothered.'

Cass heard the underlying worry in Ellie's voice. 'But you think it could be connected to Cherilyn's murder, don't you?'

'I don't know, Cass. But what if it is? There was something ... strange about the way the damage was done. It didn't strike me at the time, but I've been thinking about it this morning, and it's like some of the damage had a purpose, but some was random. I know that doesn't make sense, but that's what it felt like.'

'Well, don't you go back there again by yourself. If you have to go there and Bruce won't be there I'll go with you.'

'But -'

'No buts. I'll go with you. And stuff what my mother thinks.'

Ellie's laughter echoed over the phone, and Cass joined in. It was about time she made decisions without feeling like she should consider what Audra thought.

The pants Geoffrey had bought at the op shop didn't fit as well as he would have liked, but they'd been the best he could afford at the time. He looked at himself in the mirror glued to the old-fashioned wardrobe. The crack on one side gave him a slightly disjointed look, but overall he didn't look too bad. The jacket had been given to him when he'd left jail, but at least it was relatively modern, even if it was a bit short and the collar wouldn't straighten no matter how much he pulled at it. With a shave and his hair washed he looked presentable enough. At least the old bag should let him through the front door.

Good thing his old man was dead. The righteous old prick hadn't even let her visit him in jail. But he knew she wouldn't turn him away, not when he presented himself like the prodigal son, the repentant sinner come to plead for forgiveness. The pretence shouldn't be hard to maintain, he'd learned the art of lying and looking innocent at an early age, recognising even then the value in puppy-dog eyes and softly-curling brown hair. Charming the ladies had come easily to him. And the one he now had to convince was his mother, and he'd always been able to wrap her around his little finger.

He opened the old one-door fridge with its rust marks that had seeped through the thin layer of paint. Like everything else in his fully-furnished, self-contained bedsit, it told of a landlord whose shopping expeditions didn't go further than the cheapest second-hand stores. He reached out to grab one of the three cans of rum and coke sitting next to half a loaf of bread, a tub of margarine, and a jar of jam, and stopped. Fingers trembling, he closed the door. Not even coke could disguise the smell of rum, and he needed to appear as reformed as possible.

His nerve started to falter as he locked his door, pulled on his gloves and walked to the bus stop. Perhaps he should have phoned first? No, he didn't want to give her the chance to refuse to see him. Too much risk in that. If he turned up at her front door, surely she wouldn't turn him away?

In spite of the cold wind that buffeted the open-fronted bus shelter, he began to sweat.

Cherilyn's murder had reminded Ellie how fleeting life was, but it was with a different kind of sadness that she and Miranda drove out to the nursing home to see Damien's father Bert on Sunday afternoon. Bert and Eugenia had been one of the better things to come out of her marriage to Damien. "Salt of the earth" types, practical and non-intrusive in their support after Paul's death, adored their grand-daughters but didn't spoil them, and always made Ellie feel that she was a welcome addition to the family. She sometimes wondered how Damien had turned out to be so different.

The only blessing in Bert having Alzheimers was she wouldn't have to tell him that she and Damien had broken up.

As she and Miranda waited for the door that separated the visitors' arrival section from the Alzheimers and Dementia wing of the home to be unlocked, Ellie felt the usual tightening in her stomach she got on every visit. It wasn't just the sight of so many elderly and not-so-elderly people with minds that no longer functioned that did it, but the worry that one day she or Damien could end up in the same state and Pru and Miranda would have to make the decision that Damien had found so hard.

The large recreation room was painted in the palest of lemons, the vinyl floor covering an almost perfect imitation timber, the curtains a cheery burst of sunflowers and leaves. All designed to add some brightness to the lives of people imprisoned by diminishing memory and fading abilities.

Ellie and Miranda walked past the armchairs on wheels that held those people beyond walking or doing anything for themselves. 'Living corpses' Damien had muttered the first time they had inspected the home and she'd shushed him quickly, worried one of them might still retain enough function to hear him and be upset.

They found Bert out in the garden, sitting on the grass, a handful of weeds next to him, staring vacantly at the agapanthus plants surrounding a small gardenia bush. A carer who'd been talking to another patient came over as they approached him. 'He's a little lost today, I'm afraid,' she told them. 'You may not find you can make contact with him.'

'Has he been happy?' Miranda asked.

'We think so. He's always happier here in the garden.'

Ellie's chest tightened further. She squatted down and looked closely at Bert, trying to find some semblance, some flicker of the man she'd known for thirty years. 'Bert? Bert, it's Ellie. I've come to see you. Miranda's come too.' Miranda knelt on the grass beside her.

Dull grey eyes slowly focused. His eyebrows slowly drew together. He looked at Ellie without recognition, then frowned deeply as he looked at Miranda. 'Ellie? What are you doing here, Ellie?'

'I'm Miranda, Grandad. This is Ellie.'

Confusion showed on Bert's face. 'No. No, that's not Ellie.' He looked back at Miranda. 'Are you trying to trick me, Ellie?'

At Ellie's quick head shake, Miranda stopped her

instinctive denial. 'She's my mother,' she said instead.

Bert's expression brightened. 'I remember Ellie's mother. A lovely lady. Like my Eugenia.' Tears started to trickle down his cheeks. 'She doesn't come to see me any more. I'll have to find her.' He started to rise, then hesitated. His mouth opened, and all expression left his face. He dropped back onto the grass and stared vacantly into the distance.

As they drove away five minutes later Miranda stated flatly, 'I'm not going back there again.'

Ellie bit her lip. She wanted to say the same thing herself, but knew she couldn't. Next visit might be different, Bert might recognise her, but if not she would still go back. Even when he became one of Damien's "living corpses" she knew she would go and hold his hand and tell him Eugenia still loved him and she was waiting to see him. She knew she would do for him what she hoped someone she once loved would do for her.

This was only a second date, Ellie told herself that evening as she waited for Chris to arrive. She shouldn't feel like there was any importance attached to it. But she couldn't calm the nerves in her stomach, the way her heartbeat accelerated at the sound of a vehicle in the street. She peered out through the gap in the loungeroom curtains, looked at her watch, then peered out again.

'Mum, you're starting to make *me* nervous,' Miranda complained and put down her book. She levered herself from the lounge and walked over and turned on the television. A current affairs program blared into the room and she lowered the sound.

'I'm sorry.' Ellie smoothed a non-existent wrinkle in her turquoise jacket and hitched at her matching skirt to ensure it sat straight. 'I shouldn't be nervous. It's only dinner.'

'And how often in the past thirty years have you gone out to dinner with a man you barely know? Even I would be nervous if someone asked me on a dinner date.'

'Mirie, I don't mean to pry, but why aren't you going out on dates? Don't you meet anyone you're interested in?'

'I don't like doing the pub and club scene and there aren't too many other places you can meet a decent man these days. And don't tell me to join a sports club, you know I'm uncoordinated.'

'What about your friends from the soup kitchen where you volunteered who used to come around here?'

'People move on, Mum,' Miranda flopped onto the lounge. 'They get different lives. And I don't often go there now I do the food van. Guess I've just got into a rut.'

'What about the church Ben runs the food van for, surely they have a club for young people?'

Miranda looked uncomfortable. 'I'm not really *churchie*, Mum. I don't mind volunteering with the van but ...'

'But you really only do it because you fancy Ben.'

Eyes widening, Miranda whipped around to stare at Ellie. 'Oh, God! I'm not that obvious, am I?'

'Only to me, dear. Ben seems to be totally oblivious to the fact that you fancy him.' Ellie tried to keep the sarcastic note from her voice but Miranda gave her look that said she'd got the implication.

'Don't you like him, Mum?'

'I think he's a very nice young man, Mirie, but he either doesn't realise that he has a chance with you or else he's simply not interested.'

Miranda sighed. 'I think he's not interested in me.'

'There's only one way to find out - ask him out. See what he says.' Ellie was tempted to say more but she heard Chris's vehicle pull up outside. She picked up her coat and purse and opened the front door. 'Be braver than I was, Mirie,' she said and walked out.

When the warden had told him his father was dying, Geoffrey had quickly concealed the pleasure surging through him. The whole time he'd been in prison, he'd worked hard at being a model prisoner, never allowing anything to jeopardise his chances of parole. Rejoicing in his father's imminent death would not project a good image.

'Your mother wanted you to know,' the warden had said. 'We could arrange a hospital visit for you to see him.'

He'd looked at the warden with what he hoped was deep sorrow etched on his features, and allowed a tear to trickle from the corner of one eye. 'My father disowned me years ago, Warden. If he's not asking to see me then I'm afraid it would only bring more pain to my mother to see him reject me again. It's better I don't go.' The words had been said with just the right amount of sadness, and he'd congratulated himself on his acting skills when he'd seen the sympathy on the warden's face.

His skills at lying had saved him on many occasions, but they wouldn't do so now. He'd pleaded coercion when the cops had picked him up with the drug shipment, and faked remorse so well during his trial his sentence was more lenient than it should have been, but he'd got word in prison that when he was released he'd better make recompense for the loss the gang had incurred or swimming with concrete boots would be the least of his worries.

Prison had provided him with time to think. Childhood memories had re-surfaced, and with them a chance to get his hands on something that would enable him to buy off his predators.

It had all seemed so easy, but he hadn't counted on death interfering, though at her age he should have. She'd been his favourite aunt, too, one that appreciated the wild streak in him, probably because she'd once shared it.

Now as he waited for his mother to return to the one-bedroom retirement unit she had moved to after his father's death, his lip curled in disgust. So much for being the faithful wife to the man-who-would-be-bishop. His father's ambition had far outstripped his abilities, and the coveted manse had remained an unfulfilled dream. His mother's meek acceptance of his father's overly-pious excuses had angered him as much as his father's failures.

The apprehension that had built in him in the hours he had spent waiting on his mother's tiny enclosed patio threatened to blow into full-scale panic. What if she didn't come home? What if she was away on holidays? She mightn't return for weeks.

He was running out of time.

The pathway and street lights in the retirement complex had been on now for several hours, and he moved out of the shadows to look at his watch. Eight o'clock. It had taken several bus connections to get here, and he wasn't sure how late they all ran. He would have to leave. Tomorrow he would phone her first, and if she answered he would hang up and make his way back.

As he walked away, he wondered if the builder would call the cops when he found the damage to the unit. Finding that red chalk had been a stroke of luck. He'd realised he could make the damage look like it had been caused by vandals who'd broken in. He'd put a few more holes in the walls for good measure. The anger in his graffitied words had been genuine - an expression of his wild frustration and almost all-consuming fear when he hadn't found it, when he'd realised that his aunt must have taken her secret with her to her grave.

His mother was his last hope.

'This must be Brisbane's best-kept secret,' Ellie murmured as she surveyed the interior of the small restaurant. She absently picked a crumb from the red and white check tablecloth and put it on her plate. 'I've never tasted a pizza so good. All those combinations. Yum.'

'Do you have room left for dessert?' Chris smiled and handed her the menu.

'I doubt it.' She scanned the list. 'But ... Tiramisu cake - how can I resist?'

'Good choice. They make the best here.'

It was easy to believe. The restaurant wasn't fancy, more traditional home-style Italian with its candles overflowing wax down the sides of Chianti bottles and grape-leaf clusters and white cement-daub walls and tubs of flowering red and white geraniums at the entrance. Families with young children and groups and couples of all ages occupied the tables that huddled close to allow maximum patronage.

Chris caught the eye of a waiter and placed their dessert order. 'Would you like more wine?' he asked Ellie as the waiter picked up their dishes and the empty bottle.

She shook her head. 'No thanks. I have to work in the morning. As it is I'll be tempted to sleep in.'

'How are the designs going?'

It was a topic she had avoided all evening, worried that if she mentioned the break-in and vandalism Chris might want to investigate it and that would really get Bruce off side. But she knew she wasn't a good liar, so she told him everything, including how Bruce wouldn't inform the police of what had happened.

'Why do I get the feeling you don't consider this a simple case of kids breaking in and vandalising the unit?' he asked when she'd finished.

'I have nothing to go on but a gut feeling.' Ellie found it difficult to express what she felt. It was like walking into a room that looked perfectly okay but knowing that something wasn't quite *right*. 'There was a lot of damage, but some of the holes in the wall looked like they'd been made carefully. They weren't just punched out. They were too uniform, too square, as though they'd been deliberately cut out, whereas the others were jagged, like they'd been punched or hit with something like a hammer.'

'Do you think I could have a look at them?'

Ellie saw the interest in his eyes, and imagined his cop brain ticking over the possibilities. She wasn't sure she wanted this date turning into an investigation, even if she had mentioned the vandalism, but she needed to talk about it, and Chris was more likely to have answers than Cass or Kandy. 'I doubt Bruce would welcome you, but I have a key to the building.' She saw his eyebrows rise. 'I can't get there during a working day so Bruce gave me a key so I could look around after work or on weekends. I might need to take more measurements and I'll need to check and see if the refurbishments are being done the way I designed them.'

'I'm working a late shift tomorrow, but what about we go there after you finish work Tuesday?'

'Okay. I'll bring a torch.' She was surprised at the relief she felt in knowing she wouldn't be going back there alone. By the time she left work and drove to the units it would be dark, and she didn't relish the idea of being there now the electricity had been disconnected. Especially when the memory of what she'd seen in unit three kept popping into her head.

She wasn't sure if it was the wine she'd consumed or the need to stop thinking about Cherilyn's murder, but her mind abruptly switched tracks and she blurted out the first thought it came up with. 'How did your wife die?'

Surprise registered in Chris's eyes, but before she could apologise and take back her question, he replied, 'Hit and run. She'd walked down to the shop to get some milk and was hit when she was crossing the road.'

'Oh, my God. I'm so sorry.' Of all the things she'd surmised - cancer, heart attack, car accident - Ellie had never considered something like that.

'We never found the car or even a witness who could

describe it. It was night and drizzling rain and she was wearing dark clothing. But it would have been impossible for the driver not to know he'd hit someone.' There was no emotion in Chris's words, and if it wasn't for the flicker of pain in his eyes, Ellie thought he could be reading out the details of a case in which he had no personal involvement. 'I was supposed to buy the milk on my way home, but I'd been delayed at a crime scene so she left Danny in the house and walked to the corner shop. It was only two hundred metres away.'

'How old was Danny?'

'Eight. Old enough to leave on his own for the ten or twelve minutes it would have taken for Angela to get the milk.'

'So he's eighteen now,' she mused. Then she frowned. 'How old are you?'

'Forty-six.'

'Hell! I'm a cradle-snatcher.'

Chris chuckled. 'Technically you're only eighteen months older than I am, and that's hardly cradle snatching.'

'How do you know how old I am?'

'You found a dead body. That immediately makes you a possible suspect until you're cleared, which means we have to check you out.'

'So,' Ellie's brain raced, but her words emerged slowly, 'you know everything about me.'

If she'd thought his eyes could twinkle before, it was nothing to the gleam she saw now. His lips curled in a half-suppressed smile. 'Not ... everything.'

The words were so blatantly suggestive the colour flamed

in her cheeks before she realised he was teasing her. 'Just as well,' she muttered, grabbing a serviette and dabbing at her face.

'I'm sorry.' He was instantly contrite. 'I didn't mean to embarrass you.'

'I'm not embarrassed,' she smiled, trying desperately but ineffectively to ignore the moisture seeping from every pore in her skin and the heat that made her body glow with colour more becoming a tomato, 'but if you know so much about me you know I'm in that horrible menopause age bracket.'

'It's a bugger, isn't it,' he sympathised. 'My sister had a hard time of it.' He gave her an appraising look. 'You don't get mood swings, do you?'

She shook her head. 'No, thank heavens. Just the odd power surge. And wine seems to make it worse.' She reached for the water jug and poured a glass. 'I think I should stick to this.'

'My sister should have,' he grimaced. 'Every time she drank she was a real pain in the butt. I even told her husband that if he strangled her I'd go to court and testify it was justifiable homicide,' he laughed. 'But she's fine now.'

'It sounds like you're quite close to her.'

'She's my older sister, always bossing me around. Good thing I was always taller or she would have been impossible to live with.'

In spite of his words, Ellie could see the love he obviously had for his sister. 'Does she live in Brisbane?'

He nodded. 'After Angela was killed, Rhonda and my mother looked after Danny when I went to work. They kept me sane too.'

'Is that why you went back to being in uniform?'

For a moment she thought he wasn't going to answer, or if he did it would just be to give a one word reply. But he picked up a serviette and folded it into ever decreasing squares that seem to require his intense concentration as he said, 'I thought I'd have a better chance of finding the car if I stayed in Homicide, but after a year Warren told me I should either take a break, give up looking, or get out of the service because I was becoming obsessive and wasn't doing my job properly. Rhonda and Mum had been trying to tell me the same thing but I hadn't listened. Danny had become withdrawn to the point of barely speaking and I hadn't really noticed, or if I did I'd put it down to the same grief I was feeling. I told Rhonda what Warren had said,' he looked up from the serviette, and his lips moved in the beginning of a wry smile, 'expecting her to sympathise, but she gave me a blast that nearly knocked my head off. The next day I asked to go back into uniform.'

'Did you regret it?'

He shook his head. 'I'd told Rhonda how guilty I felt that Angela had gone to the shop when I'd promised I would do it, and she told me guilt didn't raise a child and if I didn't start becoming a better father I'd lose Danny as well. It was the wake-up call I needed.' He placed the now extremely small serviette in the centre of the table. 'How long have you been separated from your husband?'

Separated. Such a strange word. Taken literally it could mean that she and Damien were like two people pushed apart by a frenzied crowd or a wartime battle, seeking but not finding each other. Or maybe they'd deliberately decided to go their own ways. When in actuality they'd drifted apart, becoming strangers to each other. And maybe in a way, she thought, she'd become a stranger to herself. She was still trying to find who she really wanted to be. Working again had helped restore some of her confidence, and the opportunity to get back into the designing and decorating that she loved had put her in touch with the creative side of herself she'd thought long-buried under Damien's less-than-subtle demands. But something was still missing, and she wasn't sure she was ready yet to find out what that was.

'About three months now. It wasn't anything dramatic. We hadn't really been a couple for a long time.' She was tempted to tell him that Damien already had someone new in his life, or maybe his lover had been around for longer than Ellie wanted to think about, but she didn't want him to think she was on the rebound.

'So there's no chance of getting back together?' The question was asked in such a casual tone that Ellie almost missed the stillness in his body that gave lie to his seemingly mild interest.

'None that I can see,' she said, and felt a twinge of regret for the twenty-nine years of marriage that had ended with barely a whimper. 'I phoned to tell him about Cherilyn and that was the first time we'd spoken since he'd left. I don't even know where he's staying. Thank heaven for mobile phones,' she laughed.

As though on cue, Chris's mobile rang. Annoyance flicked across his face. 'Sorry,' he said. 'But I'd better check it.'

Ellie smiled her assent. Chris looked at the screen, a frown furrowing his brow. 'Sorry. I'll have to take this. Back in a minute.' He pushed his chair from the table and walked outside, the wind whisking leaves through the entryway before the glass doors closed behind him.
The waiter returned with their dessert. Ellie viewed the delicate sponge and creamy filling and coffee-chocolate layers decorated with blueberries and raspberries and chocolates curls and discovered she didn't feel as full as she'd thought. Actually, her mouth was almost watering at the sight.

Chris strode back to the table. 'I'm sorry,' he said, not making a move to sit, 'I have to get home. Danny's had a bit of an accident.'

CHAPTER SEVENTEEN

All thoughts of cake fled from Ellie's head. Irrational as she knew it to be, images of Paul's cold little body sprang into her mind. She swallowed hard before asking, 'Is it bad?'

'No. No.' Chris must have noticed her reaction. 'He's all right. I'll explain on the way if you don't mind coming with me. Or I could call a taxi to take you home.'

'Don't be silly. Of course I'll come with you.'

He glanced down at the table. Ellie saw him hesitate. 'We can take it with us,' she said. 'Perhaps Danny might like some too?'

'I'm not sure he deserves it, but it's a nice thought. Back in a minute.' He went to the counter and spoke to the woman behind the cash register as he paid for their meals. Within moments their desserts, with an extra, were put in takeaway containers.

'So what kind of accident did Danny have?' Ellie asked as they drove away.

'We've had a possum getting into our roof,' Chris explained. 'At least we think it's a possum because of the noise it makes. We've checked but we can't find how he's getting in so we made a trap and put it in the ceiling. Apparently Danny went up there tonight when he heard the trap spring and ended up putting his foot through the ceiling.'

Ellie stifled a laugh, unsure if Chris was seeing any humour in the situation. She decided it was better to be sympathetic. 'So Danny didn't hurt himself, he's just worried about the damage to the ceiling?'

'Not quite. Apparently when his foot went through the ceiling he fell backwards and the possum trap he was holding wedged between two beams, but the rope handle twisted around his wrist and he can't reach it with his other arm to free himself because of his foot being stuck in the ceiling. And he can't get his foot out because it went in at an angle and his boot is preventing him pulling back against the plasterboard. He thought about kicking a bigger hole with his other foot but decided he was better off phoning me. Luckily he had his mobile in his pocket.'

He glanced across at her, and in the glow from the street lights he must have seen the grin she could no longer suppress. His own lips lost their sternness and his laughter mingled with hers.

They were still smiling when he pulled into the driveway of a neat, low-set pale-brick home. A small hedge took the place of a front fence, and two large shrub-filled pots guarded the entry to the path leading to the front door. After the warmth inside the vehicle, the wind seemed colder than it had when they'd left the restaurant. Chris quickly unlocked the front door and ushered Ellie into the house. She barely glanced at the comfortable lounge room with its masculine sparseness of black leather lounge, flat-screen television on a steel and glass shelving unit, neatly stacked bookcase, and newspaper and mug on the coffee table. Then her gaze swung towards the ceiling, searching for a protruding boot.

'Danny?' Chris called.

'Here, Dad.' The cry came from further inside the house. Chris walked down a hallway to the laundry, Ellie following, and they saw Danny's boot where it poked out from the ceiling, only a metre from an open manhole. Chris took the stepladder Danny must have used to climb up, reached up, untied the shoelaces, and eased the boot from his son's foot. He pulled down some of the ceiling plasterboard behind Danny's heel and slowly the sock-covered foot slid out of sight, accompanied by a faint groan of relief from its owner.

'Thanks, Dad.' A couple of seconds later a face that bore a striking resemblance to Chris's appeared in the open manhole. 'We caught him. I'll hand the trap down.'

Chris took the trap and lowered it to the floor. The contents stared at them, stunned by the sudden glare of the light. '*That's* what's been causing that racket at night?' Chris asked, incredulous.

Ellie couldn't help it. She laughed. The possum was the tiniest she'd ever seen, its little pink nose barely twitching, its long claws clutching a piece of carrot as though afraid its meal would be confiscated.

'That's the baby.' Danny lowered himself onto the ladder and climbed down, swatting dust and cobwebs from his jeans and jumper. 'It got caught and the mother was really upset, but she got away. But I saw where she went so I plugged the hole. I thought we could release the baby outside and she'd find it.'

'She might not accept it back,' Ellie said. 'But it looks old enough to be independent. Possums are territorial, so you'll have to release it here. You could make a nesting box and put it in a tree in your backyard for them so they don't try to get back in your roof.'

Danny looked at her as though seeing her for the first time. Then he grinned. 'Hello. I guess you're Ellie.' He offered his hand. 'I'm Danny.'

'Dusty Danny,' Chris reminded him. 'Why don't you get cleaned up. We brought dessert home.'

'Sorry.' Danny rubbed his palm against his thigh. 'What about the possum?'

Chris picked up the trap. 'I'll release it in the bigger tree. That's probably where its mother lives. You can make a nesting box tomorrow. Is your foot okay?'

'Just a few scratches.'

Ellie watched as Danny hurried back up the hallway. He was nearly as tall as Chris, but gangly and awkward, as though his body couldn't keep up with his enthusiasm.

'He's slightly autistic,' Chris said quietly as he turned on the outside light and opened the laundry door. 'Luckily he's very intelligent, but his social skills are on the light side.'

'How did he cope with his peer group at school?'

'Not well. He wanted to be friends but he couldn't seem to understand that they didn't have his abilities with maths and English and he used to get impatient with them. He ended up getting teased and bullied a lot.'

Ellie nodded her understanding. 'There was a boy in Miranda's class like that. Great kid, but different to the herd so he was picked on a lot. It used to upset Miranda that the other boys wouldn't just leave him alone.'

'Yeah,' Chris sighed as they walked towards a large eucalypt tree in the corner of the yard. 'Kids can be cruel.' He put the cage on the ground, the door facing the tree, and opened it. The possum didn't move.

'Back at the restaurant,' Chris said while they waited, 'you went white when I said Danny had had an accident. Were you thinking of Cherilyn Manning?'

'No.' Ellie let the word hang, pulling her coat closer against the outer chill while trying to ignore the inner one. She didn't move. Chris didn't move. Neither did the possum. She shivered. 'We had a son. Our first-born, Paul. Money was tight so I went back to work when he was a couple of weeks old and he went into crèche. He died of SIDS when he was eleven months old. They discovered he wasn't breathing when they went to wake him for his lunch-time bottle.'

Chris looked at her for a long moment, then he picked up one end of the trap and gently slid the possum onto the grass. 'Go to Mumma,' he told it, and watched as it abandoned the carrot and scampered up the tree. He shook the remaining carrot pieces onto the grass and closed the trap door. Then he put his arms around Ellie and hugged her.

There was something so intimate, so consoling, in his embrace that she sank into it as though she belonged there. And maybe she did. They'd both lost someone they loved. But though she'd shared her loss with Damien, she'd never felt the comfort from him that she was feeling now with Chris. Had they been so unable to connect with each other even back then? Before she could explore the idea further, Chris tilted his head to hers and said, 'Let's get inside where it's warm.' Then his lips touched hers in a kiss so gentle it almost brought tears to her eyes.

'Dad! Ellie! Do you want coffee with your cake? Is that third piece for me?' Danny called out, and Ellie turned to see his face at a window.

'Typical teenager,' she smiled, 'they'd find cake buried under a tonne of snow.'

'And chocolate,' Chris agreed as they walked to the door.

Several minutes later they sat at the kitchen table and watched Danny play host. There was an innocence about him that Ellie found appealing. And he looked and acted much younger than eighteen. 'Are you still at school?' she asked him.

He passed mugs of tea to her and Chris and placed spoons on the table for the three of them. 'First year at uni. IT. Information Technology.' He scooped a large spoonful of cake into his mouth.

'Do you like it?'

'Some of it's boring,' he swallowed a mouthful, 'because it's so basic. But some of the other guys there are on my wavelength and we have a lot of fun.'

With several more bites he finished his cake. 'I got study to do.' He stood up. 'Nice to meet you, Ellie,' he smiled, and trotted down the hallway.

'He seems keen,' she commented. 'I had to use bribery to get Miranda to study. Pru was the conscientious one. Still is.'

'Don't be fooled.' There was a dry edge to Chris's voice.

'He's probably playing a computer game or surfing the net or talking with mates on Facebook.'

'I like him.'

Chris looked at her, a slow smile lighting his face. 'So do I,' he admitted. A long silence followed, but it wasn't strained, and Ellie found herself searching for a word to describe it. Companionable, she finally decided. Comforting. Like having a hug. Only, and she smiled at the memory of how that had felt, not quite as good. The hug was definitely better. Thinking about it now reminded her of the smell of his skin as she'd leaned into him, her face against his chest, his neck. It wasn't aftershave or talc or anything like that, it was *him*, and something in her responded to it on a level more basic than her intellect could fathom. But she wasn't going to question it, just enjoy it.

It was funny - when she was waiting to go out with him she was as skittish as a new-born colt, but when she was with him she wasn't nervous, just ... happy. The realisation surprised her. She hadn't been happy for such a long time it was almost a shock to recognise the feeling.

'What's so amusing?' he asked.

She re-focussed to see him smiling at her. She smiled back. 'Teenage boys and possums.' She glanced at the clock on the opposite wall. 'And if I don't get to bed soon I won't wake up in time for work in the morning.'

There was a slight pulse in the air as the possibility of what her words could imply hung between them, then he stood and took their empty mugs to the sink. 'I'd better take you home,' he said.

That gleam was back in his eyes, and Ellie fought to

control her reaction to it. Oh, yes, he was tempting, all right. It had been so long since she'd enjoyed love-making that the thought of being between the sheets with him was enough to make her clench her thighs together. Not so much in anticipation as to not give in to the ache that was threatening to overcome her natural caution. She might have kissed on their first date, but she wasn't going to hop into bed on their second. Or third. No matter how appealing the thought was.

But when he walked her to her door some time later and kissed her goodnight, she wondered just how long her resolve would last.

The winds were blowing straight from the Antarctic. They had to be. Geoffrey couldn't get warm, no matter how many of the thin blankets the charity had given him were piled on top of his futon. In prison he'd hated the cold so much he'd volunteered to work in the kitchen. In summer it was a bitch, but in winter it was a welcome relief from the energy-sapping cold and the bleakness exacerbated by the stark cell that had been his home.

In that half-awake state that told him he needed more sleep but his shivering denied him, Geoffrey remembered that he had something important to do today. Once that thought focused in his mind all hope of sleep fled. He lay there a while longer, fighting the need to relieve himself, then flung the blankets aside with a curse and lumbered the ten steps to the bathroom that was so small he was surprised he didn't have to sit on the toilet to have a shower. *Compact*, the landlord had called it, and he'd only refrained from snorting his disgust because the rent was the lowest he'd been able to find and even that left him little for other needs.

It was only after he'd spent five minutes under the shower that he finally warmed up. That was another reason he was loathe to leave the bedsit - the hot water system might be old but it had been installed in an era before environmental restrictions had been placed on flow and volume. The copious amount of steaming water was the only luxury he had, and he wasn't going to lose it.

Coffee and toast was hardly filling, but he slathered on the jam to try to take the edge off the gnawing in his belly. He looked at his mother's letter and wondered again if she'd written it because she cared or because it was the Christian thing to do. Even at his worst she had still tried to convince him that God would forgive him, but he was sceptical that a supreme being would forgive someone who wasn't really sorry for his sins. And he wasn't enough of a hypocrite to pretend otherwise.

My door is always open to you, she'd written when his sentence was nearly up, but he hadn't taken up the offer. His skills at lying didn't extend to 24/7.

He brushed his teeth, knowing his mother would notice if he hadn't. Although he hated the way it flattened what was left of his curly hair, he pulled on a beanie before he left.

The phone booth wasn't occupied, and he slipped inside and shut the door to escape the wind, but it whistled under the gap. It didn't take long for his feet to lose what little warmth they had, and his mood dropped in sympathy. He automatically checked to see if any coins had been left in the change cavity. Empty. Typical. He shoved his own money in, punched the buttons, and waited. The ringing went on and on. His stomach clenched tighter with each drawn-out tone until he finally heard the long beep that told him there would be no answer.

The shiver that ran through his body had nothing to do with the cold. Fear rose in his throat like bile. He gulped it down. Where was she? He would have to go there again, make enquiries. Maybe the neighbours would know where she was.

Someone had to know.

By the time he walked from the last bus stop to his mother's unit, apprehension ate into his belly like a ravenous rat. The retirement village was more alive than it had seemed the previous day - residents were walking, or riding those four-wheeled scooters he'd been tempted to nudge in the days when he used to own a car. An old man, wizened, hunched, but obviously still determined, pushed a walker with hands so twisted with arthritis he almost couldn't grasp the handles. He watched the man's slow procession, the incapacity that age had forced upon him, and this time his shiver was not the fear of being killed by his ex-partners in crime. *Shit! I'd shoot myself if I got like that.* And then he realised that if he ever reached that stage he would no longer be able to handle a gun, let alone pull the trigger.

He nearly turned and ran, but a middle-aged woman in a pale uniform came out of a unit and noticed him. She hesitated a moment, then walked towards him and said, 'Can I help you?'

Only desperation stayed him. 'I came yesterday to see my mother, Maud Lenard, but she wasn't home. I phoned this morning and got no answer so I thought I'd come out and see if she was all right.'

Eyebrows drawing together in a frown of sympathy, the woman shook her head. 'I'm sorry, but your mother was taken to hospital two days ago with a stroke. She's still in there, I'm afraid.'

He didn't have to fake his distress at the news, but it wasn't because he felt any concern for his mother's health. 'Is she ... How is she? Can she speak?'

'I believe so, but she has been affected quite badly by the stroke and you must prepare yourself. If you walk back to the office with me I can give you all the details and let you know which ward she's in, Mr Lenard,' the woman smiled.

He smiled back. 'Please, call me Geoffrey.'

Ellie couldn't believe how happy she felt. She wasn't naive, she knew all about the physical and emotional reactions falling in love caused, and she wasn't going to be duped into thinking that Chris was the best thing since sliced bread. But she was certainly going to enjoy this euphoric sensation while it lasted. She'd even had a record day of sales at work and Richard had been extremely pleased, murmuring something about a Christmas bonus if that continued. Even the weather had improved - the westerly winds had died down by lunchtime and the sun had shared its benevolence, creating the kind of winter's day Queensland boasted about to the southern states.

By the time she battled peak-hour traffic and pulled into

her driveway, tiredness had taken some of the glow off her happiness bubble, but there was still a smile on her face when she unlocked the front door. Miranda's car wasn't in the carport, and Ellie could only assume she'd left early for her rostered shift with the food van.

Ten minutes later, changed into a tracksuit and slippers and with a pre-dinner wine in one hand and stroking Mayhem from head to tail as she lay on her lap, Ellie stretched out on the lounge to watch the television news. Nothing of great import was happening - politicians were squabbling like petulant puppies over a perceived breach of parliamentary privilege, a movie star was behaving outrageously, a car had crashed into a shopfront but no-one had been injured.

She was considering whether she felt like cooking a meal from scratch or if opening a can was a better option when the newsreader made a sudden announcement: 'A police officer has been shot while responding to an altercation near Ascot raceway.'

She watched as the screen switched to a tree-lined street blocked by police cars and swarming with officers in protective vests carrying weapons of varying firepower. Street lights broke the darkness into patches of light and shadow. Spotlights focused on a house where, according to the newsreader, the person who "allegedly shot the police officer" was holding a hostage and refusing to give himself up to the police. As the television reporter highlighted the drama of the situation, the tightness that had started in Ellie's stomach clawed its way into her chest and threatened to stop her breathing. Was Chris the police officer who'd been shot? He was on duty, she knew that, but was Ascot part of his precinct or whatever police in Australia called their area?

Her fingers curled, pulling at Mayhem's hair. The kitten meowed its displeasure and dug its claws into her leg. Ellie ignored the sting, her mind focused on the situation unfolding on the screen. She tried to tell herself that the odds were stacked in favour of Chris *not* being the officer who was now, according to the announcer, listed as critical since his recent arrival at hospital.

It didn't work. The not knowing was a pain in her gut that wouldn't go away. There was a rawness about it, as though she were feeling something she hadn't felt in a long time. Something she hadn't even felt when her father died. Cancer had taken him quickly, too far along by the time he'd gone to a doctor to even offer a hope of treatment, but still allowing enough time for the family to adjust to his early death. Not that you adjust, she remembered, but in the end it was a relief to see him free of his suffering.

This was the same agonising disbelief that had gripped her as she'd sped to the child care centre after the manager's phone call. The sheer terror that, she now realised, had led to the kind of grief that had ended up muting her feelings in the ensuing years. Feelings that Chris Ryan was slowly bringing to life again.

Mayhem jumped off her lap, claws again digging into Ellie's leg, and she jerked with the pain.

The reporter signed off and the scene switched back to the newsreader. Ellie drank her wine, her attention so inward-focused she couldn't remember if it was red or white, and caring less. She stayed on the lounge, anxiety and fear tying her stomach in knots as she waited for news updates. At the end of the program a quick segue to the hostage drama showed it hadn't been resolved and Ellie remained seated, watching but not really hearing the ensuing current affairs program and sitcom. At one stage she thought about grabbing something to eat, but was afraid she would miss an update.

Finally, just as the sitcom ended, the news came through that the gunman had freed the hostage and surrendered to the police. But no further news came about the officer who had been shot.

Ellie remained frozen a moment longer, then picked up her mobile and speed-dialled Chris's number. It went to messagebank.

'It's Ellie,' she told it, grateful her voice sounded relatively normal. 'Phone me when you can. Please.'

CHAPTER EIGHTEEN

The next few hours became a mix of a half-eaten toasted sandwich, a let-go-cold coffee, and distracted attempts to finish her designs for the units. When a vehicle pulled into the driveway she almost ran to the door, then realised the engine noise was too light for Chris's four-wheel-drive.

Miranda opened the front door a moment later. One glance at her daughter's face and Ellie's words of greeting died on her lips. 'Mirie, what's wrong?' she asked instead.

Miranda swiped at her red-rimmed eyes, threw her shoulder bag on the lounge and herself after it. 'I did what you said.'

'What I said?' Ellie hurriedly searched her memory. 'Oh. You said something to Ben?'

'Yes.' Miranda drew in a deep breath, then let it out in a long sigh. 'I told him I liked him. Liked him more than just as a friend.' She lapsed into silence.

'And?' Ellie prompted.

'And he said he likes me. But just as a friend. He said he can't think of getting into a relationship at this point in his life because he wants to focus on his work with the church. He's even considering becoming a minister.'

'Oh.'

'Yeah. Oh.'

Ellie wished she could say something wise that would help Miranda but her brain wasn't functioning well and she considered that nothing she said at the moment would alleviate Miranda's misery.

'He did say that he values my friendship and he hopes that I'll still come out on the run with him,' Miranda added.

'And will you?'

'I guess so. I - '

The sudden ringing of the phone had both their heads swivelling to stare at it. Ellie rushed over and grabbed the receiver. Miranda looked at her, head tilted in query.

'Hello?' Ellie tried to keep the hope out of her voice but it came through, thick as treacle.

'It's Chris.'

A sigh of relief escaped her. 'I was ...' she wanted to say *concerned*, wanted to appear as though she were just a casual friend with only a casual friend's depth of concern, but ... 'worried. The news. On TV. The shooting.'

'Yeah. It wasn't good.'

The bald understatement shook her. She felt like yelling at him.

'Thanks for worrying, but I'm okay.' He sounded tired. 'I have to go. I'll see you at the units tomorrow evening.'

'Okay. Bye.' Ellie placed the receiver back in the cradle.

'Mum? Was that Chris? Was he involved in that shootout? Everyone was talking about it.' Miranda pulled herself from the lounge and went over to Ellie. 'Are you all right?'

'Of course. I was just concerned. Chris has been very kind to me.'

Miranda said nothing, but if the look she gave Ellie was any indication of her thoughts, Ellie's acting talent was on equal footing with her tolerance of rats.

If tiredness was a prerequisite, Ellie should have slept soundly, but her dreams bordered on nightmares; her senses, even in sleep, seemed more acute than when she was awake, rousing her at the slightest noise. She woke to another sunny day, crisp and cold with a light breeze that wafted the faint perfume of orange jasmine through her partially-open window. A good-to-be-alive day, in spite of winter's chill.

She closed her eyes, snuggled further beneath the doona and tried to persuade herself to go back to sleep.

It didn't work.

Her mind buzzed, torn between anticipation at seeing Chris that evening and her burgeoning feelings towards him and the panic that thought elicited. She'd done a lot of thinking last night. Once she'd known he was all right, she'd analysed her reactions to the situation. In the past it had been easy for her to drift, accepting the status quo, only half-heartedly fighting Damien's control over their lives, and retreating further from a relationship that hadn't really existed for some time.

But with Chris she wanted to rush headlong into being with him. It was so easy, so companionable, but still with that frizz of excitement that made her feel alive, really alive, for the first time in years. But with that feeling came fear. The realisation and the memory of loss. Loss and grief so profound she wasn't sure she could risk feeling it again.

'Mum! You're going to be late for work!' Miranda yelled

from the hallway.

Ellie tossed the doona aside and scrambled from the bed.

Chris's Rodeo was parked outside the units when Ellie arrived that evening. He walked over and opened her car door. She shoved a torch in her pocket, stepped out and pulled her coat closer. 'Hi,' she said and the word came out all husky and sensuous. Her heart beat faster as he leaned close and kissed her. It was light, a greeting kind of kiss, but she felt it all the way to her toes. Damn, but she was lost already, heating up in ways that had nothing to do with menopause.

It scared the hell out of her.

'Hi yourself,' he smiled and put his arm around her and walked her to the footpath. Her fear ebbed, pushed away by the *rightness* of being with him.

Chris had brought his torch. It was bigger and the beam stronger than Ellie's and she was grateful for that - the darkness inside the building was deeper than outside with its glow of street and house lights. They made their way to the third floor, not speaking, shining their torches on the stairs and the landings so they could see where they were going.

The door to unit nine was open. He motioned Ellie behind him and they walked in. The closed windows and the echo of their footsteps in the darkness created a feeling that was both eerie and claustrophobic. If it hadn't been for the city lights sprinkling the horizon, Ellie would have felt almost disorientated. She swept her torch beam over the walls.

'The holes! They've been fixed.'

She examined the patched-up sections of wall. The job had been done so well there was no way to tell what shape the holes had been. Even the prised-up floorboards had been nailed down.

'If Bruce had called us in,' Chris said, 'our forensic guys might have found some clues to the perp. No use now.'

'I'm sorry to drag you all the way over here for nothing.' Ellie examined more of the patches. She was about to turn around when his arms folded her back against him.

'It's not entirely a wasted trip,' he murmured, his breath warm on her hair. 'We could grab some dinner. You must be hungry.'

She turned in his embrace and without really meaning to, she was kissing him. Kissing him with a passion she'd thought had disappeared years ago. His lips were soft but demanding on hers, rousing her further, asking for more, needing more. It would have been easy, so easy, to yield to that urgency, to offer what they both wanted, but she drew back, her breath coming in funny little puffs as she forced herself to gain control.

Chris must have done a better job at finding that control than she had. She heard the smile in his voice as he said, 'That wasn't the sort of hungry I had in mind, but it beats a pizza any day.'

Her laughter strangled in her throat. It beat a pizza by more than a country mile. But she wasn't sure if that's what she wanted. No, she wanted it all right, but could she cope with it? It would be so easy to fall in love with him, she was half-way there already, but could she live with someone whose life got put on the line every day? Who might not come home to her one night because some drunken idiot got hold of a gun and started a shoot-out with police?

She pulled away from him. 'Perhaps we should get that pizza.'

His torch beam moved so he could see her face. 'You okay? You sound ... serious.'

She took his arm and smiled. 'Pizza is serious. So many decisions - meatlovers, Hawaiian, seafood ...' She could tell he wasn't convinced, but here in this gloomy room in a building that echoed with death was not the right place to discuss what was bothering her. 'Let's go get some.'

Geoffrey Lenard smiled tiredly at the nurse who came to check on his mother. He knew the medical staff thought his bedside vigil was indicative of his devotion and tried not to dispel the illusion. He'd been shocked, more than he thought possible, by her appearance when he'd first arrived. He'd expected to find her aged, after all he hadn't seen her in years, but the tiny figure whose white hair had blended into the surrounding white sheets reminded him of a peach that had shrivelled in the hot sun.

In the previous forty-eight hours she had recognised him twice, but her mind had wandered to his childhood and stayed there. No amount of cajoling could get her to remember what had happened to her older sister.

Yesterday he'd pleaded with the retirement village manager to allow him into his mother's unit. She'd agreed, but stayed with him while he'd gathered photos he felt might help jog his mother's memory.

Now he studied the photo taken only months before his

mother's oldest sister, Fanny, had died aged forty. The three sisters smiled through faded black and white - Maud, shy and timid as always, Fanny, dutiful and serious as befitting the eldest, and Iris, the middle child, the rebel, the one whose smile barely concealed her contempt for the restrictions of her gender and family's status.

Visits to Iris's unit were a rarity in his childhood. His father disapproved of his sister-in-law's proclivity for associating with the more risqué elements of Brisbane society. As a clergyman he'd felt, as he'd so often told Geoffrey, that it was his duty to keep his son from people who might lead him into temptation to sin. Years later Geoffrey wondered if that restriction had made the temptation even more alluring.

'You should go home,' the nurse said. 'Visiting hours are nearly over, and I don't think your mother's going to wake again tonight.'

'I'll go soon,' he replied. 'Just a few more minutes.'

She nodded her sympathy and left. Geoffrey slumped further down the visitor's chair, cursing again the practicality of the straight back and vinyl seat. He'd explained the circumstances to the men to whom he owed the money, and had gained a small reprieve. But the sense of urgency hadn't left him, and he knew it wouldn't until the threat of bodily harm or death had been removed. Dying was one thing, a quick bullet to the head and lights out, but he knew the pain his associates were not only capable of inflicting but had done so to other unlucky bastards with more enthusiasm than he could comprehend, and the thought had caused more than sweat to leave his body on several occasions.

'I'm sorry.'

The soft words, slightly slurred, jerked him from his thoughts. His mother raised a crepey-skinned hand towards him. Her eyes were focused and clear for the first time since he'd been visiting her, and a strange sense of connection tugged at him. He pushed it aside. 'Sorry for what?'

'Not standing up to your father for you. I begged him to allow you to do the things that other boys your age were doing, but he was never a flexible person. My mother said he had "sinful pride" but I would never have told him that. When he found out I'd taken you to visit your Aunt Iris he made me promise I wouldn't do so again. You always wanted to go,' she sighed.

A memory flashed. His mother, finger on lips, telling him not to mention to his father that they'd been to see his aunt. 'But you still took me,' he frowned. 'Only once or twice a year, but we still went.'

'She was my sister. I loved her. She gave up a lot for me. And she loved you. I sometimes wondered why she never married and had children because I could see she loved you.'

Geoffrey felt his world tilt a little. His gentle mother, the woman he'd always considered spineless, had defied his father for him. And for the aunt his father had despised.

'What did she give up for you?'

Her eyes closed. 'Too long ago. And she's gone ...' Her voice trailed off, and he realised she'd gone back to sleep. He wanted to shake her awake, but knew from the past two days sitting with her that it would be futile. He hauled himself from the chair and stood looking at her as though seeing her for the first time - the white hair, the wrinkled skin splotched with age and sun exposure. He bent and kissed her forehead, then shook his head in surprise at himself and hurried from the room.

It was surprisingly mild for a winter's night. No westerly wind swirled its icy breath across the city, no southerly busters blew from the Antarctic. Even with her new short haircut Ellie didn't feel the need to wrap a scarf around her head to protect her ears as they walked to the same restaurant they'd been to only two nights before. It wasn't as crowded tonight, and they opted for a table in an unoccupied corner.

They'd been seated and placed their orders when Chris looked at her with a searching gaze that made her feel as though he were capable of reading her soul. 'What's wrong?' he finally asked.

She was about to say 'Nothing,' but stopped herself. She'd spent too many years avoiding anything that would expose her doubts, her insecurities, her needs. If she wasn't going to remain a coward she would have to confront her fears. 'I don't know how to explain it,' she began, then looked into his eyes and faltered. How could eyes that were the colour of clear sky appear so warm, so concerned. She could feel her worries melting under their warmth.

His hand reached across and covered her entwined fingers where they lay on the table. 'Just tell me.'

'I don't know if I can cope with the kind of work you do.'

He frowned a little. 'Do you mean dealing with murders and things like that?'

'No.' She wished his hand didn't feel so good on hers. It made it hard to think of saying that maybe they shouldn't see each other again. 'With the fact that in your job you could be killed just because some idiot objects to having his car searched by a cop and pulls a knife or some drunken husband is beating his wife and decides to shoot the cop who tries to intervene.'

The blue darkened, clouded over, as his eyebrows drew closer together. 'My wife died because some idiot was driving too fast in wet conditions. None of us know when something like that can happen. At least cops are trained to cope with the kind of situations you're talking about.'

'I know. But ...' she hesitated, 'I'm afraid. Not afraid of dying. Not myself. Afraid of having people I care about die. It's taken me a long time to realise how badly Paul's death affected me. I don't know if I could cope with that again.'

'Tell me about it.'

Simple words. Tell me about it. As though it was that easy. She'd never told anyone before, just buried the memory like she'd buried the person she once was.

Maybe it was time to bring both out into the open and see what could come of it. She tried to move her hands away so she could remain detached while she told him, but his grip tightened as though he knew her intention. 'Just tell me,' he said. 'It will be all right.'

'I got there just before the ambulance officers. The centre staff were still trying to resuscitate him but ... his ... his little body was cold ... and blue. And I grabbed him and held him and thought that if I cuddled him he would get warm and it was only a mistake or a nightmare and he would turn pink and wake up.' The words tumbled out, startling her with their intensity, as though she'd unleashed not only the memories but the feelings as well. Time might have dimmed the pain, but not the images that were seared forever in her mind. 'Then the ambulance men came and said he was dead and they took him away and it was an hour before Damien arrived. He'd been in transit from a meeting and he didn't have a mobile phone then.'

'Did you ever tell Damien that you'd held Paul's body?'

She shook her head. 'I couldn't. I didn't have the words. Saying them would have made it all too real. It was real enough as it was. I couldn't relive that again by telling him.'

'Have you ever told anyone?'

She shook her head again. 'There never seemed a good time. We had counselling, but it seemed ... I don't know - so clinical. And I think I was trying so hard not to blame Damien because I'd had to go back to work when Paul was so little that I didn't want him to feel worse. And on top of that I kept thinking that if only I'd done something differently that day or been more aware that perhaps Paul wasn't well, that I should have noticed if he'd had a fever, or a hundred other things, that he wouldn't have died. It was a day like every other day but I was sure I must have missed something.'

'Yes. Your rational brain tells you one thing, but your heart tells you something else, doesn't it.'

'Did you ...'

'Blame myself for Angela's death? Yes. I did. For a long

time.'

'Were you happy together?' The question came out before she could stop it, but it was something she needed to know, though she wasn't sure why.

'Yes, we were. She understood that being married to a cop wasn't always easy, but she dealt with it okay.'

Ellie absorbed his answer, wondering if she needed to know because she was worried he would compare her with his dead wife or because she doubted her ability to cope with what his job entailed. Right now both scenarios were more than she wanted to think about. 'I'm sorry. I don't know why I shoved all this kind of angst onto you. It's not like we're ... involved or anything.'

His hand stilled on hers. His gaze intensified, pinning her like a moth to cardboard, his voice low and almost rough with emotion as he said, 'I became *involved* with you when we sat on the stairs at the units and you didn't groan at my pathetic attempt to take your mind off what you'd just seen.'

Her heart jumped at the way he said *involved*, the emphasis he gave it, but she didn't want to delve into that, not just yet anyway. 'You mean about you fainting at your first autopsy?'

He nodded.

'Did you really faint?'

'No,' he smiled, 'but it made you feel better to think so, didn't it.'

It was her turn to smile. 'I didn't feel quite so wussy knowing I wasn't the only one.'

'So how about you don't worry about my job and we just keep dating and see how you feel about it in a few months time.'

A few months? At the rate she was falling for him, in a few months she'd be a total goner. It was too scary to contemplate. But then, not seeing him again was just as scary. For the first time in a long time she wanted something so badly she was willing to risk the type of emotional pain she'd spent most of her life avoiding. She smiled, aware that he would see the doubt in her eyes, but unable to hide it. 'I guess we could do that.'

Although Chris had seemed to accept her reluctant agreement to keep going out with him, Ellie wasn't so sure she could hold up her side of the bargain. Knowing her fear was irrational didn't make it go away. Talking to him about Paul's death had eased not just some of the pain - she'd learned to cope with that and time had helped - but the guilt she hadn't been able to lose, and the resentment towards Damien that still lingered deep in her soul. But her fear of loss had become so ingrained she questioned if she could ever really free herself of it.

Once again, the reassurance she'd felt from being with him disappeared the moment he said goodnight at her door and drove away. She watched him get into his Rodeo before walking inside.

'Hi, Mum.' Miranda looked across from the documentary she was watching on television. Mayhem was lying on her lap, asleep in the relaxed way cats have when they feel safe. 'What did Chris think of the holes?'

Ellie kicked off her shoes and flopped down on the spare chair. 'Bruce had already patched them up.'

'Bummer.'

'Tell me about it. I felt like an idiot. Chris was okay about it, but I wonder if that was because it gave him an excuse to take me to dinner again.'

'You mean he didn't believe you?'

'I think he did, but he's all cop - needs to have proof, not just my say-so.'

'Understandable.'

'I suppose it is.' She reached over and stroked the kitten. Mayhem twitched but didn't wake. 'How did you go on the van with Ben last night?'

Miranda sighed. 'I think he's avoiding me.'

'What makes you think that?'

'We had a new volunteer with us and he spent most of his time showing her what to do.'

'Understandable.'

Miranda narrowed her eyes but Ellie assumed an air of innocence. Two can play at devil's advocate, she thought.

A flickering image on the television screen caught her attention. Black and white footage of Brisbane's parks and gardens from early in the twentieth century. People moving like marionettes across leaf-strewn paths and beneath the limbs of trees already old in nature's terms. In the background were houses and buildings that had long since been demolished, and she felt again the disappointment when she'd discovered unit one had been renovated. With a jolt she remembered that she hadn't taken the opportunity tonight to finish measuring the living room. So much for trying to be professional.

'You okay?' Miranda asked.

'Why?'

'You kind of jerked up, like you'd been stung.'

'Just mentally kicking myself. I forgot to get the rest of the measurements for unit one. I'll have to go back after work tomorrow and take them.'

'You'll probably be late getting home. Do you want me to cook dinner?'

Ellie smiled. 'That would be great.'

Geoffrey Lenard stepped out of the bus onto the Translink busway station platform. He paused for a moment, wishing he could still feel the mild midday sunshine that had shone through the window on his journey to the hospital, but no warmth penetrated the modern steel and concrete structure. He pulled his coat closer and hurried into the hospital. After his mother's brief brush with reality last night he was cautiously optimistic that she might be the same way again this morning and he could obtain the information he needed.

When he'd left last night the nurse had warned him not to come in before lunch as his mother was scheduled for another scan and more blood tests. Now, as he hurried along a hallway that led to his mother's ward, the aroma of roast lamb overtook the all-pervading smell of antiseptic, and his stomach rumbled in response. The bus trips of the past few days had eaten into his dwindling money and breakfast today had consisted of a slice of toast and coffee so anaemic it barely coloured the interior of the mug.

He stopped in the doorway to the room his mother shared with several other women.

Her bed was empty.

Not only empty, but stripped of sheets, pillows, and blankets.

CHAPTER NINETEEN

Geoffrey's jaw dropped. Air gushed from his lungs. He could swear the room started to sway.

'Mr Lenard? Mr Lenard?'

A woman was speaking to him. He turned to face her, seeing but not really noticing the nurse's uniform straining across her more than generous curves. Then he remembered her face. The nurse who'd spoken to him last night. 'My mother …' his voice failed him.

'She's fine, Mr Lenard. Just a little accident. Elderly people don't always have good bladder and bowel control, I'm afraid. She's just being given a wash and a change of nightgown.'

Relief rushed through him so quickly he staggered. The nurse reached out to steady him. 'Are you all right?'

'Yes, yes. I just haven't eaten. Didn't realise how late it was getting.'

The look she gave him said she'd seen the state of his clothing and shoes and knew that time had little to do with his lack of food, but her eyes held nothing but sympathy as she said she'd try to 'rustle up something' for him. Within a few minutes she returned with a tray like those that had been placed on the stands over each patient's bed. It was only then that he noticed his mother's stand held a similar tray.

'A patient checked out this morning,' the nurse informed him, then winked conspiratorially. 'No point having her lunch go to waste.'

Just then another nurse bustled in, linen in her arms, and swiftly made his mother's bed. Geoffrey waited until she had finished, then placed his tray next to his mother's. He looked around to see two of the other patients, both women and both on the wrong side of seventy, staring at him with ill-concealed curiosity. The third patient, a younger woman, was devouring her lunch as though she'd been starved for some time. Geoffrey remembered some of the medical procedures he'd endured when he'd fallen ill once and knew that fasting was a pre-requisite for most. He closed the curtain around the bed to give himself some privacy and took the lid off the plate.

Salad. Cold meat of some to-be-guessed-at origin, and salad.

What sane person ordered salad in the middle of winter, he fumed.

He looked at his mother's lunch. Lifted the lid. Roast lamb. Dripping with gravy. Crisp potatoes. Soft pumpkin. Carrots and beans and even some broccoli.

His hesitation was brief. He swapped the trays around and wolfed down the hot meal. He was just dabbing his mouth with the paper serviette when the curtain was pushed aside and a nurse wheeled his mother over to the bed. Her face broke into a lopsided smile of pleasure and something he'd thought long gone stirred in his chest.

The nurse locked the wheelchair brakes and began to

help his mother onto the bed. The old woman faltered, her legs obviously lacking the strength to stand. Geoffrey took her arm, surprised by how thin it felt under the flannelette nightgown, and assisted the nurse.

'Sorry,' his mother apologised. 'I'm more tired than I thought.'

'It's all right, Maud,' the nurse tucked the sheet and blanket around her, plumped several pillows behind for support, and pushed the tray table over the bed. 'Just eat your lunch now, dear,' she said, and with a nod to Geoffrey, now seated on a visitor's chair, swept away.

'I'm so pleased you've come,' his mother smiled again. 'I thought I might have dreamed you were here last night. We talked about Iris, didn't we?'

She remembered! Geoffrey tried not to appear too eager. 'Yes. You were saying she gave up a lot for you. What did you mean?'

Maud looked as though she were uncertain she should talk about it. 'It was a long time ago, when I was going to be engaged to your father. It doesn't matter any more.'

Geoffrey shrugged. 'If it doesn't matter, then what's the harm in telling me. Iris is gone, and I'm the last family member alive. It's part of my history, so I probably should know.'

Maud pondered this a bit, then sighed. 'It was a scandal at the time, and it could have prevented me marrying your father.'

Geoffrey managed to stop his reactive snort. Having that sanctimonious old prick as a father had pushed him into places he may never have otherwise gone. The forbidden was always more attractive than the safe. 'I know Iris was a bit unconventional, but I didn't think she did anything scandalous.'

'Not when *you* knew her. But when she was younger,' Maud's smile replaced the tiredness in her eyes, 'she was such a tearaway. She'd always been a wilful child, but she got worse as she got older. Nothing our father said could make her change her ways. She made friends with a group of artists. They were a wild lot, and their morals weren't the best. She used to paint, but she also used to pose for artists too. Sometimes in the nude,' she whispered. 'She said that's how she made a living.' Drool slid from the corner of her lip, and she took a handkerchief from her bedside drawer and wiped it with a trembling hand. 'Your father wanted to marry me, but he said he couldn't because it wouldn't do for the wife of a minister to have a sister with the reputation Iris was getting.'

Geoffrey tried to curb his impatience. As a child, the few times he'd seen Iris she'd always been circumspect around him, but when he'd become a teenager she'd been less cautious and he'd discovered what sort of a life she really enjoyed. 'So what happened?' he prompted.

'I told Iris how heartbroken I was. She didn't like your father but she loved me, so she gave up modelling for the other artists and got a job in a shop. She left the artist's commune where she was living and moved into a flat.' She paused, leaning back against the pillows, her voice softening to a tired whisper. 'The flat where we used to visit her,' she explained.

This was more like it. The unit. The "flat" as his mother

always called it. That's what he needed to know. 'She lived in a top floor unit when you used to take me there,' he said. 'Is that where she died?'

'No. She had a fall and broke her leg and couldn't handle the stairs, so she moved into one on the bottom floor.'

No wonder he'd had no luck in the top unit! 'Which one?' He had to fight to keep his eagerness from showing.

'I forget which number but it was the front one.' The pause was longer this time, and her eyes closed briefly. 'The first on your right as you walked into the entrance.'

'What happened to all her things when she died? She had some nice paintings, if I remember?'

'She'd left them to an art foundation in her will. They weren't worth much - the solicitor had them valued before he handed them over, some sort of tax thing.'

That explained the measly $1,300 he'd received from her estate. It should have been more, but her hospital bills had had to be paid and the solicitor's fees had eaten a large hole as well.

There was another question he wanted to ask her, but he was fairly sure she wouldn't know the answer. Even if she did, he doubted she would discuss it. His parents had always been prudes, using euphemisms for body parts and functions. Hell, he'd got to grade five before he'd found out he had a penis and not a "that". His first grade schoolmate had called it a "prick" and he'd wondered how you could prick anything with flesh that was soft and rounded. His mother's choice of "nude" to describe Iris's modelling was indicative of how she was. In his whole life he'd never heard her use the word "naked".

Before he could ask her anything else, her head slipped to one side and her breathing slowed into the soft rumble of sleep.

He thought about leaving, but decided not to just yet. If he waited for a while he might score some afternoon tea from the plump nurse who'd found him some lunch. Then he'd go back to his bedsit and pick up his tools. With a bit of luck, tonight would prove a lot more rewarding than his previous visits to the units.

'Looks fabulous.'

Ellie whirled at the words coming from behind her and grinned as she saw Kandy. 'Do you really think so?'

'Absolutely.' Kandy waved a ring-clustered hand at the living room display Ellie had just finished decorating. 'You have a good eye for detail. I would never have thought to contrast that shade of orange with the green and brown.'

'Tangerine,' Ellie corrected automatically, with a smile.

'How's it all going?'

'Great. Richard and the staff are really nice and I'm getting the hang of things. My first week here I was so nervous I nearly ran away when Richard was on lunch and a customer started asking questions I didn't know the answers to.'

Kandy plonked herself down on the dark leather lounge and crossed her legs. Then grimaced and uncrossed them. 'Must remember not to do that. My chiropractor says it's bad for my back - pulls my spine out of alignment. I've had back problems recently. Too much sport.'

Ellie couldn't stop her grin. 'Perhaps too much of a

certain kind of sport?' Kandy's answering smile lacked its usual animation, and Ellie instantly apologised. 'I'm sorry. I was only joking.'

'Don't worry,' Kandy waved a dismissive hand. 'I'm not even getting any of that lately.' She stood up. 'What time do you finish work?'

Ellie looked at her watch. 'In half an hour. Why?'

'Can we meet somewhere? To talk?'

'Sure.' Alarm bells started clanging in Ellie's head. Serious talk wasn't something Kandy indulged in, but lately some chinks had started showing in her cheerful armour. 'There's a cafe two doors down. It's nothing flash but the coffee's good. I'll meet you there.'

'Thanks, Ellie. I appreciate it.'

By the time Ellie walked into the cafe thirty-five minutes later, her curiosity was such that it would have killed a hundred cats. She spied Kandy at a corner table, a coffee cup empty in front of her. The way her friend's fingers were worrying at the teaspoon, Ellie wondered if she'd taken up smoking again. She'd fidgeted like that when she'd gone through nicotine withdrawal two years ago.

Kandy saw her and waved her over, then caught the eye of the girl behind the counter and signalled. 'Coffee's coming,' she said when Ellie sat down. 'And I've ordered Black Forest cake as well. It that okay?'

'That's fine.' She was about to say that it sounded like comfort food, the kind women buy when they need to feel better about themselves or men or a doctor's report. Ellie found her chest constricting a little. Maybe Kandy had caught something from one of her lovers? Or had she fallen in love with one of them? Or had Phillip found out about her affairs and thrown her out? Kandy didn't say anything and by the time the waitress arrived Ellie had just about blown her mind with hundreds of unanswered questions.

The coffee steamed in its mug, creamy, frothy, and sprinkled with chocolate dust, the aroma wafting into Ellie's nostrils with its tantalising bitter-sweetness. If a man smelled like that, she thought, no woman could resist devouring him. The thought made her think of Chris. He didn't smell like coffee, but she felt like devouring him anyway. Perhaps Kandy had met a coffee-flavoured lover?

Kandy poured a sugar sachet into her coffee and stirred, her gaze on the mug, but Ellie doubted she saw what she was doing. The tightness in her chest increasing, Ellie waited for Kandy to start talking. But Kandy kept stirring.

'What's up?' Ellie finally asked.

'Did you suspect Damien was having an affair?'

If Kandy's question was designed to take her by surprise, it worked. Ellie stared at her, then gathered her wits. 'No. But I suppose I should have. Things had been so ... well, bad isn't the right word, more like non-existent, for so long that I guess I didn't want to think about it. Why do you ask?'

'Because I think Phillip might be having an affair.'

The absurdity of Kandy's words hit Ellie. 'But you have affairs all the time. Why would you be upset if Phillip did?'

'Because Phillip couldn't care less about sex. If he's having an affair it will be because he's fallen in love with someone.'

'But ...' Ellie tried to find the logic in Kandy's worry

about the situation, 'like I said, you have affairs all the time. What's the difference?'

'That's just sex. I *love* Phillip. Hell, I must do. Why else would I stay with a man who can't even get an erection when he sees me in a G-string and tassles?' She saw Ellie's incredulous look and explained, 'I only tried that once, when we were first married. I knew he was conservative but I thought a little titillation wouldn't hurt. I soon found out he has very set ideas on what constitutes acceptable wifely behaviour. Anyway,' she took the teaspoon out of the mug and tapped it on the table, 'for a man like Phillip who has no sex drive, if he's having an affair it's because he's in love with someone. Do you see?'

In some strange, convoluted way, Ellie *could* see what Kandy was getting at. She took a long sip of her coffee, then spooned cake into her mouth and ate it before asking, 'Why do you think he's having an affair?'

Kandy broke pieces off her cake with her fork, then pushed them around the plate. 'The usual things that make wives suspicious. Phone calls that hang up when I answer, meetings that go late into the night, that sort of thing. I called into his office unexpectedly and his secretary said he was out to lunch so I went to his usual restaurant and he wasn't there.'

'Perhaps he'd gone somewhere else?'

'Phillip is a creature of habit. He would only go somewhere else if he didn't want the staff there to see who was with him. And his mobile was turned off. He never turns that thing off.'

Ellie had to concede Phillip's behaviour did look a little

suspicious. 'What are you going to do about it?'

A frown drew Kandy's perfectly-shaped eyebrows together. 'I don't have a clue. I could hire a private investigator to find out but I don't want to do that. Phillip might find out and I don't want him to think I don't trust him.'

Again there was a crazy logic to Kandy's thinking, and Ellie thought she saw it. Well, sort of. 'Perhaps you could tell him that you feel he's avoiding you. Maybe, if he *is* having an affair, it will give him the opening he needs to confess.'

'And what if he does confess and wants to leave me? I know you and Cass think I'm a tough cookie, but I'm not really. I'm scared to be on my own again. Before I married Phillip I had lots of lovers, but I didn't have anyone who *loved* me.'

'How long have you been married?'

'Nine years, nearly ten. Long enough to know when he's lying to me.'

'I was married to Damien for nearly thirty years and I didn't have a clue what he was up to,' Ellie said, then sighed. 'But it shows just how little there was between us at the end.'

Kandy raised limpid brown eyes to Ellie. 'Makes you wonder about this whole marriage business, doesn't it.'

'But there's always Cass and Joe,' Ellie smiled. 'They're set in concrete. Shining example for the rest of us not to give up hope.'

'Let's just hope they don't fuck up. Oh. Sorry. About the swearing. You and Cass don't swear and I usually keep my tongue under control when I'm around you.'

'That's okay. It's my mother's fault - she used to say that *swearing is a crutch for a crippled conversationalist*.'

Kandy laughed. 'If that comes into your head every time you go to swear it's no wonder you can't.'

'And getting my mouth washed out with soap if I even said shit or bastard. Strict parents and a convent school upbringing,' Ellie shrugged. 'Didn't have a chance, did I.'

'Would have been better than my dead-head parents,' Kandy replied and Ellie silently agreed. At least her parents had cared about her.

In the silence that followed, Ellie finished her coffee and cake. Kandy picked the cherries out of her cake and nibbled at them. Obviously their talk had done nothing to improve her appetite, and Ellie felt less than cheerful herself when they parted company and walked back to their cars. Somehow she felt she'd let Kandy down, as though she should have been able to help her more, but she honestly had no idea what to advise.

Darkness had already fallen as she got into her car. She put the key in the ignition. And remembered she'd planned to go to the units after work and finish measuring unit one.

She hit the steering wheel.

And just to prove she could do it, she swore.

And decided to go anyway.

CHAPTER TWENTY

Only a slight breeze rustled the lasiandra leaves outside the front door of the unit building as Ellie turned the key in the lock. She switched on her torch, walked inside and locked the door behind her.

Damn, but she wished Bruce had left the electricity connected. The place was spooky with its high ceilings and dull echoes and drab colours and musty smell of old carpet and peeling wallpaper. She walked into unit one and pulled the curtains aside, grateful the glow from the nearby street light wasn't interrupted by a fence or trees. The room wasn't lit up, but at least it wasn't totally dark now.

If she didn't let herself think about it, she could almost pretend that this once-lovely old building wasn't where Cherilyn had been so brutally killed.

She took out her pad and tape. It was awkward trying to take measurements and hold the torch at the same time, but luckily she only had a few to do. By the time she'd finished she felt pleased that she hadn't succumbed to the fear that dark places usually held for her. She swept the torch beam around the lounge room, seeing in her mind how her designs would transform it. A sudden thought made her look up at the ceiling. She should have noticed it before, and cursed herself for not doing so. Unlike the foyer and unit nine, the ceiling here had been lowered, probably to fit in with the modernisation done in the 1970s. The original ceiling would have been plaster, perhaps with decorative patterns, and hopefully with ornamental cornices. It was too much to hope that it could be pressed metal - the ceiling in unit nine was plaster and she couldn't see why it would be different here. She made a note to check it out in daylight.

She packed her tape and pad into her handbag and walked into the foyer. As she passed the stairs she hesitated. If she took the measurements of unit nine now she could start work on the design for the renovations tonight. She remembered her enthusiasm when describing to Bruce her vision of how it could look, and her idea to have different themes for each unit. Her eagerness bubbled up. Shining the torch ahead of her, she climbed the stairs.

Geoffrey pushed aside the loose palings in the fence behind the units and crawled through the resulting gap.

When he'd first checked out the area with a view to breaking in, he'd realised that breaking into the front of the building would be impossible without the risk of being seen. The street light was too close and there wasn't enough shrubbery to give him cover. The house behind the units, however, provided perfect access. An elderly couple lived in the highset Queenslander, and their yard was so overgrown he could slip down the side and through their back yard without any chance of being spotted.

In seconds he scurried from the fence to the back of the unit building. He slid a piece of strong, flat steel under the hopper window he knew opened into an empty storage room. On his last visit he'd chiselled out the groove in the sill so that the latch hung loose inside it. Now he moved the steel so it pushed the latch out of the groove. He slipped a piece of wire that he'd bent to a right angle at one end between the sill and the bottom of the window, twisted it so the right angle caught against the timber, and pulled the window open. He quickly climbed inside, taking care not to make a noise.

It was going to work. Ellie knew it was. Even at night the unit had that same light, airy feel it had in the daytime. Perhaps it was the light-sprinkled view across to the river, luckily not impeded by other multi-storey buildings, although some modern high-rises dominated the skyline to the left and right. Or maybe it was that the windows were larger than most made in that era. The floor plan, too, was more open than unit one. Yes, the renovation she'd envisioned should be achievable.

Taking the measurements was harder here, with no street light to help, and took longer than she anticipated, but by the time she'd finished she almost floated on a glow of satisfaction. This unit would be the pick - even in the dark it had an ambience the others lacked.

She picked up her bag and walked out onto the landing then down the stairs. With only a small window on each floor, the stairwell was a lot darker than the rooms. The confined area felt almost oppressive, as though the air had been sucked out of it.

Her torch beam started to dull, and she remembered she had no spare batteries. The thought of being caught in there with no light made her quicken her pace.

Soft thuds on the staircase.

Footsteps?

Geoffrey whipped around, gloved fingers on the door handle of unit one. A figure rounded the first floor landing, torch pointing downwards. He turned to hurry back the way he had come, but before he could, the torch flicked towards him. The figure cried out and pitched forward, tumbling over and around until he heard a sickening thud, and then all went still.

No wonder people said they were scared shitless. His guts heaved, his bowels clamoured to be emptied. He stared down at the figure, then turned on his torch. A woman. Head twisted to one side. The beam illuminated the side of her face and the dark red blood spreading from underneath her fair hair. Her long dark coat fell around her like a shroud.

Not another one!

He hadn't really looked at the other stupid bitch, just lashed out and ran for the window, shoving his torch into his coat pocket as he did so. It had happened so quickly he was left with only fleeting impressions. Unfortunately, they were impressions that refused to go away. Now it was happening again. He stood, frozen, his brain trying to decide what to do.

A mobile began to ring.

He spun around.

No-one was there.

It kept ringing, and he realised the sound was coming

from underneath the woman.

He hurried around her and ran back to the storage room.

CHAPTER TWENTY-ONE

Miranda dialled Cass's number. She felt a bit foolish worrying about her mother; after all, she was a perfectly capable woman. But the fact that Ellie knew she was cooking dinner for her and it was now past a reasonable time to eat gave the worry a basis. And Ellie's mobile kept ringing out. Okay, if Ellie was in traffic and couldn't pull over to answer it she could understand, but she'd phoned four times in the past ten minutes and still no answer.

Cass's phone stopped ringing and the answering machine clicked in. Miranda left a brief message and hung up. She flicked through her mother's personal directory and found Kandy's number.

Kandy answered after the first ring, and Miranda quickly relayed her concern. When Kandy explained about meeting Ellie after work it seemed such a reasonable explanation she said goodbye without mentioning that Ellie wasn't answering her mobile.

A few minutes later her own mobile rang, and she sighed with relief when she recognised Ellie's number. Shit, but she was going to give her a blast for worrying her. She flicked the phone open and put it to her ear. 'Mum, I've been-'

'Miranda?' The voice was soft, hesitant, but she

recognised something in the inflection as he said her name.

'Mouse? Mouse, what are you doing with my mother's phone?' Panic inched her voice up several notches. 'What's happened to her?'

'She's not dead, but she looks hurt real bad.'

Miranda gripped her mobile so hard her hand hurt. 'Mouse! Where is she?'

'In the place where Cherilyn died.'

'Mouse, I'm going to call an ambulance. Can you stay with her please?'

'Do you want me to clean up the blood?'

Her stomach heaved, her imagination going crazy. 'Where is she bleeding?' Shit, what had happened to her?

'From her head. But I think it's stopped now.'

'That's good. Mouse, can you stay on the phone? I'm going to use the other phone to call an ambulance, okay?'

'Are you coming too, Miranda?'

'Yes, Mouse, I will but I have to phone the ambulance first.' Miranda flung down the mobile, ran to the landline and dialled triple zero, grateful she'd seen the address of the units on Ellie's sketchbook. It seemed to take an eternity for her call to be put through to the ambulance service but she knew it was only seconds. Seconds she hoped wouldn't mean the difference between life and death for her mother. As soon as she'd given them the details she grabbed Ellie's personal directory again, flicked through the pages and found Chris's home and mobile numbers. She dialled his mobile.

Minutes later she was driving far in excess of the speed limit to get to the units.

Pain. Sharp, blinding, digging into her skull like a jackhammer with a knife edge. Ellie was sure her head would explode if she opened her eyes, but she tried anyway.

Darkness. Oh, God, had she gone blind?

No, she could see outlines ... of what she wasn't sure. Then she felt movement near her head.

'Don't move. Miranda is calling an ambulance. She told me to make sure you didn't move.'

The voice. Male. Familiar, but not familiar enough that she could recognise it. If Miranda had called an ambulance then she must be hurt. That would explain why everything seemed so topsy-turvy. She moved her hands, felt coldness, hardness. Tiles. That's what it felt like. She moved her head towards the tiles, trying to get up. Pain shafted harder and nausea roiled through her stomach. She bit back the urge to vomit, but it happened anyway, half-digested food spasming out in liquid and chunks. She felt it warm the tile under her cheek. Acrid. Revolting. She had never felt so ill. 'Please.' The word rasped from her throat. 'Help me.'

Cloth that smelled like dirt and musk and kittens moved over her lips. 'It's all right, Miranda's mother. The ambulance is coming. Can't you hear it?'

She heard it then, the faint high-low rhythm of a siren. With a sigh, she closed her eyes and gave in to the need to sleep.

Miranda looked at Chris as he sat beside her in a curtained cubicle in the Emergency Room. She'd only met him a couple of times, and had thought he was fairly laid-back for a cop, but now he looked so grim she was glad she wasn't a lawbreaker.

'Are you sure they'll treat Mouse okay?' she ventured to ask him.

'They've only taken him to the station to make a statement.'

'Mum was lucky he found her. She could have been lying there for ages like that ...' Miranda couldn't finish the sentence, her mind replaying the scene that had greeted her when she'd arrived at the units at the same time as the ambulance. Chris's Rodeo had screeched to a halt as she'd run up the path ahead of the ambulance officers. Mouse had unlocked the door and she'd stopped in shock at the sight of her mother. She wasn't sure how long it took for her mother to be assessed and put in the ambulance, but it felt like she'd aged years in that time.

'How did Mouse find her, anyway?' she asked, remembering that Chris had questioned him while she stayed with Ellie and answered the ambulance officers' questions.

He ran a hand over his face, pushing at his forehead as though he too, wanted to expunge the image of Ellie that had greeted them. 'According to Mouse, he often walks the streets in the New Farm area and down by the river looking for stray animals, and he recognised Ellie's car. He wanted to ask her how the kitten was going so he knocked on the front door. When no-one answered he looked in through the glass panel next to the door and saw Ellie lying on the floor. He said he could only see her legs but she wasn't moving and he was worried.

'Apparently Mouse is also always on the lookout for a good place to doss down if he has to move in a hurry and the units were one of his regular haunts. He had no trouble breaking in through a window that had a dodgy latch. From what he said,' Chris stretched back in the hard plastic chair and flexed his shoulders, 'he nearly ran away because he thought he'd get the blame, but then he heard Ellie's mobile ring and he pulled her bag from underneath her and got it out. When he saw the missed call was from you, he hit Reply.'

'Thank heavens,' Miranda sighed. 'Mum wasn't making much sense when she woke up, she wasn't even sure where she was. Have you figured out what happened?'

'I found one of her shoes a few stairs down from the first landing. The heel had caught on a thread in the carpet runner. It looks like she tripped and hit her head on the tiled floor.' He thumped his fist on his thigh. 'She shouldn't have been there at night on her own. It's too dangerous with no lights.'

Miranda was going to tell him about Ellie's meeting with Kandy, but hesitated. Ellie could tell him if she wanted him to know.

Chris looked at his watch and frowned. 'How long do these damn scans take? You'd think she'd be back by now.'

Miranda shared his impatience. After an initial examination, the ER doctor had sent Ellie for a scan. He hadn't said anything, but Miranda felt he was worried Ellie might have a skull fracture. Considering her vagueness, lethargy and obvious pain, it was a possibility, and Miranda couldn't subdue the worry that gnawed at her. She'd been horrified by the amount of blood Ellie had lost, but the doctor had reassured her that scalp wounds bled a lot but weren't necessarily serious.

'I guess we're lucky it wasn't Saturday night. They'd probably be twice as busy in here then.'

'More than twice,' he muttered.

Rubber wheels squeaked on the vinyl floor and Ellie's bed was wheeled into the cubicle where they waited. Both of them sprang to their feet, their gazes directed to the doctor who walked behind the bed, chart in hand. 'No fractures,' he said as though anticipating their question, 'and no bleeding into the brain. Severe concussion, but she'll be all right. We'll keep her in for a day or two to make sure nothing else crops up.'

'But I have work,' Ellie protested weakly, her eyes partially closed to cope with the brightness of the lights.

'I'll write you out a certificate,' the doctor smiled. 'You'll be lucky if you're back at work in a week. You're going to have quite a headache for a while. I've stitched the wound in your scalp and you'll have to get those out in five to seven days.' He turned to a nearby orderly. 'Mrs Brighton is ready to go up to the ward now, please.'

'Can we go with her?' Miranda asked.

The doctor shook his head. 'It's past visiting hours and we don't want to disturb the other patients. You can see her tomorrow.' He beamed at them, hooked the chart on the bed end, and walked away. The orderly hovered, obviously waiting for Miranda and Chris to say goodbye to Ellie.

Miranda kissed her mother softly on the forehead. 'I'll see you in the morning,' she said and walked out of the way. She watched Chris take Ellie's hand and put it to his lips. Brief though the kiss was, in that instant she realised that Chris Ryan was in love with her mother.

CHAPTER TWENTY-TWO

If she moved slowly and kept her head fixed in the one direction, Ellie discovered, it eliminated the shafts of pain through her head. The overall ache didn't go away, in spite of the painkillers, but at least it was bearable. And being propped up on several pillows helped.

She'd vomited again, but this time a quick-thinking nurse with a pan had saved her from wearing it. When the noise of clanging trolleys, chatty patients and morning television had become too much for her to cope with, and the nursing staff realised she was covered by health insurance, they'd moved her to a private room.

The hospital gown she wore was definitely of the one-size-fits-all variety, and she hoped Miranda would soon arrive with her pyjamas. When she'd asked the nurse this morning what had happened to her clothes and bag she'd been informed that her clothes were in the cupboard and Miranda had taken the bag home, and she worried that her notepad might have fallen out. She remembered going to the units, but everything after that was so hazy she wasn't sure if she was remembering last night or other visits there.

A soft knock sounded on the door and she called out, equally softly, 'Come in.'

Miranda poked her head around the door and grinned.

'Wasn't sure what you said.'

Ellie felt her answering smile lacked the cheerfulness of Miranda's but it was all she could muster. Her head ached, bruises covered half her body, and she felt like crap. A nurse had cleaned her face and hair last night but she was sure she didn't smell too good either.

'PJs, underwear, clothing, toiletries.' Miranda held up an overnight bag. 'The nurse said it's okay if you want to have a shower.'

'Thank heavens.' Ellie tried to push herself into a sitting position, but the room started to sway and she dropped back against the pillows.

'Wait on, I'll give you a hand.' Miranda walked over, put the bag down and helped her move, cautiously, so that she sat upright. It was a relief when the walls stayed where she knew they should be. 'Think I'd better help you into the shower,' Miranda said.

Fifteen minutes, hot water and shampoo later, Ellie felt more human and less like a punching bag. She even thought she could eat something. 'Something dry,' she told Miranda. 'Nothing dairy - don't think I can handle that yet.'

Miranda went to see what she could find, and left Ellie sitting on the bed, brushing her wet hair carefully to avoid the stitches. The wound was just inside the hairline close to her temple, and if she brushed her hair carefully the stitches couldn't be seen. She tried to remember what had happened to her at the units, but gave up in disgust. Thinking made her head hurt.

A flash of blue in the doorway made her heart thump. Chris. Oh, God, but he looked good, standing there, all lean but solid at the same time, a bunch of roses in one hand, police cap in the other, and a look in his eyes that said "caring" more than any words could.

'You look better than you did last night,' he said, and walked in, closing the door behind him.

'I hope so.' Hell, she'd seen herself in the mirror - she still looked like crap, only a better version. 'I still can't remember what happened. Miranda told me about Mouse finding me. Was he able to give you a clue?'

Chris shook his head. He placed the roses on the bed and gently kissed her. Ellie gave silent thanks that she'd cleaned her teeth before melting into the warmth of his lips. When he moved back, she breathed, 'Thank you,' and wasn't thinking of the flowers.

He looked like he was going to kiss her again, but sat on the visitor's chair instead. 'From what we can work out, your heel caught in the carpet on the stairs and you fell onto the tiled floor and hit your head.'

Something flicked in Ellie's mind at his words, but it quickly went. 'I must thank Mouse for calling Miranda. I could have been lying there a lot longer.'

A smile made its way across Chris's face. 'I think you and Miranda have a friend for life there. And I gained a few brownie points by suggesting to him that if he had anything on him he didn't want the attending police to see then he might want to leave it in the garden before they arrived to take him to the station to make a statement.'

'You did?' Ellie smiled. 'That was very un-cop-like of you.'

'I've attended a lot of crime scenes, and it was pretty

obvious that you'd fallen and not been pushed or hit. I figured I owed Mouse a favour. He could have left you there and no-one would have known, but he didn't.'

'Maybe you should offer to take one of his kittens. You'd join his friends-for-life club.'

Before he could reply, the door opened.

Damien walked into the room.

Ellie stared. She felt her jaw drop.

He'd lost weight, his expensive suit tailored to fit his trimmer physique. In one hand he carried an overnight bag. The other held a bouquet of flowers that screamed ostentatious. She found her voice. 'Damien. What are you doing here?'

He glared at Chris before striding over to the bed and thrusting the flowers at Ellie. 'Miranda called and told me about your accident. I caught the first plane I could.' He glared at Chris again. 'I'm Damien Cummins, Ellie's husband.'

Ellie almost groaned. Damien had made the statement sound like a challenge. She saw the gleam of battle in Chris's eyes as he stood.

'Separated husband,' Chris reminded him.

It was like a rag waved at a bull. Damien clenched his teeth, and Ellie wouldn't have been surprised if his eyes bulged. 'We're still *married*,' he ground out.

'That's only a legality.' Chris's tone was mild, but Ellie could see the tension in his body and the way his fingers gripped his cap.

'I came here to be with my *wife*, and would appreciate some privacy, if you don't mind.'

'Perhaps Ellie minds.'

Both men held each other's gaze for a few more seconds, then turned to look at her. It was like being confronted by the headmistress when you knew you had to take the blame or rat on your friends - dead whichever way she went. Then anger bubbled up. She tossed the flowers to the end of the bed. 'What about your girlfriend, Damien? How does she feel about this?'

Damien didn't look exactly sheepish, but about as close to it as he could get. 'That was a mistake. I realise that. I should never have let you go.'

'You tossed me away,' Ellie heard her voice rise. The ache in her head worsened. 'Like ... like unopened junk mail.'

'I think you should leave.' Chris's tone made it obvious it wasn't a suggestion.

Damien spun around to face him. 'I think *you* should be the one to leave.'

Ellie watched in horror, sure that a fight was only a breath away. Her patience snapped. 'Both of you leave!' she yelled, and shuddered at the pounding in her brain. 'Please!'

'Do what she says.' Kandy marched into the room, her lack of height more than compensated by the fierce determination in her stride. She waved an angry hand at the two men. 'She's got concussion. She doesn't need all this shit. Piss off and leave her be.'

Damien looked astounded. Ellie thought it was probably the first time any woman had spoken to him like that. She suppressed a giggle that had the potential to turn hysterical.

Chris nodded his acquiescence. 'I'll see you later,' he

said to Ellie, and strode out, giving Damien a look that would have cowered a criminal suspect.

Damien flinched, but didn't walk away. 'We need to talk, Ellie.'

Kandy walked in front of Ellie, cutting him off. 'Bugger off, Damien. Ellie will talk to you when and *if* she wants to.'

Ellie closed her eyes and gingerly eased her head onto the pillows. The sound of Damien's retreating footsteps brought more relief than any painkiller. 'Thanks, Kandy,' she whispered.

'Unbutton your pyjama top and lie face down.'

Ellie opened one eye. 'Why?'

'Your muscles will be as tight as wires after that little scene, let alone what happened to you last night. I do a fabulous relaxing massage. No,' she grinned, 'don't ask me where I learned.'

It didn't take long for Kandy to rearrange the pillows and for Ellie to position herself to cause the least pain to her head. When she felt Kandy drop oil on her back and begin to smooth it across her skin she tried to make her body relax. Kandy's hands applied gentle pressure, and after a few minutes Ellie's shoulders loosened, the knots in her neck started to unravel, and the pain in her head began to ease. Kandy worked in silence, and Ellie was grateful she didn't have to discuss Damien's sudden re-appearance. Ten minutes later she was drifting into an almost-doze when Miranda came back.

Ellie saw the furtive way she looked around, as though wondering if she was going to be welcome or not.

'Hello, Kandy,' Miranda said, forcing brightness, then

put a packet on the side table. 'I got you some potato crisps, Mum.' Ellie noticed that she didn't look at her.

Kandy's fingers didn't stop weaving their magic. 'Hi, Miranda.'

Miranda stood, shifting her weight from one leg to the other. 'I saw Dad in the foyer.' She let the statement hang, as though waiting for someone to take up the conversation.

It wasn't really something Ellie felt like tackling now, but she thought it was better to clear the air rather than stew on it. 'Why did you phone him?'

Miranda shrugged, but said, 'I thought he should know.'

'Why? He didn't care about me when he was with his girlfriend, what made you think he would care now?'

'He phoned me last week and asked how you were. He asked me not to tell you. His girlfriend had left him and he was pretty depressed.'

Ellie went to rise, but Kandy's hands pressed her back into the bed and kept massaging. Anger started to boil in Ellie's gut. 'So you thought you'd tell him I was hurt so he could come waltzing back into my life and play the distraught, caring husband and I'd be so grateful I'd take him back.'

'Not really.' Miranda slumped into the visitor's chair. 'I thought that if there was a chance you could salvage your marriage then you should have the opportunity. You're not as ... as *door matty* as you used to be and ... well, he is my Dad, and it wasn't like he hit you or anything.' She sniffled, and scrabbled in her pocket for a tissue.

The anger seeped out of Ellie as quickly as it had come. She'd thought Miranda had taken the breakup well, but it seemed like she still had issues with divided loyalties. 'Mirie,' she reached out and touched Miranda's arm, 'our marriage was over a long time ago. I should have been more open with you and told you that, but I don't think I realised it myself until Damien's business crisis forced me to confront it. I'm sorry.'

'That's okay,' Miranda snuffled into the tissue, then blew her nose hard. She got up, walked over to the bin and threw the tissue in. 'I'm sorry I interfered. I thought I was helping. But there's something I think you should know.'

What now, Ellie wondered, unsure if she really wanted to hear. Her head was hurting again, and Kandy's gentle kneading at the base of her skull wasn't doing as much good as it had before. She waited for Miranda to continue.

'Chris Ryan is in love with you.'

Kandy's fingers stilled. 'Oh,' she muttered.

Ellie felt her mouth open but no words came out.

Cass poked her head around the half-open door.

She took one look at the stunned tableau in the room, and tentatively asked, 'Anyone for chocolate brownies?'

CHAPTER TWENTY-THREE

Kandy made tea and coffee in the visitors' lounge and brought them back to Ellie's room after Miranda left. Cass sat on the visitor's chair and Kandy perched on the end of the bed while Ellie leaned against her propped-up pillows and sipped her tea. Cass insisted Ellie couldn't have coffee - she didn't need the caffeine stimulant.

'What do I do now?' Ellie felt like shaking her head, but thought better of it. 'Do I believe Miranda?' She bit into a chocolate brownie.

'She's only basing it on how Chris looked at you. That doesn't mean he's in love with you, it could just be the way it seemed to her.'

Ellie thought back to her last conversation with him and his conviction they would still be together in a few months time. Was it possible he loved her? She was certainly falling for him, but that could be a rebound effect. Or hormones. Oh, yeah, hormones. She was definitely in lust with him, she just hadn't done anything about it. Yet.

'What about Damien?' Cass asked. 'How do you feel about him?'

'Good question. He's Miranda and Pru's father and there's shared history, and for a moment when I saw him there was a twinge of something, but it could have been shock. He does look a lot better now he's lost weight though,' she mused.

'You're not going soft on the prick, are you?' Kandy snorted.

Ellie tried not to laugh at Kandy's choice of words. 'No. You can't resurrect the dead. What Damien and I had died a slow death years ago. Though until I heard his girlfriend's voice on the phone I had had a few fantasies about him coming back and declaring his undying love for me.'

'So what are you going to do about Chris? If the man's in love with you and there's no hope you're going to reciprocate it would be kinder to put him out of his misery now.'

What *was* she going to do? She didn't have the energy at the moment to tell Cass and Kandy her fears about falling in love with him and then losing him. She didn't even want to think about it at the moment. Maybe she needed advice. 'What do you think I should do?'

'Don't look at me.' Cass said. 'If I tell you what to do and it goes wrong you'll never forgive me.'

Ellie looked at Kandy, who shook her head. 'Your call.'

'Then I'm not going to do anything. I'll just see what happens and worry about it when the time comes. I know that's procrastinating, but right now that's the best I can do.'

'If they handed out awards for procrastination,' Cass sighed, 'Joe would need a trophy room.'

The three of them laughed, aware of Cass's complaint that Joe was always "going to" fix something in the house. One Christmas she'd even bought him a brass circle labelled "A Round Tuit" that came with the explanation it was for those men who, when asked to do something by their wives, said they would get around to it and never did.

Their laughter died as a doctor walked into the room. Ellie blinked. He was almost a George Clooney lookalike. She glanced at Kandy, expecting to see her positively salivating. And blinked again. Kandy was showing only a cursory interest in the gorgeous specimen. Alarm bells went off in Ellie's brain. Whatever was happening with Kandy and Phillip was more serious than she'd thought.

Geoffrey had watched every television news bulletin from 6am and had also listened to the radio, and when no mention of the woman was made by midday, he even went and bought a newspaper to see if anything was in there. But there was nothing about her anywhere.
She must still be alive. If she wasn't, the workmen would have found her this morning and something should have come out in the news.

He made a cup of coffee and tried to drink it, but he'd run out of sugar and milk and the bitterness was too great. Or maybe it was the acid pouring into his gut from what had happened last night. He poured the coffee down the sink.

He was sure the woman had seen him. She'd cried out when she'd spotted him, and surprise must have made her lose her footing. There'd be no physical evidence to place him at the scene, his gloves saw to that, but he still worried. What the hell was the woman doing there? The other one would have been a squatter, but the woman last night wore a coat that said she shopped in stores most women couldn't afford to look in. He cursed that he hadn't had the presence of mind to search for her bag and take her money - the bitch was probably loaded.

Should he go back there tonight? He might have been given a slight reprieve by his "associates", but they wouldn't extend that again. Instinct warned him against going back too soon after last night's bungle. He now knew where Iris had lived before she died. Maybe he should see if his mother knew more than she realised she did.

He pulled out his wallet. He'd need more money if he was to keep going to see his mother.

Gazza. Gazza owed him a favour. Gazza should have been the one doing the drop-off the night Geoffrey had been caught by the cops, but he'd been too hung over to even get off his couch. Yeah, Gazza owed him all right.

An hour later Geoffrey was knocking on the front door of a fibro cottage that was more dilapidated than his bedsit. A growled obscenity filtered through a cracked window pane, then the door was pulled open.

The man who stood there in a worn grey pants and sweater needed a shave, dental work, and a haircut. He stared at Geoffrey, swore, then pulled him inside and slammed the door. 'You shouldn't have come here, mate. It's good to see ya, but ya can't stay. You're dead meat, and I will be too if they see me with ya.'

'It's okay, Gaz. I made a deal with the boss. I'm going to get the money for him - get him off my back.'

Gazza's eyes narrowed. 'How ya gonna do that?'

'I know where something valuable is hidden. As soon as I can get hold of it and sell it, I'll give him the money and be in the clear.'

'So what's that got to do with me?'

'I need some money, just a bit to see me through until I can get this thing.'

Gazza laughed, spittle forming on rotten teeth stumps. 'Does it look like I got money?'

Geoffrey looked around the room, seeing the torn curtains, the battered furniture, and sighed. He'd wasted money getting here, and now it looked like he'd have to go to a charity and beg for some food to see him through the week. 'I was stupid to come,' he muttered, and turned to leave but Gazza grabbed his arm. 'Wait a sec.' He scurried towards another room. Geoffrey heard what sounded like furniture being moved, then scrunching plastic, then Gazza came back and shoved something at him.

A gun. Small. No bigger than his hand. 'Take it,' Gazza pushed it into Geoffrey's hand. 'If the word on the street is kosher, you're gonna need it.'

Pain gnawed at Geoffrey's belly, and it wasn't from hunger. Gazza must have heard wrong. He had a deal with the boss. Give him the money from the painting and all would be forgiven. What he would get for the painting wouldn't make up for all the money he'd lost but a few hundred thousand was better than nothing.

But even as he tried to convince himself, doubt crept up his back like ants on a honey jar.

He managed to wangle an almost-decent cup of coffee from the hospital domestic who brought the patients' lunches. Getting some lunch as well didn't happen this time, but his mother said she was too tired after doing her physiotherapy to eat her lamb chops and vegetables and told him to have them. He watched her eat the thin soup that had come with the meal and wondered if she'd told the truth or if she'd realised how hungry he was. He felt a twinge of gratitude. It had been a long time since anyone had done anything for him without expecting something in return.

'Did you see much of Iris before she died?' he asked.

'Only when she was in hospital. She hired a removalist to move her to the bottom flat. I didn't see her a lot after that, though I felt terrible when I learned she had died alone like she did. But the doctor said it was quick. A heart attack while she was sitting watching television.'

'What about her friends? Didn't they come around?'

'They'd all died. Poor Iris. For someone who'd enjoyed such a full life, she'd become somewhat of a recluse in the end.'

That was a relief. For a while he'd considered that perhaps she'd given what he was looking for to a friend, but doubted she would do that while his mother still lived. If Iris had hidden it all these years there was a good chance it still remained that way. All he had to do was find it.

Ellie was given the okay to go home, and it didn't taken long for Kandy and Cass to get her ready.

Cass insisted on driving her, obviously concerned that Kandy's expertise behind the wheel didn't extend to slow and careful. Ellie had to smile as Cass dawdled along at just below the speed limit. It didn't surprise her to see Kandy's Porsche speed past, any more than it did to see the Porsche parked outside Miranda's house when they arrived.

As Cass helped her from the car, she had to admit her head wasn't in the best shape. The ache persisted, although the dizziness only happened now if she moved fast. The stitches pulled a little and she'd have to remember them when she brushed her hair. She'd texted Chris that she was leaving the hospital, and then phoned Miranda to let her know. Now Miranda opened the front door and came out to meet them. 'You still mad at me, Mum?' she asked.

'No, Mirie, and I wasn't really mad at you. It was just such a shock to see your father arrive, and I really couldn't handle the way he fronted up to Chris as though he was some kind of home-wrecker.'

'I thought Chris handled the situation rather well,' Kandy chuckled.

'*You* handled the situation better than *I* did,' Ellie muttered.

Cass hauled Ellie's bag from the back seat and place her other hand under Ellie's elbow. 'Let's get the patient inside.'

They'd almost made it to the front door when a taxi pulled up and Damien got out. Ellie shot Miranda a suspicious look.

Miranda made an "I'm sorry" face and said, 'Dad's flying back to Sydney this evening and he wanted to see you before he left. I told him what you said about it being all over between the two of you but he wanted to talk to you anyway.'

A sigh rippled through Ellie's body but she simply said, 'Okay. I guess I owe him that.'

'I'll leave you to it,' Kandy said. 'Make sure you look

after your mother, Miranda,' she added with well-restrained emphasis. 'Coming, Cass?'

Cass looked from Ellie to Damien's approaching figure and reluctantly handed Ellie's bag to Miranda. She gave Ellie a gentle hug, whispered, 'Don't let the bastard wear you down,' and walked back to her car.

Ellie noticed that Damien had lost his usual confident swagger. She thought Kandy's and Cass's curt nod and brief greeting of 'Damien' could have contributed to that but wouldn't have been the cause. No, something else had happened. Even during his misery over losing his business he hadn't lost that streak of arrogance she'd found so masculine when they'd first met but had soon come to find tiring.

Mayhem ran to greet her, rubbing against her legs and purring loudly. Ellie wanted to pick her up, but knew bending down wasn't a good idea at the moment.

Damien followed them into the lounge room. Mayhem ran and hid behind the lounge. Damien stood looking around for a moment, then said, 'I see you've made a few changes. Has Dad escaped lately? He would have cracked up.'

There was no rancour in his tone, so Ellie decided not to take offence. Besides, she didn't need the aggro. She lowered herself carefully onto the lounge. 'Bert hasn't been here. Have you seen him yet?'

'I went this morning, after ... He's deteriorated a lot, hasn't he.' He looked away, and Ellie saw the faint sheen of tears in his eyes. 'He didn't know me, Ellie. I told him who I was but ... he said I was lying, that ... that Damien was at school and Eugenia - Mum - had gone to pick him up.'

Ellie noticed the distress on Miranda's face as she hurried off to the bedroom with her bag. 'He was like that when Miranda and I saw him last.' Sadness washed over Ellie. It must have been a shock for Damien to see how badly his father had deteriorated. When Damien had visited Bert before leaving for Sydney, Bert had been having many lucid moments.

'Will you do me a favour?' Damien asked. 'Will you try to get to see him every so often and let me know how he is? I phone the nursing home and they're sympathetic, but it's not like seeing him.'

'I'll see him as often as I can. And it would be a good idea if you could visit a bit more.'

'Hotel rooms aren't cheap. I can't afford to come up too often. Perhaps I could stay here?'

Ellie was sure the innocent, hopeful look in his eyes was false. It was typical of Damien to revert to charm to get his own way. Well, she was too tired, too sore, and too thoroughly pissed at him to play his game. 'The lounge is probably a bit lumpy, but if you don't mind squeezing into it you can stay here.'

Disappointment - or was it frustration - flashed in his eyes. 'Ellie, I know you told Miranda it was all over between us, but surely you're not going to throw away nearly thirty years of marriage just because I made one little mistake?'

Suspicion that had been lurking since she'd phoned Damien and heard his lover murmuring bed-talk in the background abruptly surfaced. 'Was it only one mistake,

Damien? Was that the first time you'd strayed?'

'Of course.' He held out his hands in supplication, but she caught his blink and the involuntary twitch of his cheek that told her he was lying even as the denial left his mouth. 'I've always loved you, Ellie. We just got into a rough patch and I didn't handle it well. I was under too much stress with the business failing.'

She refrained from pointing out that the business hadn't *failed*, but that his greed and arrogance had made him easy prey for a clever con artist.

'It's too late, Damien. It's over. We can't go back. I don't love you anymore.' There. The words were out. Some of the pain still lingered, and she guessed it always would, but it was cathartic saying the words. She wasn't vindictive by nature, but the exasperation that showed on his face caused her immediate pleasure. He was so used to her falling in with his wishes that he wasn't coping well with this new version of her.

'I suppose it's too much to ask if we could be friends?'

She wasn't too sure what "friends" meant, but she was prepared to be civil. 'We can be friends.'

He looked at his watch. 'I'd better go. Airport traffic can get pretty heavy.' He stood, then hesitated. 'Are you involved with that cop?'

Irritation inched its way up Ellie's back. 'Not that it's any of your business, but we've only been seeing each other a few weeks. I'd hardly call that involved.'

'Miranda said he's in love with you.'

'No, I didn't.' Miranda walked into the room. 'I said I *think* he's in love with Mum. I could be wrong.'

'And whether he is or he isn't is definitely none of your business, Damien. Have a safe trip back to Sydney.' Ellie smiled, grateful to see him leave, but saddened by the whole situation.

Miranda walked him to the door and hugged him goodbye. When she closed the front door, it sounded to Ellie like it was closing on the end of an era.

Kandy wasn't sure if she wanted to go home. Her doubts about Phillip had been eating into her for days now, and she kept thinking that each time he came home from work he was going to tell her he had fallen in love with someone else and was going to leave her. It didn't matter how many times she told herself that was ridiculous, the doubt still lingered.

You can take the girl out of the background, she mused, *but you can't take the background out of the girl.* She'd come a long way from the homeless, street-wise young woman who'd lied to get a waitressing job to escape a life that had no future, but the insecurities of that life had left their mark. Sometimes she wondered if the sexual encounters she indulged in really happened because she was sexually frustrated or because she needed the constant reassurance that even Phillip's solid presence couldn't give. She enjoyed the sex, had always had a good appetite for it, but occasionally it felt like she was looking for something she would never find.

Her Porsche Boxster negotiated the two-lane road leading to Bridgeman Downs on Brisbane's northern outskirts. She could have driven on the Bruce Highway and turned off, but she liked the way the Roadster hugged the narrow bitumen, the way the powerful engine felt like it had to be reined in so the vehicle wouldn't take off when it rounded tight curves or crested hills. She didn't exceed the speed limit by a lot, but the traffic would soon increase to school-pick-up frenzy, and she took advantage of the relatively clear lane.

Suburban houses soon changed to five and ten-acre bushland blocks that sheltered sprawling ranch-style homes, mansions surrounded by perfectly-landscaped gardens, and double-storey, marble-pillared edifices with tennis courts and swimming pools. Kandy watched a car leave the driveway of one of those edifices, and realised it had come from her house. She braked, slowed almost to a crawl, and looked intently at the driver as the car went past.

A woman. Blonde. Slight build. About her age, maybe younger.

Kandy's stomach sank so low she felt sick from the drag of it. She turned into the driveway, still going at a snail's pace, her mind whirling. This morning she'd told Phillip she was going to see Ellie in the hospital and would do some shopping afterwards, so she would be gone all day. It was now two-twenty. Phillip never left the office before five o'clock. Was he home? Had the woman come here to meet him or had she simply made a mistake and driven into the wrong place?

As she pressed the remote and the garage roller-door revealed Phillip's BMW, she thought she might throw up. In the ten years she'd been married to Phillip she'd convinced herself she'd buried her past. Now it only took the possibility of betrayal and she was once again the scared fifteen-year-old packing her bag and sneaking out the back door, hoping her father wouldn't wake and start beating her.

She parked the Porsche and sat for a few minutes, gathering her strength for what she expected would come.

A bright smile plastered on her face, she walked through the gleaming tiled laundry to the kitchen. A glass sat on the bench, a smidgen of amber liquid in the bottom. Funny. Phillip was usually quite fastidious about rinsing glasses and cups as soon as he'd used them. She picked it up and sniffed. Scotch. Even stranger. Drinking in the afternoon wasn't something Phillip normally did either. A shiver of apprehension ran down her spine. Perhaps he was too preoccupied with how he was going to break up with her to be his usual predictable self.

With its tiles and stainless steel and numerous appliances, the kitchen was almost commercial in appearance, but Kandy loved it, delighting in cooking for Phillip's many business dinners at home. Few of the guests were close enough to him to be called friends, but Kandy understood that. In their own ways, they were both private persons.

She dropped her handbag on the bench and walked into the dining room, her boots clacking on the tiles like slow castanets, then into the carpeted quietness of the formal living room. Tension winding ever tighter, she hesitated in front of Phillip's office door. It was open just enough that she could see Phillip seated at his desk, staring past the rolling lawns and clipped-hedge boundary to the cloud-sloughed sky. Slivers of sunshine highlighted the grey in his fair hair and emphasised the fine lines in his face and neck.

His usual calm expression was gone. What she saw now was the face of man in emotional pain.

CHAPTER TWENTY-FOUR

In spite of the anxiety tearing her apart, Kandy felt a rush of sympathy for Phillip. She loved him, and she wanted him to be happy. But she also wanted to be happy. Steeling herself for the hurt she was now sure would come, she walked into the room and said, 'Hello, Phillip.'

His head whipped around as though he'd been slapped. 'Kandy,' he said, but the sadness in his eyes gave lie to the smile on his lips.

She decided this wasn't the time for subtlety. 'Are you having an affair with the woman I just saw leaving here?'

Now he looked more than slapped. He was obviously stunned. She hoped it was because she was wrong and not because he was shocked that she'd found him out. 'Woman?' He said the word as though it was foreign to him, then seemed to recover himself. 'Kandy, please sit down. I was hoping to be able to tell you this later, but ...' he gestured to the other dark leather chair.

'I'd rather stand.' *That way I can run when it gets too much.*

'Please.'

She couldn't bear the distress in his eyes. She sat.

'I was married when I was nineteen.'

Kandy gaped. Before she could berate him for not telling

her before this, he continued. 'She was seventeen. We'd had sex once, she fell pregnant, and our parents insisted we get married. It wasn't a love match, but we pottered along reasonably well for twenty years, then broke up. It wasn't pleasant. I left Victoria and came here to Queensland and started a new life.'

'Phillip, you're sixty-four, you can't tell me that woman was your wife. Not unless she's had great plastic surgery.'

'No. She's my daughter.'

Relief and anger flooded through Kandy in equal measure. 'And you didn't think having a daughter was important enough to tell me about? Or did you think she wouldn't approve of me?'

'There wasn't any need to tell you about her or her about you. I haven't seen her since I left Melbourne.'

A horrible thought filtered into Kandy's mind. 'Haven't you been in touch with her at all? Birthdays? Christmas?'

Phillip shook his head. 'That was one thing my wife insisted on - I wasn't to have any contact with the children.'

'Children?' Kandy's head started to spin. 'How many do you have?'

'Just Vanessa and my son Joshua.'

Kandy stared at him. What kind of woman would insist her husband have no contact with their children? And what kind of a father was Phillip that he would agree to that? 'Why wouldn't she let you see your own children?'

'It doesn't matter now. It was a long time ago. I set up a trust fund to ensure they were always financially well off, and even my grandchildren will benefit.' Phillip's face had resumed its usual placidity, but she was beginning to see how deceptive that was. 'I'm sorry you had to find out like this. I should have told you before.'

Whether it was the last couple of days of anxiety or her shock at Phillip's revelation she wasn't sure, but Kandy felt like the stuffing had been knocked out of her. 'I think I need a drink,' she muttered. Phillip reached over as though to pat her hand, but she snatched it away and stood up. 'Actually, I think I'll have a swim.'

She almost ran upstairs to their bedroom and into the dressing room. She grabbed one of her one-piece swimsuits from a drawer and hastily stripped. As she pulled the swimsuit up over her legs she saw herself in the full-length mirror. Saw her tanned and toned body with its curvaceous hips and still-high breasts that had never suckled a child. And her ever-so-slightly-rounded barren belly. A sob caught in her throat and she roughly tugged the swimsuit into place, pulled on a bathing cap, and hurried down to the enclosed entertainment area with its heated pool and two spas. Her dive was concise and clean, not at all indicative of the emotions that churned inside her as she powered from one end of the pool to the other and back, again and again.

It was only as she began to tire that she realised that she hadn't asked Phillip if all those late-night meetings and hung-up phone calls involved Vanessa. And why had Vanessa come to see him after all those years with no contact?

She left the pool, pulled a towelling robe and slippers from the built-in wardrobe in the changing room, and went to find him.

He was gone, and so was his BMW.

It was amazing what a good sleep could do, Ellie thought. She stretched her arms gingerly above her head, easing some of the aches caused by bruised muscles. She looked at her bedside clock. Six pm. Four hours since Damien had left and she'd crept into bed and felt the bliss of relaxing into a painkiller-induced sleep.

Carefully, she moved her head from side to side. It still hurt, but the dizziness wasn't as bad as it had been. And the nausea had gone. The room was cold, and her pyjamas weren't thick enough on their own. She snuggled back under the doona. She wanted to sleep again, but her stomach growled in a way that convinced her that would be impossible. With a sigh of resignation, she got out of bed and pulled on her fleecy dressing gown. Although the floor was carpeted, it had worn with age, and she quickly shuffled into her slippers.

An appetising aroma was drifting up the hallway. She detoured to the bathroom, then walked to the kitchen. Miranda was standing at the stove, stirring something in a large saucepan. 'Smells good,' Ellie commented.

Miranda turned towards her and smiled. 'Chicken soup.'

Ellie returned the smile. 'Eugenia would be proud. And crunchy bread rolls?'

'In the oven, keeping warm.'

A knock sounded at the front door. 'Sit down Mum,' Miranda put the spoon on the sink. 'I'll get it.'

A moment later Ellie heard Chris's voice, then Miranda's, then Chris's again, and she wondered if Miranda had gone into protection mode. A moment later both of them walked into the kitchen. 'Chris's come straight off his shift, Mum. I told him there's plenty of soup if he wants some but he said that's up to you.'

Ellie had wondered how she would feel when she saw him again, especially after Miranda's surprising revelation. Right now he didn't look like a man in love, but rather a man in doubt. His quiet confidence seemed to have deserted him. He held his police cap in such a tight grip she was sure his fingerprints would be embedded in the cloth. Without a single doubt she knew her appetite wasn't just for the chicken soup. Whether she could cope with loving a man whose job put him in more danger than most was something she didn't even want to consider at the moment. She just knew she wanted him.

'Pull up a chair,' she smiled. 'Miranda's used her grandmother's recipe. You're in for a treat.'

Her smile must have conveyed more than thoughts of food. Chris's tense expression eased and a gleam lit his eyes. 'I'm sure I am,' he said.

Half an hour and several bowls of soup later, Miranda said she wanted to watch her favourite television show and went to the lounge room. Ellie tried not to smile. As far as she was aware, Miranda watched little television, and had never mentioned having a favourite show.

'Ellie,' Chris said, face serious, 'I want to apologise. I wasn't very polite to Damien. And it wasn't fair to you. He *is* still your husband.'

'Like you said, it's only a legality.'

'It seems like he wants you back in his life.' He picked a crumb off the table and put it on his plate and pushed it around.

Ellie watched him watching the progress of the crumb. If he didn't love her, why was he acting like her reply didn't interest him in the slightest? Men. Sometimes they were so easy to read. Then she thought of Damien. Maybe not. She remembered Kandy's advice about putting Chris out of his misery. Okay, it wasn't quite what Kandy meant, but she could at least tell him what she'd decided about Damien. 'He's got Buckley's.'

The crumb stopped moving. Chris's confidence seemed to soak back into him like water into a sponge. His smile almost made her heart stop beating. 'I'm not working this weekend,' he said. 'Would you like to go up to Montville or Maleny with me? Only if you feel up to it. We could stay Saturday night and come back Sunday. No pressure - just two friends spending some time together.'

He was lying and they both knew it. What was between them had gone way past friendship. He was right about the "no pressure" thing though - he wouldn't have to ask. She was already mentally picking out her sexiest lingerie. It might have been wasted on Damien, but she was sure Chris would find it very interesting indeed.

Geoffrey shivered as he walked from the bus stop to his flat. He hunched deeper into his coat and pushed his gloved hands into the pockets. His right hand touched the gun he'd kept there since Gazza had given it to him. He'd never owned a gun before, didn't really know if he could use one, but it made him feel better just to know it was there.

The street light shortened his shadow as he hurried past,

then stretched it to a jagged line as he continued along the broken pavement. Just as he turned into the gateway to his building, the light emitted a loud pop and went out. He jerked in sudden fear. His hip hit the brickwork, his sneaker caught on the bottom of the gate and he fell forward. He pulled his hands from his pockets, thrust them out to break his fall, but wasn't quick enough.

Pain knifed through his right wrist as it twisted under him.

It was nearly midnight before Phillip returned home. Kandy was lying in their super king-size bed, still awake, but pretending to be asleep. Phillip didn't turn on the light, but she heard him move to his dressing room and close the door. She heard the faint click of the light switch. A minute later it was turned off and the door opened. The bed was so big that even though he made no effort to lie down gently, she didn't feel the dip of springs or pull of the sheet and doona. She looked across at him, at the relaxed line of his body as he lay on his back. When she'd first seen his bed, she'd thought how wonderful it was, but soon came to realise that its huge size did little to promote intimacy. You almost needed to pack a lunch to crawl from one side to the other, she'd once told him.

The lack of intimacy was even more pronounced tonight. The gap between them was more emotional than the doona-covered physical space. She lay still, chewing over the questions she wanted to ask him, trying to work out phrasing that wouldn't sound accusative. Just when she opened her mouth to speak, she heard a gentle snore. He was asleep!

Anger raced through her. How could he sleep when she was a frayed mess of doubts and questions and worries and misery?

It was a long time before her mind finally succumbed to exhaustion and allowed her to sleep.

Geoffrey didn't have any painkillers except cheap scotch. It wasn't his favourite brand, but when he'd bought it last week the difference in price had allowed him to buy a few more groceries. Now he drank it not because he enjoyed it, but because he needed the freedom from pain he hoped it would bring.

His wrist was a swollen lump of blue-black bruising and agony. He'd chipped ice from the freezer of his old fridge and folded it in a tea towel and wrapped it gingerly around his wrist, but it provided only a little relief from the pain. He suspected a bone was broken, but knew he couldn't get to the hospital tonight. He was sure the last bus had run and he didn't have enough money for a taxi fare. Tomorrow he'd work out how to get there. Tonight he'd just have to drink enough scotch to wipe himself out and hope to sleep.

It was bliss not to have to leave the warm cocoon of her bed and get ready for work. Ellie snuggled even further under the covers and tried to get back to sleep. It didn't work. The sound of Miranda showering seemed to hum through the walls. The sun was shining too, and the glow seeping through the curtains was enough to lighten the room and take the edge off her determination not to face the day.

The shower stopped, but it was too late. Ellie was very definitely awake now. The bedside clock flicked a new red number at her and she blinked. Seven o'clock. What was Miranda doing up so early?

Now that she was fully awake, her toileting needs couldn't be put off, so she slipped the doona back and gently eased herself into a sitting position. And smiled. She felt a lot better this morning. The headache had eased to a dull nagging shadow. She could cope with that. Dressing gown, slippers, a trip to the loo and the bathroom, followed by a cup of hot tea, and the morning would be distinctly rosy.

She got to the bathroom part only to discover Miranda was still in there. Stranger still. She knocked on the door. 'Mirie? Are you okay?'

'Sure, Mum. Come in.'

Ellie did. And blinked in surprise. Miranda was carefully applying eye-liner, her face a picture of intense concentration, her long blonde hair swirled at the back of her head in some complicated knot. An white tailored blouse was tucked into a black skirt that hugged her hips. Her pyjamas were draped over the bath and her sloppy Ugg boots flopped against the side as though feeling abandoned.

'Where are you going?' The question popped out before Ellie could stop it.

'Sorry. In all the excitement yesterday I forgot to tell you that I have a job interview today.' She slid the eye-liner into her make-up bag and careful unscrewed her mascara and applied it. 'Which lipstick?' She held up two.

'The one in your left hand,' Ellie answered. 'Mirie, I'm

so pleased for you. What's the job?'

'Just a shop assistant, but it's with a store that sells scientific equipment and books. The employment agency phoned yesterday. I'm so nervous I couldn't eat breakfast.' She glanced at Ellie. 'Don't worry, I had some fruit juice. That will keep me going until after the interview.'

She blotted her lips, smiled at the mirror and checked her teeth. Satisfied, she gave Ellie a quick hug. 'Wish me luck.'

'I'll cross my fingers for you.'

Miranda went to her bedroom and came out wearing a black jacket and clutching her handbag. She grabbed her car keys from the kitchen and called out 'Bye,' when she opened the front door.

'Mirie!' Ellie called and watched her daughter turn. 'You look great. You'll knock them dead.'

Miranda laughed, as Ellie knew she would, and left.

The house now seemed too quiet, and Ellie realised she'd become used to sharing breakfast with her daughter, or at least having her around before she left for work.

Work. Something pinged in Ellie's mind, and she realised that with all the kerfuffle with Damien and Chris she hadn't asked Miranda for the bag she'd been carrying when she'd fallen down the stairs at the units. She was sure she had to do something there, but couldn't remember what it was.

She found her handbag on a shelf in her wardrobe and hauled it down. And grunted at the weight of it. No wonder her shoulders sometimes ached. She really should get a smaller one. But then it wouldn't hold her notebook and sketch pad, would it. She took out the notebook and leafed through it. That was it. The last notation. False ceiling in unit one. She needed to see if the original ceiling was good enough to warrant the time and effort of removing the false one. Perhaps she could do that today.

As though anticipating that thought, the ache that had settled dully in the back of her head increased.

She frowned. Perhaps she'd think about going to the units again after some tea and toast and painkillers. And maybe some more sleep.

When Kandy woke she saw that Phillip's side of the bed was empty. She checked the time. He shouldn't have left for work yet. But lately he wasn't doing anything he usually did, was he.

She dressed in a dark blue pants suit and went downstairs. Phillip was sitting in the dining room, coffee and croissant half devoured, the Courier-Mail spread across the pale oak table. He looked up, pushed his reading glasses further down his nose, and smiled. 'Good morning, darling.'

It was obvious his world was back on track. But hers was out of kilter. She wanted to ask him about the late meetings and hanging-up phone calls but somehow the words wouldn't come. She knew she was being a coward, but her insecurities ran deep, and after yesterday's revelations she didn't feel ready for a full-on confrontation. 'Good morning.' She wanted to kiss him on the cheek as she did every morning, and as he expected every morning, but she glided past him to the kitchen and poured herself a large coffee. She noticed another croissant warming in the oven, took it out and slid it on a plate, picked up that and her coffee, and went back to the dining room and sat down.

'Are you going into work today, dear?' Phillip enquired.

Kandy had hired a manager for her catering firm several years ago, and her presence at the office wasn't as essential as it used to be, but she still averaged at least three days there each week. She was proud of what she'd built up and wasn't about to give it up. Besides, although the manager was extremely competent, he lacked Kandy's entrepreneurial skills, and Kandy enjoyed the cut-and-thrust of decision-making and business politics. 'I haven't decided yet,' she replied.

The croissant oozed butter over her fingers as she picked it up and bit into it. Phillip continued to read the paper. Kandy finished the croissant and wiped her fingers on a serviette from the holder Phillip had placed on the table. She'd grown used to his fastidiousness over the years but now it bothered her. Like his emotions. Why did he have to be so controlled all the time? Why couldn't he let his feelings erupt like hers did sometimes?

She sipped her coffee. 'When will I get to meet Vanessa?'

Phillip lowered the paper. 'I'm afraid that won't be possible. She's flying back to Melbourne today.'

'Already? That was a short visit. Why did she come to see you? Especially after all these years.' Kandy tried to sound casual but she heard the tone in her voice and knew he wouldn't be fooled.

'Her mother isn't well and she wanted to tell me herself. Vanessa was always considerate like that.'

Kandy wanted to say that Vanessa could have easily done that by phone, but she didn't. 'What's wrong with ... What's your ex-wife's name?'

'Mary.' Phillip smiled and pushed the paper aside. 'I'd better get to work. I might be the boss but it doesn't set a good example if I'm late.'

'No,' she agreed, but suspected his conscientiousness had more to do with avoiding any more questions she might ask.

He stood up, leaned over and kissed her on the cheek, and walked to the downstairs bathroom. She knew he would brush his teeth, comb his hair, put on his suit jacket and adjust his tie, get his car keys and drive his BMW to his office. Phillip was a man who lived by habits, which was why it had become so obvious to her when those habits had been broken.

His explanation of why his daughter had visited didn't convince her he was telling the truth. Vanessa could have easily phoned to tell him about her mother. And did 'isn't well' translate to something life-threatening? Just how serious was Mary's illness? Phillip didn't seem overly concerned. It might be his *ex*-wife, but he was usually a sympathetic person and she couldn't believe he would describe her condition so casually. Kandy's street instincts had been honed further with the cut-and-thrust of business negotiations, and right now she smelled a tall, fair-haired, fashionable rat. Unfortunately she loved him.

Ten minutes later she was accessing the Yellow Pages on-line. She had always known that money could get you most things you wanted, but being married to Phillip and having access to what she considered an almost unlimited supply made her realise just how easy it could be. Now she called the number of the private investigation service that seemed best equipped to handle her needs, and offered them double their usual fee to get certain information to her within the next couple of hours.

CHAPTER TWENTY-FIVE

The hospital Emergency Department was a mix of crying kids and whinging adults and patient patients and those too sick to bother making any noise or eye contact or even attempt to watch the morning show on television.

Geoffrey watched the never-ceasing flow of humanity through pain-hazed eyes. Only some of the pain was from his wrist, the rest was a hangover of enormous proportions. His name was finally called and he stumbled into the next two hours of his life. He emerged with a sling holding his strapped-up wrist to his chest, a box of paracetamol in his pocket, and a disbelief in the x-ray that showed no bone was broken.

'Sometimes a bad sprain can be more painful than a break,' the doctor had told him. Geoffrey had been tempted to offer him both so he could make a comparison. Only discretion and the knowledge he was physically incapable of doing so kept his mouth shut.

He caught a glimpse of his reflection in a glass panel. Shit! He looked bloody awful. Shaving had been out of the question. Not only was he right-handed, but he couldn't be sure his left hand would be steady enough to hold a razor without cutting himself. He stood in the hallway and debated what to do. Almost without conscious thought, he started walking to his mother's ward.

Ellie couldn't believe she'd gone back to bed and slept for three hours. Sleeping in the mornings wasn't something she'd done before, but as she wriggled her feet into slippers and pulled on her gown, she realised her body had needed it.

Twenty minutes later she emerged from the bathroom dressed in a cerise velour pants and jacket that was a lot newer than her favourite tracksuit and almost as comfortable. She heated up some of Miranda's chicken soup and buttered a bread roll and was about to sit down to eat it when a knock came at the door. Her heart beat a little faster at the thought it might be Chris taking a break from his shift to check on her.

When she opened the door she tried to hide her disappointment, but Cass quickly picked up on it. 'Guess you were expecting a certain man in blue,' she quipped with a grin.

'I wasn't sure,' Ellie said as she indicated for her friend to come in. 'We're going away this weekend and -'

'Away? As in spending the night together?'

'Get that gleam out of your eyes, Cass Brighton,' Ellie tried not to laugh. 'He said there's no pressure on me, we can just go as friends.'

Cass started to laugh. 'That's a good one. The man fairly eats you up every time he looks at you, and he reckons you can just be friends?'

'Don't worry,' Ellie rolled her eyes. 'There's no hope of that. The eating up is mutual. The man turns me on like I haven't been turned on for years.'

'Sounds like you need an electrician, not a cop.'

'I was just having lunch,' Ellie deflected. 'Would you like some?'

'No, thanks. I've already eaten. But I'll have a cuppa.'

'Why aren't you at work? You usually work Fridays.'

'Slow day, so I took the afternoon off. I'd done some overtime last week so it evens out. Thought I'd come and see how you're doing.' Cass waved Ellie to the table and went to fill up the kettle. 'And what happened with Damien after Kandy and I left yesterday.'

Between mouthfuls of food Ellie told her. And added details of Chris's suggestion of a weekend in the mountains.

'Montville and Maleny are so pretty,' Cass sighed in envy. 'All the hinterland behind the Sunshine Coast is beautiful. Joe and I went years ago.'

'Speaking of Joe,' Ellie put down her spoon. 'Would he be working on the units this afternoon?'

Cass poured two cups of tea and brought them to the table. 'Why?' She raised a suspicious eyebrow. 'You're not thinking of going there again, are you?'

Ellie explained about the false ceiling in unit one and how she needed to find out if the original ceiling was worth restoring. 'So I thought if I borrowed a ladder from Joe I could have a look through the manhole. I'd still need a torch, but it would be safer in the day time.'

'You're crazy. You could have been killed when you fell down those stairs, and now you want to go climbing a ladder. Are you sure you didn't dislodge something when you hit your head? You used to be so sensible.'

'You could come with me to make sure I stay safe,' Ellie

cajoled.

Cass looked at her with mock severity. 'Emotional blackmail.' She smiled. 'Guess I'm an easy mark.'

Twenty minutes later they were on their way to the units in Cass's car. Cass had refused to let Ellie drive her own car, declaring that she wasn't going to risk her passing out at the wheel and turning them both into road accident statistics. Ellie was actually relieved. She didn't feel as good as she'd made out to Cass she did.

As they arrived at the units, Ellie was surprised by the number of tradesmen's trucks parked in the driveway and on the road. They walked through the front door, and when Ellie looked at the stairs, she had a flash of memory that startled her. A man ... A shadow ... Something she'd seen, but only fleetingly. Somewhere here. But it was gone as quickly as it had come.

'G'day, love,' Joe called out from the top of the stairs. 'Saw you pull up. Hi, Ellie. How are you?' His boots clomped on the stairs as he walked down to them. 'What's the problem?'

Cass explained their need to borrow a ladder and within a few minutes, Joe had positioned his ladder in the unit one hallway and was pushing the manhole open. He wrinkled his nose. 'Bit dusty in here.' He climbed down. 'Use my torch, it's more powerful than your little one. I've got to get back to work. Give me a yell when you're finished.'

'Thanks, Joe,' Ellie said, and took the torch. With Cass holding the ladder, she climbed up until her head and shoulders were in the false cavity. She switched on the torch and shone it upwards. And felt the kind of disappointment that comes when you pin your hopes on something and it doesn't measure up. Through the battens and beams that held the false ceiling in place, she could see no fancy cornices, no intricate designs, no patterns or swirls or decoration of any kind on the original plaster. She turned slightly so she could shine the beam through to the lounge room section. No different. It would be a waste of time and money to remove the false ceiling.

She turned around so she could step back down the ladder. As she did so, her arm brushed something and she almost dropped the torch when it moved. She eased away as far as she could and shone the torch at it. A large rectangular object. Covered in cloth, or thin canvas. She reached out carefully and touched it. It didn't move, and she realised it had only done so when she'd bumped it because it had been placed between two beams and she'd knocked it off. A thick layer of dust made it impossible to see if there were any markings on it. Careful not to disturb too much of the dust, she picked it up, manoeuvred it out of the manhole and handed it down to Cass.

As soon as Ellie got to the floor, they took the bag outside to brush the dust off by rubbing it gently over the grass. They discovered it was actually a thick cloth drawstring bag. Once they'd removed enough dust, Ellie opened it and drew out a flat parcel covered in brown paper and tied with string. She pulled the string aside and unwrapped the paper.

'Wow!' Cass breathed over her shoulder. 'She's beautiful.'

Ellie stared at the painting. 'This isn't an amateur's

work.' She peered at the signature on the bottom right-hand corner and felt her heart beat faster. She turned the frame around and saw an inscription and two initials on the back.

Her mouth opened, but for a moment her voice seemed to desert her. Then she whispered, 'Oh ... my ... God.'

CHAPTER TWENTY-SIX

The private investigation agency phoned Kandy back within a couple of hours.

She expected her hand to tremble as she answered the phone, and was surprised when it didn't. She'd had nearly ten years of security with Phillip, and what she planned to do could put that at risk. She gave her credit card details, waited while they made sure the transaction had gone through, then wrote down the information as they told it to her.

After she'd hung up the phone, she threw on a coat and grabbed her handbag. What she needed to do now couldn't be done with a phone call. People lied too easily through the distance of a phone line. No, when she spoke with Vanessa Olden it had to be face to face.

As she drove into the city, she had to fight the doubts that wriggled into her mind. She couldn't believe that Phillip had betrayed her. Apart from sex, they'd shared so much together. She knew that he knew about her affairs. They'd never discussed it, but he'd made veiled references that indicated they didn't worry him. Sex had been infrequent during the first few months of their marriage, then had dwindled to many months when a cuddle was as intimate as he preferred to get. But she'd remained faithful for three years, until a couple of after-lessons drinks with her tennis coach had ended in the most erotic, satisfying sex she'd ever experienced. The pleasure had been matched by her guilt and shame, and she'd switched the next day to piano lessons. They were next on Phillip's list of things she should learn.

All her attempts to get Phillip to discuss their differing sexual needs ended in failure. He simply stated that he wasn't highly sexed and saw no need to do anything about it. It was then he had hinted that he didn't mind if she found her own answers for her needs. And so her sexual liaisons with other men began.

Almost as though the fates were determined to make sure she didn't miss meeting with Vanessa before she left for the airport, the traffic flowed smoothly all the way into town.

'If this is as valuable as you think it is,' Cass said as Ellie carefully re-wrapped the painting, 'what are we going to do with it?'

Ellie had been considering just that as she'd gazed at the painting and tried to remember what she could about the artist. 'If it's genuine, it will be worth a fortune, and it looks pretty genuine to me. But I think we have to find the owner first. This Iris that he dedicated it to, she might have been the person who lived in the unit.'

'I could ask the property manager where I work if she can find out who used to manage the rentals for the units,' Cass suggested.

'That's probably our best option. I could ask Bruce who he bought the units from but that might make him wonder why I need to know, and I'd like to try to find the owner first.'

Cass nodded. 'Good idea. Knowing Bruce, he'd probably say that whatever was in the building when he bought it is his now. But where are we going to put it until we track Iris down?'

'Well, it's been safe in the ceiling for years, so why don't we put it back there?' Ellie slid the painting back into the bag Cass held open. Her excitement about discovering the painting was slowly ebbing, but she was intrigued by the beautiful woman portrayed in it. And for an artist of such renown to write something so personal on the back was a mystery she wanted to resolve.

With the painting secure in its hiding place, they drove back to Ellie's house. Cass phoned her property manager friend who promised to get back to her as soon as she'd found out anything, then said goodbye to Ellie and drove home.

Ellie looked at her watch - she thought Miranda would be home by now. She hoped nothing had gone wrong with the job interview.

Geoffrey wondered whether it was because he was seeing her through eyes that tended to haze over in bright light, but he thought his mother seemed better today than she had all week. She greeted him with a smile that reminded him of how she'd been in the years before his father's overwhelming dominance and pomposity had drained her of the ability to have fun.

But at the sight of his arm her face clouded over and he

felt an unfamiliar twinge of remorse at having caused her happiness to dim.

'It's not broken,' he said before she could ask. 'I slipped over last night and sprained my wrist.'

'Oh, dear. That will make it hard for you to keep looking for work.'

He'd forgotten he'd lied about what he was currently doing. His guilt deepened, but he shook it away. It must be the grog, he thought. Guilt was an emotion he hadn't experienced in a long, long time. Probably not since his early teens. He must be getting soft.

'Geoffrey,' Maud said as he sat down next to the bed, 'the manager at the retirement village did me a favour and went to the bank for me.' She pointed to the bedside cupboard. 'Can you get my handbag out for me, please?'

With a barely-restrained groan at having to move when he'd just relaxed, Geoffrey did as she asked. Maud fumbled at the handbag catch, her fingers trembling. Geoffrey was just about to help her when she flicked it open. She drew out a bank passbook, opened it and handed him a wad of fifty dollar notes. 'I want you to have this. I don't have much, but it will be yours when I die. But I thought you might need a little to tide you over until you find work.'

Geoffrey's hand shook as he took the money. He didn't count it, just shoved it into his pocket, but he could tell there was about five hundred dollars there. In other times it would have been an insignificant amount, but right now it meant decent food and a new pair of shoes. And maybe a coat that really kept out the cold. 'Thanks.' His voice sounded gruff, but Maud beamed, her eyes lighting up as though he'd paid her a wonderful compliment. 'I appreciate it.' The words seemed to slip from him, but when he saw the sheen of happy tears in her eyes, he was strangely pleased that they had.

'Five star luxury,' Kandy murmured as she walked into the Sofitel Brisbane Hotel. 'Must have the same taste as her father.'

She'd dressed with care, black pants and a burgundy and black swirled-patterned clinging blouse under a tailored black jacket. Her black boots had heels so high they almost made her totter, but she needed the height - her confidence was in inverse proportion to her anxiety, and she was a mass of that.

Two young female clerks were behind the reception counter, but she walked over to where a middle-aged man, whose badge said he was some kind of manager, was accessing one of the check-in computers.

'Hello,' she smiled, and waited for the reaction she got from most males. He didn't disappoint. He abandoned the computer and beamed at her. 'Can I help you, madam?'

It still irked her that men always seemed to assess her physical attributes and rarely anything else. It was Phillip's interest in her personality and intelligence that had attracted her to him and led her to love him. 'You have a guest here, a Mrs Vanessa Olden. Could you please let her know that Kandy Breckham wishes to speak with her?'

'Certainly, Madam,' he beamed again, and hit the computer keys like it was the most important thing in his day. He picked up the phone, dialled the room number, and, after a few seconds' wait, repeated Kandy's request. After a few moments he frowned, and said, 'Mrs Olden, are you still there?'

Kandy's stomach lurched. Was Vanessa going to refuse to see her? She crossed her fingers.

'Very well, Madam. Thank you.' The manager returned the phone to its cradle and smiled with a little less enthusiasm than before. 'Mrs Olden said she will be down shortly. If you'd care to wait.' He indicated the groups of lounge chairs in the spacious foyer.

'Thank you.' As Kandy walked away she could feel his eyes on her, but when she turned he moved back to his computer. She chose a seat that gave her a clear view of the lifts. She didn't want Vanessa catching her off guard.

The detective agency had informed her that Vanessa had married nineteen years ago and had had two children. It seemed to Kandy that everyone was capable of having children except her.

As the minutes ticked by she began to worry that Vanessa had changed her mind, or maybe she'd lied about coming down and hadn't really intended seeing her at all. By the time Vanessa emerged from the lift Kandy's stomach had almost knotted in anxiety. Vanessa strode straight towards where she was sitting. It took an effort for Kandy to remain seated until Vanessa was almost in front of her, then stand and smiled pleasantly. 'Thank you for agreeing to see me, Vanessa.'

The guarded look in Vanessa's eyes didn't dissipate. 'How can I help you, Kandy?'

'Could we talk in private, please?' Kandy couldn't stop

the pleading tone in her voice.

Vanessa hesitated for only a moment. 'Come up to my room.'

Although they were the only people in the lift, they rode in silence, and walked the corridor to Vanessa's room in silence.

It wasn't just a hotel room, but a suite that was bigger than some of the bedsits Kandy had called home as a teenager. Vanessa nodded to the brown leather lounge and said, 'Please sit down. Would you like a coffee or tea?'

Kandy craved the warmth a coffee would bring to the coldness sitting in her chest, but she was afraid her hand would shake. 'No, thanks.'

Vanessa sat on an adjoining lounge chair, back stiff, hands spread on her thighs as though looking for somewhere to grip. 'Did Phillip tell you where to find me?'

'No. I hired a private investigator. Phillip only told me about you because I saw you leaving our house as I was driving in.'

'Ah. I wondered why that car slammed on the brakes and slowed down as I drove out. What else has Phillip told you?'

'Not a lot. How is your mother?'

Vanessa frowned. 'She's fine. Why?'

'Phillip said she's ill and that's why you came to see him. To tell him.'

It was as though the words had pricked the bubble of Vanessa's defences. With a long sigh she leaned back in the chair, her shoulders slumping. 'My father's not a bad man, Kandy. He simply doesn't cope with reality.'

It was Kandy's turn to frown. 'He owns a financial investment company and is the director on the boards of half a dozen other companies. Are you saying that's not reality?'

'It's about the only reality he handles well. I'm talking about his private life. I gather you knew nothing about me until yesterday?'

'That's right. Phillip said he married your mother because he got her pregnant but the marriage didn't end well and she insisted he didn't have any more contact with you and your brother.'

'And he didn't tell you why?'

The knots in Kandy's stomach tightened all the way to her throat. 'No,' she whispered.

'Kandy, it's not my place to tell you. Dad should.' She looked at Kandy, eyes sympathetic, then sighed again. 'But he won't, will he.' Now her hands gripped the sides of the lounge chair as she leaned forward, voice soft, face contorted with emotion.

'Kandy, Phillip ... my father ... is gay.'

CHAPTER TWENTY-SEVEN

Of all the things Kandy had imagined that Vanessa might tell her, saying that Phillip was gay wasn't one of them. 'Gay,' she echoed.

'I'm so sorry,' Vanessa reached out a comforting hand, then let it drop. 'I wouldn't have told you, but ...'

Kandy was too stunned to ask what Vanessa was about to insinuate with "but". 'How do you know?' she finally asked.

Vanessa stood up. 'I think we could both do with a coffee now. Or maybe something stronger?'

The temptation to raid the mini bar and fortify herself with enough alcohol to numb the pain and disbelief she was now feeling was almost overwhelming, but Kandy wanted to be clear-headed when she heard what Vanessa had to say. 'Coffee, thanks. Strong. White. One sugar.'

When Vanessa went to make the coffee, Kandy stared through the large windows at the inner city skyline with its mix of high-rise architecture. A kaleidoscope of memories raced through her mind, but now suspicion tinged each one. Her world was cracking open and she wasn't sure she would be able to keep a grip on it. She barely heard Vanessa come back. But as Vanessa placed two mugs on the coffee table, she said, 'Your plane. You'll be late.'

'It's all right. I changed to a later flight before I went down to meet you.'

The hot coffee sped through Kandy's system, relaxing tense muscles and loosening stomach knots, but it didn't ease the pain in her heart. 'Would you please tell me everything?' she finally asked.

Vanessa nodded. 'I wasn't going to tell you, I remember what finding out did to Mum. But you have a right to know. Apparently Dad had always suspected he was gay, but because his parents were such self-righteous people who were always more worried about what other people thought than their own children's happiness, he denied it to himself. He even started a relationship with Mum to prove to himself that he wasn't gay. Then Mum got pregnant, and they married.'

'He told me that bit. He also said that when they broke up your mother said he wasn't to have any further contact with you and your brother.'

'Mum was completely shocked by what she'd seen and what Dad confessed about always believing he was homosexual. And terribly hurt.'

'I know how she felt,' Kandy muttered.

'We were all pretty devastated. Even Phillip. He'd fallen in love for the first time in his life and I guess it was too much temptation for him to resist. Mum found them together.'

'Hell! How *Brokeback Mountain*.' Kandy wavered between laughing and crying. It all felt so surreal.

'Worse than that. Apparently she found them in bed. Unfortunately the sheet had slipped off and ...' Vanessa wrinkled her nose as though unable to even contemplate the scene. 'To make things worse,' she continued, 'the other man was a friend of mine from university.'

'So he would have been ...' Kandy found she couldn't complete the sentence.

Vanessa did it for her. 'My age at the time. Nineteen.'

If Kandy's world had tilted before, it did a complete 180 degrees now. 'Nineteen,' she repeated as though the word was foreign to her. She looked at the coffee cup in her hand, at the dark depths of it, realising that Phillip's depths were just as dark. After a while she asked, 'What happened then?'

'Well, as you can imagine, the proverbial hit the fan. Mum went nearly hysterical. Josh and I arrived home from uni when she was still ranting at Dad and Nathan. I had to stop Josh from punching Dad, Nathan was blubbering how sorry he was for upsetting everyone but he was in love with Dad, and Mum collapsed. It was such a terrible mess. Both Mum and Dad had always been so proper, so conventional, I don't think any of us knew how to handle the situation. That's when Dad confessed that he'd always felt he was homosexual but had tried not to be because of his family. And Mum's family were so straitlaced they would never have understood Dad's predicament.'

'It sounds like you were sympathetic to Phillip and ...Nathan?'

'I wasn't at the time. When Mum told Dad to leave, Josh and I were on her side. It was like he had betrayed us all. But a year later he wrote to each of us and said how sorry he was and that he still loved us but understood if we didn't want to see him again.'

'But you didn't see him again. Until now.'

'No. We thought it would hurt Mum if we did.'

'What happened to Nathan?'

'He got into another relationship a couple of months later.'

'So much for undying love.' Kandy knew she sounded bitter, but she couldn't help it. Phillip might have been to blame for his betrayal of his marriage, but this Nathan wasn't entirely guiltless.

Vanessa put her cup back onto its saucer. 'Nathan is still in love with my father.'

'What?' Kandy felt her body jerk back, a purely physical reaction to Vanessa's statement. Emotionally she felt stunned, as though her mind couldn't absorb any more shocks.

'Kandy, I know how hard this must be for you to cope with all this. You obviously love my father, and he's probably been a good husband, like he was when he was married to my mother. But Nathan's partner died last year, and a month or so ago he started talking about finding Phillip. He wanted to know if Phillip still loved him. It didn't take him long to track him down.' She hesitated, and the compassion in her eyes told Kandy that what else she had to say wasn't going to be something Kandy would like to hear.

So Kandy said it for her. 'And start up their affair again.' She didn't need to see Vanessa's nod to know her life was tumbling into ruin like an ill-constructed building in an earthquake. All her hypothesising about Phillip being in love with someone else was suddenly true, but not in the way she'd imagined. 'How do you know this?'

'I married Nathan's older brother.'

'Nothing like keeping it all in the family,' Kandy muttered. 'Why did you come to see Phillip, Vanessa? To stop him making the same mistake twice?'

'Something like that. When my husband told me that Nathan had gone to Brisbane to see my father I wasn't concerned, but then I discovered Dad had re-married.' She frowned in the same eyebrows-together, forehead-raising way that Phillip did and Kandy's heart lurched. She wondered if Vanessa realised how much she looked like her father. 'Kandy, he didn't want to meet me at his house, but I insisted. I told him I wanted to see how he lived, to see if I connected with him the way I used to when I was growing up. It was selfish of me, I know, but he was a wonderful father, and I was bitterly hurt when he left. I'm sorry that you saw me leave.'

'Don't be. I'd already suspected he was having an affair. I just didn't think ...' She didn't state the obvious, but it actually made little difference that his lover was a man. Her years on the streets had made her more tolerant than most.

She was struggling to deal with the reality of Phillip's behaviour. This was no one-night stand, no fling with a dancer at a club, no shag with the tennis instructor because he was frustrated and three-parts pissed. This was a love affair that had started twenty-five years ago and had apparently never really ended. She remembered the pain she had seen in his eyes after Vanessa had left yesterday and felt a sharp stab of sympathy. She knew he was a good man, his kindness and compassion had drawn her to him when they'd first met. He was generous, not just with his money, but his time, and he genuinely cared about people. Finding out he really was gay, and not just suspecting it, must have been very hard for him to deal with. No wonder he had meekly accepted his wife's demands and stayed away from his children.

She could even understand why he hadn't told her about his marriage and children because she handled painful memories the same way - just buried them and pretended they'd never existed. Hell, she didn't even know if her parents were still alive. And she cared even less. She wondered if it might have been different if she'd had siblings, someone who cared about her or whom she cared about. But there wasn't. There was only Phillip. And now it looked like she was going to lose him.

And the thought of it was breaking her heart.

Ellie jerked awake when the front door opened. For a second she had trouble orientating herself, then remembered she'd lain on the lounge to rest for a few minutes after Cass had dropped her home. She must have fallen asleep.

'Mum? Are you all right?' Miranda hurried into the room.

'I'm fine.' Ellie glanced at her watch. A "few minutes" had become nearly two hours. Mayhem was curled up beside her, face tucked between her paws, body relaxed, but the slight twitch of her ears told Ellie she wasn't fully asleep. 'How did the interview go?'

Miranda's smile could have lit a tennis court. 'I got the

job! They want me to start Monday. They showed me around the store and gave me an idea of my duties. I'm going to love it.'

'That's fantastic! I'm so pleased for you.' Ellie jumped off the lounge to hug her, but the room swayed and she plopped down again. 'Not a good idea,' she muttered. 'Should have done that slowly.'

'Are you sure you're okay enough to go away with Chris this weekend?' Miranda gave her a look that Ellie recognised as one of her own. She was tempted to reply, 'Yes, Mum,' but stifled the urge, and said instead, 'I'll be fine. I'll take it easy.'

Miranda didn't look convinced, and Ellie nearly laughed at the role switch that was happening. Then she remembered something she'd been meaning to ask Miranda. 'Mirie, I want to do something to thank Mouse for what he did for me. From what Chris said, Mouse took a risk staying with me until the police came. Is there something I could do for him, or something I could get him that he needs?'

'I'm sure he could do with some warm blankets. They're something that's always in short supply on the street. But,' she glanced down at Mayhem, 'how about some cat food? Feeding all those kittens must be expensive. I'm sure he takes the meat out of the sandwiches we give him and feeds them with it.'

'Blankets and cat food it is.' Ellie stretched gently, pleased that her aches and pains were lessening, but aware there was still some stiffness in her muscles. 'If I buy them on Monday morning, would you be able to give them to Mouse when you go on the van Monday night?'

'Sure.'

'How about we open a bottle of wine to celebrate your job? You can tell me all the details. And then I'll tell you what Cass and I discovered at the units today.'

One hour and a bottle of wine later, Ellie went to pack her overnight bag while Miranda hummed her way through cooking dinner. Ellie couldn't help smiling. It was good to see Miranda so happy. She just hoped the job was all Miranda seemed to think it was. At least it was taking her mind off Ben's rejection.

She shuffled through the clothing in her wardrobe. After the roominess of her walk-in robe, it had been difficult getting used to the ornate, silky oak monster that dominated the bedroom with its height and breadth. The mirror on the panel between the two doors was handy, because it was the only full-length one in the house. Unfortunately there wasn't enough room between it and the bed to get a full-length view. When she wanted to see if her shoes matched her clothes she had to sit on the bed.

Packing. She hated it. Even if she was excited about going on a holiday, it didn't stop the nervous knot in her stomach that formed as she decided what to take. She always felt sure she would forget something she would need. Once she was in the car or on the plane, there was a certain inevitability about it all and she could relax. Perhaps she'd lost too many things that were important to her in her childhood as her father moved around, seeking the job that was going to give him the money and status he seemed to think he deserved. It was the only explanation she could come up with for feeling like she did.

Warmth - courtesy of new, winter-weight clothes, a fan heater and a doona, good food, and a bottle of decent scotch. They might not stop the pain, but at least they made it easier to bear.

Geoffrey kept his sprained wrist cocooned on his new pillow and leaned back against the metal bed-head. For the first time since he'd walked out of prison he was able to enjoy the things that made his life bearable. That it was his mother's money that had brought about this happy state wasn't something he chose to acknowledge. Any more than he wanted to think about how his attitude to her was changing. As a boy he'd adored her, thought she was the sweetest, kindest person alive. But as a teenager he'd perceived those same qualities as weakness and despised her for it. Now he realised she had been just as intimidated by his over-bearing father as he had been. And the knowledge didn't sit well with him.

Kandy dimmed her headlights and turned into her driveway. She watched the branches on the eucalypt trees bordering the property sway gently in the breeze and knew if she lowered the car window the sound of their leaves rustling would be like waves shimmering over a pebbled beach. Knew the sharp tang of their oil would be faint on the winter's night. Knew the parakeets that drank the grevilleas' nectar had abandoned their feasting and screeching at dusk.

Knew that after tonight her world would never be the same again.

She had ignored the two calls from Phillip on her mobile.

She knew he would be worried about her, about why she was so late getting home. But she'd needed time to think, to come to terms with what Vanessa had revealed.

The temptation to go to a bar and drink away her pain had been strong. Instead she'd bought an all-day ticket and sat on the River Cat for hours, staring out the window but not seeing the houses, the parks, the apartment buildings, the wharves, the industries that edged the river's meandering width. She'd needed the time to think, to absorb the body-aching shock.

As a teenager, 'time to think' would have meant time to get drunk or stoned so she wouldn't have to think. It had taken a lot of courage to abandon that way of life and she wasn't going to slide back into it now.

The ferry had plied its course back and forth, passengers had embarked and disembarked, and still she'd sat and stared, until, finally, she'd worked out what she thought was the only possible solution to the situation.

Now she parked her Porsche in the garage and gathered her courage for the emotional minefield that lay ahead of her.

CHAPTER TWENTY-EIGHT

Miranda's call that dinner was ready came as Ellie was trying to decide if she should pack the demure full-length nightie she'd bought for a short hospital stay some years ago or the sexy, almost see-through one she'd worn to try to entice Damien into remembering she was more than the woman who kept his home running efficiently.

She had the feeling that if she chose 'demure' she would feel like a born-again virgin, something that didn't sit very well with her. She'd read about women getting plastic surgery to have their hymen re-attached for their second "de-flowering" and wondered how a doctor would find the damn thing in some of them. Wouldn't it have worn away with so much use?

And the more she looked at the sexy little number, the more she thought it shrieked "desperate". She'd been there, done that, had the rejection to prove it.

Nope. She wasn't going into this relationship pretending to be something she wasn't. Luckily she'd bought some new pyjamas when the weather had turned cold. They might be flannelette but at least they were pretty in a "I just want to snuggle up to you" kind of way. They also covered her bruises. She placed them in her small suitcase and zipped it closed.

Her mind was buzzing with the possible scenarios of how the weekend would turn out. More accurately, how the night would turn out. From Kandy's descriptions of some of her flings, a sexy smile and a great body didn't guarantee sexual satisfaction. She appeared to have run the gamut from thirty-second squib to the body-builder who took the expression "pumping iron" too seriously.

She wondered what Chris would think when he saw her naked. She had a few stretch marks, and her breasts weren't what you'd call "perky", but at least she didn't have to roll them up to get them into her bra. Surely at their ages he wouldn't be looking for perfection. Too bad if he was, she huffed at the thought, but a little doubt lingered.

The worry was starting to bring her headache back, so she shoved all bed-time thoughts aside and went to the kitchen. Food and sleep was what she needed, not worry. But she knew she was going to have trouble convincing herself it was that simple.

Phillip was sitting on one of the six black leather recliners in the lounge room, newspaper open on his lap, head slumped sideways, eyes closed behind his reading glasses. Kandy stood in the doorway and watched him. And wondered how she had not realised his true sexual orientation before this. She'd come across all types in her life - homosexual, heterosexual, bi-sexual, trans-sexual, even the occasional man she'd consider a-sexual. Perhaps what had confused her about Phillip was that he was first and foremost a *good* man. Until she had met him it had been easy for her to believe such men didn't exist. And maybe she'd wanted to believe so badly that he was everything she'd dreamed she'd wanted in a husband that she'd dismissed any doubts that may have arisen.

As though sensing her presence, he pulled himself upright in the chair, took off his glasses and rubbed his eyes and looked at her. He started to smile, but her mood must have been conveyed in the way she stood, unmoving, gazing back at him, and his lips lost their upward slant.

'I talked to Vanessa this morning.'

Her words weren't the bombshell she thought they might have been. Phillip said nothing, but his body seemed to shrink into the plump black leather, his face showing a sadness that wrenched at her heart.

All the sensible, dispassionate words she'd planned to say flew from her mind, and she heard herself wail like heartbroken teenager. 'Why? Why, Phillip? I thought you loved me.'

'I do love you, Kandy. But not in the way a man should love a woman. I thought I could. God help me, I tried. When we first met I found you so ... so refreshing, so different to anyone I'd ever come across before. When I found out your background I admired you even more. You have the courage I lack. The strength I lack.'

It was true. She'd always known it. Phillip had a flair for business, for making intuitive decisions that resulted in success, but he'd always hired people who had the grit to carry out the hard options. In a way, even choosing her as his wife was a good business move. She had learned the skills to move in different social circles, and had the ability to deflect unwanted attention without giving offence. As his hostess she was impeccable, as his wife she was charming without being flirtatious. She knew men were attracted to her, and if she were tall and blonde their wives would probably have carved her to pieces with looks alone, but her ability to come across as sisterly rather than as a threat had kept her safe from female talons.

She walked over and sat on one of the other lounge chairs, almost facing him, but not quite. 'What do you want to do?' she asked, her voice even, but the stiffness in her body betrayed her anxiety.

'I suppose Vanessa told you everything?'

Kandy nodded. 'She said Nathan is still in love with you. How do you feel about him?'

He didn't reply, but his expression told her what she needed to know. 'You love him, don't you?' she pressed.

He nodded, but quickly said, 'I don't want to lose you, Kandy. But I can't give Nathan up. Not now. We should have stayed together years ago, but I pushed him away when I saw the pain it had caused my family. Until I saw him a few weeks back I thought that being with you was enough, but ...'

'But it's not.'

Phillip shook his head, then looked at her with such desperation in his eyes that she couldn't help feeling sorry for him. 'What do we do now?' he asked.

'I guess,' the words dragged out reluctantly, 'it's time for me to meet Nathan.'

When Ellie woke on Saturday morning it was with the same sense of fear and anticipation she used to feel the first day at a new school. Then, the fear of the unknown would always outweigh the possibility that this would be the start of a new way of life for her. Maybe this time her father would stay in the same job, and this time she would make friends she didn't have to say goodbye to after a couple of years or sometimes only months.

But now the anticipation beat the fear hands down. Well, it did until she heard the knock on the front door. She looked at her watch. Hell! She'd slept in. Damn red wine. She scrambled from bed, yelled 'Just a minute,' at the same time as Miranda called, 'I'll get it,' and hurried to the bathroom. By the time she emerged, showered and dressed in jeans, cotton blouse, jacket and sneakers, Miranda had let Chris in, made breakfast and put it on the kitchen table.

Twenty minutes later she sat in his Rodeo and watched the northern suburbs fade away behind them.

Geoffrey knew his former boss would be getting even more impatient, but he didn't have any enthusiasm for breaking into the units again at the moment. The almost-forgotten experience of comfort, and food that was tasty rather than just filling, of alcohol that soothed rather than burned his oesophagus, was so enjoyable he wanted to savour it for as long as he could. Besides, his wrist was still so painful it was almost useless. Only the painkillers made it possible to use it to do basic toileting and personal chores. Breaking into a building was beyond him at the moment.

He briefly wondered if the codeine in the tablets he was taking was behind the numbness his brain seemed to be experiencing at the moment. He knew he should be shit-scared that he had gone beyond the deadline imposed on him for getting hold of the painting, but somehow he didn't seem to care. It was as though the danger was hidden by fluffy barriers of cotton wool.

He carefully eased into his new, full-length coat, looked at himself in the mirror and smiled. Now he looked more like himself. He glanced down at his too-short jacket with its stupid collar that now hung on the back of the kitchen chair. He should throw it in the garbage. Then he remembered the gun he'd shoved in the pocket after Gazza had forced it on him. He bent over to take it out to transfer to his new coat, but decided it would ruin the cut of the pocket. Besides, he shouldn't need it just to go to the hospital.

Ellie gazed at the tapestry of rolling green fields and tree-studded farmlets and quaint family dwellings and European-styled guest-houses designed to lure tourists into believing they were far removed from south-east Queensland with its mild winters and hot summers. It might be a few degrees cooler here in the hinterland, but the sun shone brightly in a cloud-puffed blue sky and when, through a gap in the trees, she saw across the valleys and hills to the Sunshine Coast, she was sure she could see the ocean sparkle with the intensity of it.

She shifted her gaze from the scenery for a moment to watch Chris as he negotiated the winding mountain road. He drove with the easy confidence of a man for whom a car was almost an extension of his body, and for a moment she envied his self-assurance. But the moment was fleeting. She remembered his uncertainty when he'd asked about Damien, and his quickness to brush aside her doubts about being able to cope with the dangers of his job. If he was in love with her then he would be just as tentative about their relationship as she was.

'Penny for them.' His words broke into her reverie. She saw the twinkle in his eyes and her heart jolted in a way that told her this was going to be quite a weekend.

'You can't buy anything for a penny these days,' she joked, then asked 'How's Danny? Solved all the possum problems?'

Chris chuckled. 'The nesting box worked. He now has two possums relying on him for nightly feeds. It's giving him a good idea what being a parent is like.'

'I don't think anything can prepare you for that.'

She didn't realise how her words sounded until he reached over and squeezed her hand where it lay on her lap. The feeling of being cherished almost overwhelmed her. It had been a long time since she'd felt that from a man. She clasped his hand tightly for a moment, then released it.

They drifted back to the companionable silence that had marked most of their trip. By nature Ellie wasn't a "chatty" person, and she sensed that Chris appreciated not having to talk while he was driving.

When they reached the turnoff to Montville, he ignored it and continued on the road to Maleny. 'I thought we're staying in Montville?' she asked.

'I thought you might like to look around the shops in Maleny first.'

'You want to go shopping?' She couldn't keep the

surprise from her voice.

'Well, no, I thought you might like to,' he replied in the cautious tone of a man who wasn't sure if he'd said the right thing or not.

'Well, how about we have a quick look through a couple of the shops then grab some lunch and go to Lake Baroon and have a picnic? Do you have a blanket in the back?' She wasn't sure if the smile that accompanied his nod was because he'd been spared hours of shopping or because he thought sharing a blanket hinted at more than devouring food.

Yep. It was going to be quite a weekend.

The sound of the doorbell echoed in Kandy's chest with a similar resounding emptiness. She looked at her watch. Midday.

Guess who's coming to dinner?

She tried to smile at her mental joke, but couldn't do it. She knew who would be standing on the other side of the door. She watched Phillip walk across the foyer and open it, and felt a rush of gratitude that he didn't greet the man who stood there with anything more than friendly politeness. Knowing that they'd explored each other's bodies, that they'd touched each other with love was one thing, seeing any expression of that love was more than she could cope with yet.

'Kandy,' Phillip turned towards her. 'This is Nathan Olden.'

'Hello, Nathan. Please come in.'

He gave her a wary look, and she felt like the spider to

his fly. She almost said, 'I won't bite you,' but couldn't be sure she wasn't lying.

She assessed him as he walked towards her. He was slightly taller than Phillip, but slimmer, his dark brown hair flopping into eyes that had the kind of lost puppy-dog look that appealed to motherly women and romantic teenage girls. *And gay lovers.*

He moved with an appealing grace, his designer jeans accentuating rather than detracting from his long, lithe look. His grey jacket said trendy, not sporty. His shoulders squared in a way that told her he was here to do battle, not beg.

'Thank you for inviting me to lunch, Kandy.'

She was grateful he didn't offer her his hand. She was trying not to resent him, but the effort was costing her. 'I thought it would be a good idea for us to meet,' she said. 'Perhaps you'd like a drink before lunch?'

He nodded, and she led the way to the lounge room.

Phillip hurried to the kitchen and returned with three glasses on a tray. Kandy noted that he hadn't had to ask what Nathan drank. It seemed he knew his tastes as well as he knew hers.

'What do you do for work, Nathan?' she asked.

'I'm in merchant banking. It's very challenging.' He waited for Kandy to sit before occupying another chair. Phillip sat a discrete distance from them both. 'Phillip tells me you have your own catering firm. He speaks very highly of you.'

'We've always had a lot of respect for each other's abilities. I've always thought we make a good team.' Oh, shit, that was more pointed than she meant it to be. From the corner of her eye she saw Phillip flinch. Anger flared. Bugger him! He deserved to flinch.

Nathan had seen Phillip's reaction too, but he seemed to square his shoulders even more. 'I've always admired Phillip's ability to bring out the best in people. And his integrity.'

Kandy was about to respond but found no words would come. How could she be so polite when she felt like shredding him with her tongue, or maybe her fingernails. She couldn't do it. Couldn't pretend to be so bloody civilised about it all. Her mind ran through a dozen different rejoinders but she heard herself say, 'I love him, Nathan.'

Phillip stood abruptly, sloshing his drink onto the floor. Kandy stilled him with a hand movement.

Nathan bit his lip, then blurted, 'I'm so sorry, Kandy. I didn't mean to hurt you. I only came looking for Phillip to find out ... I don't really know what. I wanted to come to terms with the past. Years ago Phillip had pushed me away and I rebounded into another relationship, and I needed ... Hell! I don't know. I just wanted to see if what I've always felt for him, what I still felt for him, was real. But when I saw him again it was as though only days and not years had passed. What we'd shared was still there.'

Kandy wanted to lash out, to hurt him like she'd been hurt, but what would be the point. Enough people had been hurt over the years. She looked at Phillip, felt the tension emanating from him, but also felt his yearning, his need, and knew it wasn't for her. Accepting her loss seemed her only option.

Her desire to fight for his love evaporated.

Maybe it was time for everyone to find some happiness. Well, almost everyone. She knew she should feel devastated by the decision she had contemplated yesterday, but instead she felt a sad acceptance. It wasn't going to be easy, but she felt it was the only thing she could do.

She stood up, finished her drink, and said, 'We have a lot to discuss, but I think it will be a lot more pleasant if we do so over lunch.'

Cass put down the phone and returned to the kitchen table. Joe had already finished lunch and was putting the kettle on, but now she had lost her appetite.

'My mother has absolutely no concept of who I am,' she grumbled. 'She sees me as the dutiful daughter she wants me to be, and not as the person I really am.'

'I told you not to answer the phone,' Joe said. 'That's what Caller ID is for.'

'That's all right for you to say.' On principal Cass didn't want to tell him he was right. 'You never answer the phone, even when it's your family.'

'I talk to them when I've got something to say.' He opened the container and cut himself a slice of orange cake.

He was so maddeningly calm that Cass wanted to hit him. She was angry, and she knew it. Not at him, but it did irk her that his family so easily accepted his reluctance to communicate on a regular basis. They reacted to his spasmodic phone calls with the kind of joy she was sure the prodigal son had had showered on him in the bible story.

'So what did Audra want?' he asked.

'She wants you to build a granny flat behind our house so she and Gerry can live close to us.'

Joe's eyes bulged and he choked on his cake. Cass immediately felt better.

'Tell me you're kidding,' he managed to splutter.

The sigh that huffed from deep in Cass's chest was tinged with resignation. 'I wish I was. She was dead serious. Said that as Gerry gets older she's finding it hard to cope with him and thinks that I should *take some of the stress off her.*'

'Holy shit! I hope you told her it was impossible.'

'I explained that we couldn't afford to do it. She said they could live with us while they sold their house and the money would pay for the granny flat.'

Panic flared in Joe's eyes. For a moment she thought he was going to bolt from the room. 'It's all right,' she reassured him. 'I also told her that although it looks like we have enough room we don't because the council knocked us back when we wanted to build another shed in the back yard.'

'But that was because they said what we were proposing would be classified as light industrial and we're not zoned for that.'

'I know that. But Audra doesn't.'

His relief was so comical Cass nearly laughed. He might not have a great deal of imagination and his tastes in food were so basic she could cook for him with her eyes closed, but she could always count on him giving her funny bone a tickle.

Her appetite returned, but before she could pick up her

knife and fork the phone rang again. She looked at Joe. He stared back, daring her to answer it. It kept ringing. She picked up her fork. The ringing continued. 'Damn!' She slammed down the fork and walked into the lounge room and stared at the Caller ID.

She quickly picked up the phone.

Five minutes later her mood had lifted considerably. She walked back into the kitchen. Joe had gone. Probably retreated to his shed to recover from his near miss with Audra and Gerry. Damn. She wanted to share her news with someone. She couldn't phone Ellie. A smile curved her mouth. She didn't want to risk interrupting ... anything.

She looked at the empty plate and mug Joe had left on the table and sighed.

CHAPTER TWENTY-NINE

Blanket *and* pillows. Well, cushions really. The kind that made Ellie wonder what a single man had in the back of his four-wheel-drive. Chris took them out when they parked at the lake to have lunch.

He must have seen her expression because he sheepishly explained that Danny had dragged them out of storage when he had told him where he was taking Ellie. 'They were Angela's favourite cushions and Danny couldn't bear to throw them out when we got a new lounge a few years ago. He remembered coming to the mountains when he was a kid and thought you might appreciate sitting on these rather than a park bench.'

Ellie didn't know whether to be flattered that Danny had thought of her comfort, or worried that he might be looking for a replacement mother. 'Does he mind us going away for the weekend?'

'No, he's fine.'

'I guess you've done this kind of thing a few times since ... you've been on your own.'

'Ellie, it's okay to say Angela's death. I came to terms with that years ago. It took me a long time to be able to say it without almost breaking down, but I eventually did. And, yes, I have dated since.'

'Anyone serious?' She tried to sound casual. Or indifferent. But the look in his eyes told her she hadn't succeeded at either.

'There was one woman who wanted it to be, but I didn't feel the same way.' He spread the blanket on the grass and placed the cushions on it. 'Besides, Danny didn't like her.'

'Oh.'

'You, however, get a very big tick of approval from him.'

'How come?'

Chris pretended to think. 'Something to do with bringing him cake and knowing about possum nesting boxes.' He grinned as she mock-punched him, then caught her hand and drew her to him. 'I should arrest you for assault,' he joked, but the humour on his face turned to something far more serious as her sneaker caught on his and her body tipped full length against his in all the right places. The result was spontaneous combustion of the best kind.

Their kisses had been of the shooting sparks variety, but because of the way he'd held her, she had suspected he'd been trying to be a gentleman. This time there was no restraint in the way he held her against him, so tight she could feel her breasts tingle as they rubbed against his chest, and the bulge in his jeans that told her the thrumming in her blood wasn't one-sided.

She tilted her head so their lips could meet, but he leant his forehead on hers and murmured, 'If I kiss you now, I will end up getting arrested.'

His words were a low, sexy rumble in his throat. She shivered with the anticipation of what they promised. She took a deep breath. 'Perhaps we should eat?'

He moved away a little. 'I'm beginning to think a cold salad might have been a better choice than a curried beef pie.'

'It's winter,' she smiled, deliberately misinterpreting his words, 'something hot is good for you.'

He groaned and pulled at his jeans to adjust them, and she lost the battle to keep a straight face. It had been so long since she'd flirted with a man that she'd almost forgotten what fun it could be. 'I'll get the pies while you get that thermos of coffee you brought along,' she said and walked to the Rodeo.

She glanced back to see him turn towards the lake and take a deep breath. His tall, lean silhouette against the backdrop of blue water extending to thickly wooded slopes on the far shore nearly made her weak at the knees. If she hadn't discovered the wonderful, compassionate core of him that attracted her soul, she would be tempted to think what she felt was simply lust, a frustrated and neglected woman's need to have a good-looking man desire her.

Okay, so she wasn't exactly in the desperate category, but she sure wasn't in the confident woman of the noughties class either. And frustrated was a very accurate word to describe what she was feeling at the moment. Hopefully that would change tonight.

With a smile that echoed in her heart, she gathered their lunch and walked back to the cushion-covered blanket.

Although Geoffrey knew he had no further need to go to see his mother, he told himself that it was a wise move to stay in touch with her. She might come good with some more money, or even remember something that could give him a clue to the whereabouts of the painting.

On his last couple of visits she had reminisced about her family. He remembered his mother's parents, a cheerful working class couple whose house always smelled of freshly-baked bread and biscuits. They'd always kept some home-made ginger beer in the fridge in case Maud brought him for a visit. Yesterday Maud had told him that his father had disapproved of her parents and had limited her visits there. He'd looked into her eyes, sad with the memory of what she'd been denied, and wondered how she had remained as optimistic and loving as she had when his father had tried to grind down her spirit.

For one brief moment, he'd wanted to put his arm around her and reassure her that she was still loved, that he was still her family, but years of habitually rejecting her stopped him.

The moment passed as quickly as it had come.

He thought about it now as he walked past a florist, and before he could argue himself out of it, he picked a bunch of roses from a bucket on the pavement and walked inside to pay.

Something was tickling Ellie's face. The irritation registered in her brain the same moment she emerged from a warm cocoon of sleep and opened her eyes to green. Green grass, green shrubs, green trees. And warmth. The kind that came from sunlight.

For a very long moment she stared at the scenery in her line of vision and tried to remember where she was. A light breeze blew strands of her hair across her cheek and she realised that's what had disturbed her. Her brain felt fuzzy, as though it needed more sleep and was trying to shut down again.

Maleny. Chris. The words seeped in and memory returned with a rush. She pushed herself to a sitting position and looked around. And felt the world spin.

'Whoa!' Chris caught her from behind as she started to topple sideways. She rested back against him, grateful for the support. She closed her eyes. Gradually the spinning stopped. She opened them. The world was still again.

'You still have concussion,' he admonished. 'You shouldn't try to sit up in a hurry.'

'How long have I been asleep?'

'A couple of hours. Apparently my company wasn't exciting enough to keep you awake.'

She could hear the smile in his voice. Then his lips pressed warm, gentle kisses against her neck and she tingled all the way to her toes.

'Another hour and it will start to get cold,' he murmured, his breath whispering softly against her cheek. 'I think we should get to the cabin and settle in and then go out for dinner.'

'Sounds good.' She wasn't sure if she was referring to the meal or settling in. The only thing she was hungry for was a large helping of Chris. Preferably naked. And doing things with her that she'd only dared dream about in the past couple of weeks.

As they drove towards Montville, she pondered how easily she had made up her mind to sleep with him. Seeing

Damien again had done it. Even after the hurt of discovering he had another woman in his life, a tiny glimmer of hope for a reconciliation had lingered deep in her heart. But his arrogance in the way he had swept into her hospital room and practically insisted that he still had a claim on her had effectively killed that.

It had been years since she had been to Montville, and her memories were of a quaint village with flower-strewn gardens tumbling around timber and sandstone shops and people strolling paved footpaths and aromas of exotic food. It hadn't changed. For some reason that made her feel pleased. Perhaps, she mused, after the turmoil of the past few months she needed to see that some things could stay constant. Sure, some shops had been spruced up and some advertising signs seemed to intrude on the genteel atmosphere of the place, but the last-century feel of leisureliness remained.

They drove through the village and turned into a tree-lined driveway meandering through lush gardens that ended at a timber building. Ellie gazed at it in disbelief. It appeared to have started its existence as a cottage then attempted to become a castle. Four towers topped with turrets had been joined to the corners of the square structure. Creepers climbed the towers, leaving windows to peek through their foliage like the eyes of a shy animal.

'Mmmm,' Chris frowned. 'It's not *really* what I imagined when I booked.'

'Do you mean we're staying ... there?'

'No, they have cabins. Apparently.'

Just then a small, white-haired man emerged from the

middle door of the building and came over to the Rodeo. Chris lowered the window.

'Guess you must be Mr Ryan,' the man flashed a broad grin. 'I'm Ronnie. The wife and I were beginning to think you mightn't be coming. Come on in and do the paperwork and I'll show you to your cabin. There's plenty of firewood so you should be cosy tonight. It's going to be a cold one.' He grinned again and returned to the house.

Chris flashed her an apologetic look. 'We can always try somewhere else.'

Ellie took another look at the cottage-castle and laughed. 'It'll be okay. If nothing else, it should be an experience.'

'One I hope you don't remember for all the wrong reasons,' he muttered, but got out of the car and followed their host.

Ellie lowered her window and breathed in the scents of winter in the mountains. There was a sharpness to the air here, a cleanness not found in Brisbane. The sun had lost its warmth now and she realised they would be grateful for the firewood Ronnie had mentioned, especially if it went in a fireplace and not a wood stove. She was prepared to rough it a little, but there was a limit.

Ronnie was still talking as he and Chris emerged from the cottage-castle. When Chris got back into the driver's seat, Ronnie walked down a well-maintained track leading down the hillside. Chris started the Rodeo and followed. The track led to half a dozen cabins scattered across the curve of the hill, each surrounded by paths and shrubbery, and each, Ellie realised in awe, with a stupendous view of the Sunshine Coast.

She looked at Chris, and saw that he, too, was registering the vista of rolling hills and deep valleys leading to a distant band of houses and high-rises flanked by deep blue ocean and endless sky.

Ronnie stopped in front of the third cabin and beckoned for them to park in a small gravelled area.

'Great view, hey?' He grinned as though he were responsible for it. 'You'll wake up to that in the morning. Key's in the door, breakfast's in the fridge. Just give me a call if you need anything.' He nodded a goodbye and walked back up the track.

'Cabin looks okay,' Chris said, but Ellie heard the hope in his voice. Timber, with a rustic look that said serviceable rather than fancy, it had a porch big enough to allow guests to stay out of the weather while unlocking the door and transferring their luggage. The lushness of the countryside seemed to indicate rain was normal weather here.

'Well, let's go in,' she said.

She unlocked the door and walked in while Chris came behind with their bags. Her mouth opened in surprised delight. The "rustic" look had been continued on the inside, but she recognised quality rustic when she saw it. The two-piece beige lounge had leather that looked as soft as kid; the peach-and-umber-swirled rugs on the timber floor were toe-drowning thick; and the plump cream doona and pillows on the queen-sized bed hadn't come from your average department store.

A box of firewood lay beside a pot-bellied heater in the corner. Ellie hoped Chris's fire-making skills were more up-to-date than hers. Her one week stint at Brownie camp was too long ago to remember well.

A small but well-appointed kitchen took up an opposite corner, and Ellie was relieved to see the stove was electric. Further along a door opened into a bathroom that had the kind of rustic look found in home beautiful magazines. Large glass doors on the eastern wall led to a timber verandah with outdoor table and chairs where you could sit and enjoy the glorious views to the coastline.

Ellie could almost feel Chris's relief as he looked around. He placed their bags on the luggage rack. She smiled. 'I see there's only one bed.' She saw the confusion on his face, the look that asked if he'd missed something somewhere. 'You did say there'd be no pressure,' she reminded him.

'Yes, well ...'

'I guess we can always put cushions down the middle,' she mused, then laughed at his expression as he realised she was teasing him. 'I have concussion, remember,' she laughed as he advanced on her. Oh, but it was so wonderful to laugh like this with a man. She'd almost forgotten how it felt.

He scooped her into his arms and strode to the bed. 'Give me a good reason why I shouldn't drop you,' he growled.

With a smile that should have signified surrender but instead felt like seduction, Ellie wound her arms around his neck and kissed him.

Tingling changed to melting. Not the slow, liquid kind rich with the familiarity of a long-time lover's caress, but molten fire that burned and made her feel more alive than she could remember.

Chris broke the kiss, but only long enough so he could

place her on the bed with care. He knelt over her, eyes brilliant, breathing laboured. 'Last chance if you want to back out.'

She wanted to say something flippant, tease him again, but she was lost in the need she read on his face. 'I think you'd better read me my rights,' she whispered, her voice tight with equal need.

This time his kiss seemed to go on forever.

He was a skilful lover, fingers teasing across her breasts as he unbuttoned her blouse, hands caressing as he unzipped her pants and slipped them down. When he unhooked her bra and dropped it to the floor, his fingers trembled as they moved, feather-light, across her nipples. She felt her breasts swell, her skin goose-bump.

'You're cold,' he frowned. 'I should light the fire.'

'We - ' her voice was husky, but it wasn't from the cold. She cleared her throat. 'We should get under the doona.'

He smiled, and she saw love in the brilliant blue of his eyes. He pulled back the doona and rolled her underneath it, then quickly shucked his clothing. While he pulled off his boots, Ellie slipped off her panties. He slid under the covers and reached for her. 'That was quick,' he said as his hands skimmed her hips. 'I was going to take those off.'

She snuggled against him, savouring the feel of skin on skin, his warmth, the unique masculine smell of him. The erection that pressed against her stomach. 'I'm an older woman,' she said, mock serious. 'I don't have time to waste.'

'We've got all night.'

'Is that a threat or a promise?'

His hand moved to her breast, slowly teasing; his lips lingered on her neck. She shivered, eager, greedy, wanting more. And when his lips moved to draw her nipple into his mouth, she knew it was definitely a promise.

Half an hour later Ellie stood, hands plunged into her dressing gown pockets, and gazed out at the lights starting to sprinkle across the encroaching darkness on the horizon.

'Coffee's ready.' Chris placed two mugs on the table, walked behind her and wrapped his arms around her.

'This definitely proves God is a man,' she grumped. 'No female deity would let a woman reach the age when pregnancy is no longer an issue and then give her vaginal dryness.'

His chest rippled with laughter and she felt his smile where his cheek lay against the side of her head. 'I thought lubricated condoms would be enough.' There was an even broader smile in his voice. 'Perhaps we should have used salad dressing.'

She chuckled at the image, her crankiness dispelled by his good humour. She turned in his arms and snuggled into his chest. 'All the chemists will be closed by now so we can't buy some lubricant. And it's a pity Ronnie left spray cooking oil with the bacon and eggs instead of the bottled stuff.' A memory tugged. 'Years ago one of the restaurants in Montville used to sell its own brand of avocado oil.' She looked up at him, half serious, half joking. 'We could buy some and use that as a lubricant.'

'I'm game if you are.'

'Then I guess we'd better get ready for an evening on the

town.' She kissed him, briefly, hungrily, and walked to the bathroom. As she showered she made a mental note to talk to Kandy about the qualities of lubricants.

And wondered about the friction-withstanding capabilities of avocado oil.

CHAPTER THIRTY

There was something almost magical about the mountains at night. Ellie gazed at the stars and wondered if they shone that brightly in Brisbane and she simply hadn't noticed, or if the clear mountain air allowed their brilliance to show through. Or, she smiled as she looked across at Chris as he drove, was it because she felt so happy. Even her bruises didn't seem to hurt as much. He had kissed them so gently, so tenderly, that she thought she would curl up and die with the pleasure of it.

Oh, but he made her feel good. Although she hadn't been able to lose herself in their love-making as completely as she would have liked, his caring and his desire to please her had compensated for her lack of fulfilment. She didn't have any experience with him to go by, but she was sure he had taken it slowly for her sake.

She was glad he had lit the fire in the heater before they'd left. Even the short walk between the cabin and the vehicle had her gasping as the cold air knifed into her lungs.

'The cold doesn't seem to stop people eating out,' she observed as they came into the village and saw that the restaurants appeared to be well patronised.

'They're either mad Queenslanders,' he observed, 'Victorians who think it's still summer, or the food's too good to miss.'

'Let's hope it's the latter. I'm starving.'

'How's your head?'

'Fine. The headache came back for a while earlier today but paracetamol shifted it.'

He frowned. 'I wasn't too rough with you, was I?'

'Of course not. But I did wonder if you were taking it easy because you were worried about me.'

'Well, maybe. But I'm not a wham, bam, thank you ma'am kind of bloke anyway.' He gave her a lecherous wink. 'I like to savour all the tasty dishes on the menu.'

'Then you'd better pull into that parking spot,' she pointed to the only vacant space she'd seen since entering the village. 'I don't know what the menu's like but it's the closest walking distance to a restaurant.'

Five minutes later they were seated at a table for two and enjoying the warmth emanating from the restaurant's air-conditioners while waiting for the drinks they'd ordered.

'What would you like to do tomorrow?' Chris asked. 'Have a look at Kondalilla Falls? Browse the shops? Take a drive to the Sunshine Coast?'

'Would I be terrible if I said sleep in, then look at the shops after we've checked out? There used to be a great shop here that sold the most beautiful leather handbags and shoes. Not that I can afford to shop there now, but it would be nice to look.'

'Do you miss that? Being able to buy whatever you like?'

'Just a little. I really miss being able to buy nice gifts for Miranda and Pru. But I don't miss the lifestyle I had with Damien. It wasn't the kind of life I wanted. I often felt like a fake. I know I bought all the high-end clothes and accessories, but I felt far more comfortable mucking around in the garden in an old pair of jeans.'

'Designer jeans,' he smiled.

'Actually,' she returned the smile, 'I bought my gardening jeans at the op shop. My conscience wouldn't let me wear expensive clothes when I was digging around in the dirt. We were pretty poor when I was growing up and Mum expected my brother and me to look after our clothes because they had to last.'

'What was your father like?'

'Lately I've come to realise that he was an older version of Damien. Poor background, desperate to make something of himself. Only he lacked Damien's knack for falling on his feet. When Dad crashed, we all burned.'

'But Damien almost went bankrupt.'

'True. He lost everything. But look at him now. He's pulled himself together, got a great job, he's looking the best he has in years.'

'But he lost you.'

Ellie sighed, but with resignation, not regret. 'I think we lost each other years ago.'

'I might sound like a bastard, but I'm happy he lost you. One man's loss ...'

He didn't finish the saying. The look on his face said it all. Miranda was probably right about him being in love with her. It was a heady thought. Particularly as she was halfway towards loving him back. 'What about your father?' she changed the subject. 'You've mentioned your mother and sister, but not your father.'

'Dad was a cop too, but he was a cranky old bastard. He died when I was thirty-four. Mum told me once that when men reach fifty, they either get worse or they mellow. From the way Mum tells it, Dad got worse. When I hit forty-five I decided to start mellowing early so I'd be easy to put up with.'

The waiter appeared with their drinks before Ellie could think of a suitable response.

It could have been the red wine, but Ellie was more inclined to believe it was Chris's company that caused the wonderful sense of warmth and contentment that enveloped her as the evening went on.

The macadamia crumbed cod was cooked to perfection, the chocolate cream mousse was velvet smooth on her tongue, and the only flaw in the evening was the awareness that this particular restaurant didn't sell avocado oil of any description. The vision she had of Chris making passionate love to her all night was swiftly turning into a nightmare of painful penetration and unbelievable frustration. She'd even fleetingly contemplated a late-night dash to the Sunshine Coast to find a twenty-four hour chemist, something the small hinterland villages didn't have.

By the time they decided to leave, she had resigned herself to a night of very careful love-making. Her earlier crack about cushions down the middle of the bed might turn out to be prophetic.

She stood to the side as Chris went to the small reception desk to pay the bill. As he paid, he murmured something to the maître d', and she saw the man's eyebrows lift in surprise, then he smiled, gave a knowing wink, and walked to the kitchen. Ellie looked after him, puzzled, then felt a flush of embarrassment as he came back with a small bottle in a white paper bag. He handed it to Chris, who put it in his coat pocket, thanked the man, and walked towards her.

The flush turned into a fire. Perspiration oozed from every pore. She was sure her face could beat Rudolph's nose for leading Santa's sleigh through the night. She almost ran out the front door when Chris opened it for her, grateful for the icy air that hit them as they walked to the Rodeo.

She didn't speak as he opened the door for her. She didn't speak as he started to drive away, but she soon couldn't contain herself. 'How could you?' Her voice was a disbelieving squeak.

'What?'

'Ask that man for avocado oil! I saw him wink. *What* did you tell him?'

'That I'd brought my girlfriend up to the mountains for a romantic weekend away and I'd promised her I'd cook her a great breakfast but I forgot to bring oil to cook the eggs and spray didn't do it the way she liked them.' In spite of the innocence in his voice, there was enough illumination from the street lights for her to see how hard it was for him to keep his amusement under control. 'He was sympathetic to my plight and said he was happy to help me out.'

Ellie was starting to see the funny side herself, but she didn't believe his smooth spiel. 'What did he really say?'

Chris laughed then. 'He said, mate, you're either in love or you're in the doghouse so far you'll have to dig your way out with an excavator.'

The temptation to ask was too great to resist. 'So which did you tell him it was?'

'I told him that one doesn't necessarily preclude the other.'

She couldn't be sure, but she thought his voice no longer held any amusement.

Kandy wondered if removing herself physically from Phillip's bedroom would lessen the pain of knowing she no longer held the prime position in his heart. She'd believed him when he'd told her he loved her, and believed even more when he'd said that that love wasn't enough. She'd packed her toiletries, most of her clothes, some of her shoes, and some odds and ends and moved into the guest wing. Gradually she would remove all traces of herself from the bedroom she now considered to be his. She wondered if she would ever accept Nathan taking her place there, but after tomorrow she would never see the room again so it was better not to imagine that.

The guest wing was totally self-contained, even to the fully-equipped kitchen and media room, and as it had its own attached garage there would be no need for her to go into the main house if she didn't want to.

She opened the bedroom curtain and gazed out at the stars. A deep, aching loneliness threatened to engulf her.

She told herself it was something she was going to have to get used to.

Sleeping in was doubly enjoyable when a strong masculine

body spooned around you and a warm hand stroked lazily over your breast, Ellie thought. The fire had gone out during the night, and although she'd done a quick sprint to the bathroom earlier on, she didn't feel like getting out into the cold again.

She squinted at her watch on the bedside drawers. Darn, they only had an hour before check-out time. Her stomach rumbled.

'Time I cooked that breakfast,' Chris murmured into her hair.

'I don't think there's any oil left,' she smiled.

He chuckled, kissed her neck and climbed out of bed. She watched his naked back as he walked to the bathroom and couldn't help the cat-licking-cream smile the sight evoked. Her body ached, but not from the bruises from her fall at the units. No, the ache was a pleasant one, one that came from making love passionately and thoroughly. She had discovered she was capable not just of having an orgasm, but having one that lasted longer than the audience response to a lousy comedian. Her thighs twitched at the memory. Memories, she corrected herself. Her smile widened. No wonder they'd slept in.

They left the cabin with five minutes to spare. Chris dropped the key in the box outside the cottage-castle door and waved to Ronnie when he opened a window in one of the towers and called out goodbye.

It was a perfect winter's day, bright sunshine with a touch of warmth and a light breeze. No wonder the main street of Montville was crowded. With its many and varied shops and great restaurants it was a tourist favourite.

Ellie thought she'd have to chisel the smile off her face when they returned to Brisbane. Chris held her hand, admired the tiny statue of a cat carved from agate that she purchased for Miranda, and laughed with her at the African carving of a native with an erect penis as long as his legs that she was tempted to buy Pru just for the shock value but decided on a letter-opener instead. She bought Cass and Kandy soaps perfumed with pure oils, and a hand-made woollen scarf for her mother for her birthday in a few weeks' time.

They were emerging from the third shop when a loud rumbling noise heralded a convoy of about twenty motorcycles coming into the village. Chris didn't grip her hand harder, but Ellie felt a distinct change in him as the black-leather-clad riders came into view. They had no gaudy drawings on their jackets, no over-abundance of chains and studs, nothing to indicate they were anything other than a group of motorcycle enthusiasts enjoying a Sunday ride, but the mood of the crowd dulled as though clouds had covered the sun and heads turned to watch the procession.

The group pulled into a parking lot near a cafe at the far end of the street and dismounted. Ellie saw the way Chris watched them, assessing, calculating, then relaxing as helmets came off and the riders trooped into the cafe.

Her head started to ache. She reached up under the hair that feathered across her forehead and gently massaged her scalp close to the stitches.

'Is your head hurting?' he asked, his attention now solely

on her. 'Are you dizzy?'

'Headache's back. I need to take something for it. And a cup of tea would be good.'

He took her arm and they walked to a coffee shop. 'I know we had a late breakfast,' he said, 'but it's lunch time. Perhaps you need something to eat.'

She wasn't sure eating was a good idea, but they ordered toasted sandwiches.

By the time she'd taken the paracetamol and drunk half her tea, she felt a lot better. When the toasted sandwiches arrived she discovered her appetite had returned. Fifteen minutes later she conceded that the most appealing option now was a drive to the Kondalilla Falls and a repeat of yesterday's afternoon nap. She was about to suggest this to Chris when the sound of motorcycle engines firing up filtered into the building. One by one the bikes roared down the road towards Maleny.

She knew Chris was listening to the noise, knew he had switched to cop-mode the moment the group had arrived, and had only switched off once he thought there was no threat being posed.

When they walked outside, the sound of raised voices carried to them on the breeze. They looked up to where the motorcyclists had been. Two big bikes remained. And next to them stood two young men.

Angry young men.

If Ellie had thought Chris had gone into cop-mode before, it was nothing to what she saw now. His whole demeanour changed. His smile disappeared; his body tensed; his focus centred on the altercation that seemed to be showing signs of becoming physical.

Ellie couldn't make out all the words, but the bikers appeared to be arguing over a television that one had sold the other and had stopped working within a day of the sale. It appeared the seller had no intention of returning the other man's money. The buyer was shorter and stockier than his bigger, ginger-haired mate, but he was just as belligerent in asserting his claim that he was entitled to get his money back. Ellie almost cringed at the language both men were using.

People coming out of the cafe were quickly giving them a wide berth. A couple of backpackers looked at them in amusement, then shrugged and walked past.

The smaller man took a swing at Ginger-hair. The punch connected with Ginger's shoulder. He stumbled, bellowed his rage and hit back. His fist slammed into the smaller man's face and knocked him to the ground. Ginger sneered something unintelligible and the smaller man sprang to his feet and pushed his hand into his jacket pocket.

With a smile that sent Ellie's blood cold, he flicked out a long-bladed knife and advanced on Ginger.

CHAPTER THIRTY-ONE

'Stay here,' Chris said to her, and his tone made it a command rather than a request. With a quick glance to check she wasn't following, he ran up the street towards the two men.

'I'm a police officer, mate.' his voice was calm but deep with authority as he stopped about a metre from them. 'You'd better put that knife down.'

They both glanced at him.

'Fuck off,' the smaller man spat, and returned his attention to Ginger.

Whether it was bravado or not, Ellie didn't know, but Ginger again taunted the man with a string of insults.

With the kind of fear that almost paralyses the thought processes, Ellie watched as Chris tried to reason with the men. Watched the way he tried to talk them down, using reason, threats of arrest, offering leniency for compliance.

Ginger started to back away, but the smaller man became more enraged.

Ellie watched Chris, her heart constricted, knowing he was going to try to get the knife away from the man, knowing that one wrong move meant the knife, gleaming sharp and deadly in the sunshine, could easily kill him. She felt herself sway with terror at the thought.

A siren sounded, the noise drawing closer.

The smaller man sprang, knife arm outstretched, at Ginger.

Chris lunged for him.

Ginger dived towards Chris.

It was like watching a football tackle that didn't co-ordinate. The three men fell to the ground, Ginger trying to get away, the smaller man kicking, screaming, lashing out with fist and feet, Chris clutching his right arm, trying to break his grip on the knife.

A police car screamed into the parking lot. A sergeant jumped out and ran towards the trio.

She knew it was only seconds, but to Ellie it seemed like minutes before the knife hit the ground, Chris hauled the biker to his feet and the sergeant restrained Ginger. After a conversation with Chris and several of the bystanders, the sergeant put the now-handcuffed bikers in the police car and drove off.

As Chris walked back to her, Ellie realised that she was still standing in the same position she had been when the bikers' argument had started. Exhaling a breath that was as much perplexity as relief, she walked to meet him.

'Are you okay? You look pale,' he frowned.

The absurdity of his concern almost made her laugh. 'You've just tackled a man who could have killed you and you're worried that *I'm* pale?'

'I'm trained for that kind of thing,' he replied. 'It's part of the job.'

And that was exactly the problem, she thought. Risking his life *was* part of the job. A part she doubted she'd ever get used to. Even now she could still feel the terror that had seized her when the knife flicked out. Loving Chris left her vulnerable to the kind of loss she never again wanted to experience.

But another thing worried her as well. If she loved him, why hadn't she tried to help him? Why had she remained rooted to the spot, watching the scene as though a barrier stopped her from running to his side? Surely she should have tried to help - thrown something at the biker to distract him so Chris could disarm him, yell out that his mates were coming back, offer him money to buy another television set? She knew Chris was trained for that kind of thing, but he was unarmed and both bikers were so angry she couldn't have been sure they mightn't have turned on him because he'd intervened. She'd never thought of herself as a coward before, but then she'd never been in a really dangerous situation before. But it puzzled her to think she had simply stood there, frozen, when someone she loved was in danger.

'I have to go to the Maleny police station and make a statement,' Chris said.

'Of course,' she replied, but noticed he was still looking at her a little strangely.

They walked back to his vehicle in silence, but when they were on the road, Ellie asked, 'How do you feel?'

'What do you mean?'

'That man could have killed you. You handled it, you did what had to be done. But how did it make you feel? I've never experienced anything like that. I'm trying to comprehend how you cope with it.'

He nodded his understanding. 'That's where the training

comes in. I've been in a few situations like that and each time you assess the best way to handle it, but when something happens you're just grateful you instinctively know what to do.'

It wasn't the explanation she wanted. 'I can understand that, but how do you *feel*? Does it upset you? Do you want to run away?'

He laughed. 'Anyone with half a brain would want to run away from an angry man with a weapon, but the adrenaline kicks in, your senses seem to sharpen, and you do what you can under the circumstances.'

'And afterwards?'

'That depends. In Homicide you deal with some pretty horrible stuff. Everyone reacts differently after seeing death. With something like what just happened, I feel relief that no-one got hurt, that *I* didn't get hurt. And sometimes I feel angry that idiots like that think they can resolve their problems with violence.'

She noticed that he was driving a little slower than usual, and his hands gripped the steering wheel tightly, as though he was having trouble staying in control. 'Do you feel angry now?'

There was a long pause before he answered. 'Yes. Because now you're running away from me and there's nothing I can do to stop you.'

The truth in his words hit her like a blow. She *was* running away. Emotionally. She should have hugged him, assured him she cared, that she was grateful he'd not been hurt, but instead she'd held herself rigid, not reaching out, not touching him, afraid to let him completely into her heart in case she lost him and had to suffer the pain that had devastated her once before.

'Am I wrong?' His words were tinged with equal despair and hope.

'I'm sorry, Chris.' She couldn't give him what he wanted. 'I want to ... I want to stop ... running, but I don't know how. If you were an accountant, or a carpenter, or a salesman, it might be different. At least you wouldn't face potential death every time you went to work.'

'But then I wouldn't be me, would I?' he asked softly, his face grim.

She wanted to cry. Wanted to make him pull the car off the road and throw herself into his arms and say that she didn't care what he did, she would love him anyway. But she couldn't. She wanted to fight back the fear that held her like a prison, but she didn't know how. 'Perhaps I just need some time. So much has happened in such a short space of time - finding Cherilyn's body, meeting you, getting concussion, having Damien come back. Even losing a way of life I was used to. Even though I wasn't happy in it, at least it was familiar.'

'Are you happy in your current life?'

She thought about that for a while. 'Yes. Yes, I am. Most of the time. I'm discovering myself again. That might sound strange, but it's true.'

His expression softened. 'No. I can understand that. Grief changes people, not always for the better.'

'I ... I didn't so much *change*.' There were tears in her eyes now, blurring the scenery into passing blobs. 'I just lost myself. Maybe I did become someone else. Someone who wasn't really me.' She brushed away the tears. 'Perhaps I just need time to find out who I am now.' She thought about telling him that they shouldn't see each other anymore, but doubted she could do it. Wanting him made her weak, but there was a strange kind of strength in that. It gave her the courage to be honest with him, to recognise that she needed to be happy in herself before she could make anyone else happy.

The silence that filled the vehicle now wasn't the companionable silence they'd previously shared. It was brittle with fragile hopes and even more fragile despair. When Chris parked in front of the Maleny police station, he switched off the engine and turned to her. 'Do you want to come in with me?'

She shook her head. 'You do what you have to do.' She opened her door. 'I'll go for a walk. Call my mobile when you're finished.'

She heard his door slam and the vehicle lock as she walked away, but it was a while before his footsteps sounded on the path into the building.

Although separated by only 15 kilometres, Maleny and Montville were worlds apart in atmosphere, Ellie decided. Montville's reputation as an up-market tourism destination was well-deserved, with a plethora of resorts, restaurants, and shops selling crafts you wouldn't find in most markets. Maleny looked like the kind of village people lived in. The types of shops showed that some had a more alternative bent than others, but the general feeling here was that the town belonged to the residents, not the visitors.

As she walked down the main street, glancing in shop windows, Ellie tried to control her fluctuating emotions. When Chris wasn't with her, it was easy to give in to all her fears for his safety. Or should that be all her fears about loss of someone she loved? Damnit! She couldn't deny she loved him, but she also knew that love could wither, could die, could be destroyed by neglect. And life could be so easily snuffed out.

The image of Cherilyn's body flashed through her mind. Dead. Un-mourned by those who should have loved her. The sadness, the futility, of Cherilyn's wasted life washed through Ellie. Her eyes filled with tears. She tried to brush them away, but more appeared, spilling onto her cheeks, soaking into her blouse. She pulled a tissue from her bag and tried to stop the flow. It didn't work. People started to look at her, curious, sympathetic, apprehensive.

She stumbled into a side street, away from the shops, and stopped under a large tree that shaded the footpath. Her breath came in choking sobs that ripped from her chest and ricocheted through her head until it started to pound.

As quickly as her crying had begun, it stopped. She leaned against a paling fence, drawing in deep breaths, trying to make sense of what had just happened. Had Cherilyn's death affected her that badly? Or was she reacting to seeing Chris in danger? Maybe it was all simply part of the concussion.

Her headache returned with an intensity that made her stomach heave. She grabbed hold of the fence, took some deep breaths, and tried to stop her lunch from coming up. After a minute or two the churning eased. On less than steady legs she walked back to the main street, bought a bottle of cold spring water, took two painkillers from her bag and swigged them down.

She found a quiet spot in a park and sat on a bench and waited for Chris to phone.

Telling herself she was going to have to get used to being alone and lonely was one thing, Kandy discovered. Doing so was another. Playing a classical music CD and then an Enya album hadn't helped. Innumerable laps in the pool made her exhausted but no less miserable. Two glasses of wine only added to her melancholy, and as she started to pour a third she realised what she needed.

She grabbed the phone and started to press Ellie's number before remembering Ellie wouldn't be home. She changed the last four digits and waited for Cass to answer.

To Ellie's relief the traffic heading back to Brisbane was relatively light. She wanted to get home quickly. The joy she had experienced in the past twenty-four hours had gone, replaced by a terrible sense of inadequacy. What was wrong with her that she could let fear overshadow the wonderful relationship she was developing with Chris?

She kept sneaking glances at him, hoping to see something other than the frustration and disappointment he had shown as she'd walked back to his vehicle. She knew her expression had said that all was not right between them.

Miranda's car wasn't in the yard when they arrived, and Ellie didn't know whether to be grateful she wasn't there to see the tension she thought was obvious between her and

Chris or disappointed there wasn't a buffer to ease that tension.

'Would you like a drink?' she asked as she unlocked the front door and walked inside.

He placed her overnight bag on the lounge room floor and shook his head. 'I'd better go home and get ready for work tomorrow. Besides, you look like you could do with a rest. Are you working tomorrow?'

'No. Richard said not to come back until I have the stitches out.' She tried to muster a smile. 'Maybe he thinks I'll scare the customers.'

Chris's answering smile showed as little amusement as hers had. 'Oh, you're scary, all right.' The smile faded. 'But not because of your stitches.' He moved closer, took her into his arms and kissed her.

It was a kiss filled with passion, with possession, with love and longing. A fiery branding that seared and weakened her so that she melded into him, aching with need, desperate to blot out the fear that stopped her from giving herself to him completely.

It was a kiss that should have been the start of lovemaking so deep and fervent it would have swept away all doubt, all fear.

But desperation, subtle as a summer haze, threaded its way between them.

Chris broke the kiss, eyes blazing, body trembling with emotion, arms still enfolding her. 'I don't normally play dirty,' he said, voice gravelly with control, 'but if I have to use sex to keep you with me I will. I don't want to lose you.'

The words of reassurance Ellie wanted to say wouldn't come. She reached up, stroked his cheek, tried to convey her churning emotions through her touch. He turned his head and kissed her palm, his eyes not leaving hers.

It would have been so easy to give in to him, to tell him what he wanted to hear, but she knew she couldn't. Knew it wouldn't be fair to either of them. 'You promised me time,' she whispered. 'Remember?'

He dipped his head in acknowledgement. 'You can have all the time you need.'

She felt the "but" behind the words, but he didn't say any more, just dropped his arms from around her and walked to the door. 'Chris,' she called to him, and he turned and looked at her. 'Call me,' she said. 'Please.'

He nodded, then walked out.

CHAPTER THIRTY-TWO

'They're very happy with my progress,' Maud beamed as the nurse helped her back into bed after taking her to the bathroom.

'That's good, Mum.' Geoffrey had to admit that his mother did seem to be improving. She was able to walk a few steps now, not unaided, but at least one foot no longer dragged across the floor like she was wearing a concrete boot. The other foot was a different matter, and he wondered how much physiotherapy would be needed to fix that. Or if it could be fixed.

'How is your wrist?' Maud asked.

'Not too bad.' He wanted to say how it really felt, but he knew she would be shocked by that kind of language. Once it wouldn't have bothered him, but somehow, in the past week, he had gained a respect for her that he'd never had before.

He had actually come to look forward to his visits to the hospital, and wondered if he might have been taking too many painkillers. His desperate need to find the painting had eased, replaced by a deep resentment that it hadn't been his fault that the cops had picked him up with the consignment. His boss had given him the time and place - how was he to know that arriving early would land him in the middle of a police sting meant for an illegal arms dealer. But the boss didn't see it that way. Geoffrey had the drugs, he was supposed to deliver them safely and get the cash. The cops got the drugs, the boss didn't get his money, and Geoffrey was on a short slide down the slippery slope to oblivion if he couldn't make up the loss. But each day it was getting harder to find the energy to even think about going back to the units to search for the painting.

His pretext of getting his mother to talk about Iris so he could find a clue to the painting's whereabouts had turned into a genuine interest in his aunt's life and that of his mother's. It had been a long time since he had cared about anyone other than himself, but his gentle little mother had revealed strengths that had surprised him. He couldn't understand why she had remained devoted to his pompous over-bearing father, but he had to give her points for loyalty.

'Tell me more about how Iris discovered she had a talent for art,' he encouraged her now, and settled back in the hospital visitor's chair to listen.

It was only when Ellie went into the kitchen after unpacking her overnight bag that she noticed Miranda's note on the bench. She picked it up and read:

> *Mum, Ben has asked me out to dinner!!! I shouldn't be late –have work ☺ in the morning. Cass phoned, said Kandy needs to talk. Didn't say what about.*
>
> *Love you*
> *M*

Ellie smiled at Miranda's obvious reaction to Ben's invitation. Maybe things were finally turning around for Miranda on the romance side as well as the work side. She did a quick finger cross, then went into the lounge room to phone Cass. A few minutes later she hung up the phone, no more enlightened than she had been before about what Kandy needed to talk about, but worried that it was important enough that both friends were coming around to discuss it with her.

Several hours later she opened the door to Cass, Kandy, Chinese takeaway containers and two bottles of wine. 'What are we celebrating this time?' she asked.

'Love, loss and the whole damn thing,' Kandy chortled, and threw her arms around Ellie, wine bottles thumping into Ellie's back. Ellie threw a 'What the?' glance at Cass but Cass just shook her head and mouthed, 'I don't know.' Then she took Kandy and guided her towards the lounge. 'Let's sit down,' she suggested.

Although she could see that Kandy was already on the path to a mammoth hangover, Ellie got wine glasses as well as plates and forks for the Chinese food. As soon as she placed these on the coffee table in front of the other two, Kandy said, 'Phillip is gay,' and burst into tears.

Ellie didn't know if she was more shocked by Kandy's announcement or the fact that crying was the last thing she could imagine Kandy doing. She looked at Cass. Her jaw had dropped so far Ellie could see the fillings in her back teeth.

Kandy's tears kept streaming down her face. Ellie rushed into the bathroom and grabbed a box of tissues and gave it to her. Kandy wiped her eyes and blew her nose and balled the tissues in her fists.

Ellie couldn't bear to see her looking so miserable. She put her arms around Kandy's shoulders and hugged her. Kandy returned the hug, her tears starting again. She pulled back and dabbed at her eyes. 'And to think I worried about another woman,' she muttered.

'How do you know Phillip is gay?' Ellie asked, and sat on the opposite lounge chair.

Kandy told them. Told them everything. Told them how she'd remained celibate for years, how Phillip seemed to give tacit approval to her affairs, how they still got on so well together and still loved each other, and how Vanessa's arrival had confirmed her recent suspicions that Phillip had fallen in love with someone else. 'I've moved into the guest wing,' she said between blowing her nose and opening one of the wine bottles. 'Nathan has gone back to Sydney to arrange his re-location to Brisbane and he'll move in with Phillip.'

'Just like that?' Ellie couldn't control her anger. 'Phillip's kicked you out?'

Kandy shook her head. 'No. It was my idea. He did what he thought was the right thing once before and broke off with Nathan. Now he's been given a second chance. I saw how much he loves Nathan, and decided I couldn't stand in the way of him being happy. I know he still loves me, but, like he said, not in the way a man should love a woman.'

'Perhaps he's bi-sexual?' Cass suggested.

Kandy shook her head. 'I doubt it.'

'Are you going to divorce him?'

'Probably. In time. I still love him, but it's not easy knowing he's not the man I thought he was. But he's still a good person,' she quickly added, as though she thought they would assume otherwise. Crying seemed to have sobered her a lot, but now she filled a glass and drank a few mouthfuls. 'We're going to keep it quiet for a while. Give ourselves time to adjust.'

'What's Nathan like?' Ellie asked.

'That's the funny part. I wanted to hate him, and he was so stiff and defensive when we met that it was easy. But once he knew I wasn't going to stand in their way, he relaxed and was really quite nice. I didn't want to, but I ended up liking him.'

Ellie poured wine into the other two glasses and passed one to Cass. She doubted that she could have been as magnanimous as Kandy, but Kandy appeared to have the kind of emotional courage she lacked. At least where Chris was concerned.

Thinking about him must have tapped into some telepathic link because Kandy asked, 'How did your weekend with the law go?'

Ellie hesitated for a moment, torn between memories of yesterday and today, then gave a rambling account about shopping in Maleny, their picnic at the lake, the unusual residence of the owner at their accommodation.

'Great travelogue, Ellie,' Kandy interrupted, 'but what about your boy in blue? Was he good in bed?'

'Great. And very understanding when I discovered that the old adage *if you don't use it you lose it* is definitely true when it comes to vaginas. Bloody menopause,' she growled.

'*That* would have stuffed up your weekend,' Cass said.

'Aaah, no. Chris is very resourceful.' Ellie recounted how he asked the restaurant maître d' for avocado oil.

'You're kidding!' Kandy laughed. 'What did you do?'

'Turned three shades of scarlet and sweated my way out the door.'

'But did the avocado oil work?' Kandy was doubly interested now, red-rimmed eyes gleaming with amusement and anticipation.

Ellie did a mock swoon. 'Tres magnifique,' she gushed in her best high school French.

Kandy giggled her appreciation. 'Sounds like that's one cop whose penis should be classified as a lethal weapon.'

'So is he in love with you?' Cass asked as she took the lids off the takeaway containers.

The laughter left Ellie as quickly as it had come. 'I think so.'

'What about you? How do you feel about him?'

It was a question Ellie didn't want to answer. But maybe if she put her doubts into words they might reveal an answer. 'I'm falling in love with him, but I don't know if I can cope with his job. This afternoon two bikers had an argument and Chris went to calm them down, and one took out a knife.' She described what happened. 'I was so terrified he would get hurt I couldn't even move.'

'Seems a fairly normal reaction.' Cass spooned food onto her plate.

'It didn't feel like it. It freaked me out.'

'So are you going to see him again?'

The question was casual enough, but Ellie didn't know

how to answer. She shrugged and countered with a question of her own. 'How did your property manager friend go with finding out who rented unit one?'

'Pretty good. I told her that the new owner of the building had found something he believed was quite valuable and he'd like to return it to the person it belonged to. Because of the inscription we found on the back of the painting I was also able to tell her that we thought that person's name was Iris.'

'So she found Iris?'

'No. Iris died not long before the building was sold.'

Ellie was surprised by how disappointed she felt. She wanted to meet the mysterious Iris and find out the origin of the painting.

'But,' Cass continued, 'my friend was able to give me the name of her sister, who was the person Iris had named as her next of kin.'

'That's great. Who is she?'

'Her name's Maud Lenard and she lives in a retirement centre about thirty minutes drive from the units. I've written down the details.' She took a piece of paper from her pocket and gave it to Ellie.

'What's this about a painting?' Kandy asked between mouthfuls of Honey Chicken.

Ellie and Cass explained about the painting they'd found in the false ceiling cavity.

'Why do you think it's valuable?'

'There was some writing on the back. It said, *To Iris. I hope your sacrifice is worth it. NL.*'

'Norman Lindsay?' Kandy's face shone with a reverence

Ellie and Cass had never seen before. 'It was signed by Norman Lindsay?'

'We think so,' Ellie said. 'It's a nude, and in his style. I studied art at school, and when I was doing interior decorating one of the clients had two of his paintings and I got a close up look. And then there was that movie about him, remember.'

'I think art was the only subject at school that didn't shit me to tears. I even stole one of the rich kid's lunch money so I could buy some extra paints. Had to hide them from my old man, though. The bastard used to trash my stuff when he got drunk.'

'Were you any good?' Ellie asked. 'At painting, I mean?'

'Let's just say I was better in bed than I was on canvas. The teacher never liked what I did.' Kandy tried to laugh, but her tone was too sad to be humorous. 'But I really loved art. Even used to borrow art books from the school library so I could look at the paintings. Nothing else in my life had any beauty.'

'Why didn't you start painting again if you loved it that much? When you married Phillip, I mean. You would have had more time, and certainly more money.'

'I couldn't.' Kandy shook her head as though denying it to herself. 'It belonged to a different lifetime.'

'And you didn't want to go back to that.' Cass made it sound like a statement rather than a question, but Kandy whispered, 'I never wanted to go back to that.'

'But you still love art,' Ellie said. 'You have some great paintings in your house. You don't have to paint yourself, but you can still admire someone else's talent.'

Kandy pointed her fork at Ellie. 'I'd like to see *this* painting before you give it back.'

Ellie smiled, please to see that some of Kandy's spark had returned. 'Okay. I'll go and see this Maud Lenard tomorrow and make sure the painting really belonged to her sister. If it does, I'll get it out of the unit and take it to her. I'll phone you and you can meet me at the units and have a look.' She turned to Cass. 'Would Joe mind me borrowing his ladder again?'

'I'm sure it won't be a problem. I'll give you his mobile number. Just let him know when you're going to be there.'

The anticipation of finding the possible owner of the painting helped to dispel some of Ellie's previous depression about her relationship with Chris. Kandy looked happier now than when she'd first arrived, but Ellie was sure that was mainly due to being with friends and a serious nudge at the wine bottle.

When Cass and Kandy left an hour later, Ellie was relieved to know that Cass had insisted Kandy wasn't driving home but staying with her.

Ellie was brushing her teeth when she heard the sound of Miranda's key in the front door. She stopped brushing and kicked her mother antennae up a notch, trying to decide if the footsteps coming down the hallway were slow from tiredness or disappointment. The footsteps went into Miranda's bedroom. The door didn't close - a good sign. She resumed brushing. When she'd finished she turned out the light, hesitated, then walked to Miranda's door. Miranda was sitting cross-legged on the bed, black skirt flowing over her knees, multi-hued lilac blouse crushing as she hunched over, face in hands, elbows on her thighs. Her boots and jacket lay in a heap on the floor.

'Didn't it go well?' Ellie ventured, not sure if she should move into the room or if it might be construed as invasion of space.

'I don't know.' A deep sigh followed the words.

Ellie edged towards the bed. 'What happened?'

'He's having a *crisis of faith*. He wanted to talk to me about it. He said he could trust me because I'm such a good friend.'

Ellie sat on the end of the bed. 'What sort of crisis of faith?' Heavens, she thought, we're all having bloody crises of some kind.

'He's not sure now if he really wants to become a minister. Says he doesn't know if that's what God wants him to do. I asked him if he thought God wants him to do something else, but he said he didn't know.'

'So what did you say?'

Miranda straightened up and dropped her hands onto her knees. 'I nearly said that I think he needs a good dose of sex, but that was only me feeling so damn frustrated, so I said he should just wait for a sign from God. And *that*,' she nearly spat the word, 'was when the new volunteer he'd been so keen to show around the other night walked past and said hello.'

Ellie was picking up "uh-oh" vibes, but simply asked, 'What's she like?'

'She had dark brown lipliner and orange lipstick,' Miranda snorted. 'She looked like an exploded Jaffa.'

'Apart from her obvious makeup blunders,' Ellie had

trouble keeping her tongue from planting firmly in her cheek, 'what's she like as a person?'

'Nice. Unfortunately. If she wasn't so obviously chasing after Ben I could like her.'

'Do you think Ben likes her?'

'You mean as more than a friend? I don't know. It's hard to tell with Ben, he's so good at projecting a calm exterior. You know,' she leaned forward again and stared at Ellie as though she'd only just realised something, 'I don't know if I *really* know Ben that well. Tonight's the first time he's ever spoken about his feelings. I reckon ...' she sat up, head cocked to one side, 'I reckon I've been too nice to him. Too willing to go along with whatever he wanted.'

'A bit *door matty*?' Ellie suggested, tongue firmly in cheek this time.

Miranda laughed and threw a pillow at her. Ellie caught and hugged it.

'What about you, Mum? How was your weekend?'

Before this, Ellie had decided not to worry Miranda with her doubts about coping with Chris's job, but as Miranda now seemed to see their relationship as more woman-to-woman than mother-daughter, she thought she'd better respect the friendship her daughter was offering. So she told her about the weekend, omitting her discovery of the lubricating properties of avocado oil.

'Oh, you've got a problem, Mum.' Miranda wrinkled her nose. 'I don't know what you're going to do about it. Is he in love with you? Are you in love with him?'

'He hasn't said anything, but he could be in love with me. He acts like it, but I'm a little rusty in that area so I could be kidding myself. And I think I could be happy with him if I could just get past this crazy fear that if I do let myself love him without reserve I'll end up losing him.'

'It's not crazy, Mum. Paul died, Dad left you, your father was a judgemental prick who made you doubt you were worthy of being loved. It's no wonder you feel like that.'

'But ...' Ellie stopped. Miranda was right. But knowing the reasons for a problem didn't make it go away.

'Give yourself time, Mum. You haven't known him that long. Just have fun and see where it goes.' Miranda smiled. 'And give me back my pillow. I have my first day of work tomorrow and I need to get some sleep.'

Ellie threw the pillow back. 'Good luck tomorrow. I'll be thinking of you.'

'Oh, God.' Kandy pressed the heels of her palms into her eyes and tried to push away the steel bands threatening to splinter her skull. It didn't work. She opened one eye, then the other, saw a pale pink ceiling she didn't recognise.

She groaned, feeling as rotten as she had the first time she'd got drunk and cheated on Phillip. For a second she thought she must have done it again, then memory returned. She carefully moved onto her side and stared at a row of mismatched toy bears sitting on a pink plastic toy box. Cass's grand-daughter. This was her room during family visits.

Misery almost overwhelmed her. Her disappointment over not having children had always been tempered by the love she had for Phillip and the life they shared, but now even that was gone. For a long moment she felt the weight of her loss drag at her soul, then the instinct for survival that had enabled her to make a better life for herself took over. She still had a business to run. And maybe she should look into starting up another one - give herself a challenge, keep her occupied so the days wouldn't be so lonely.

Or the nights.

Ellie's phone calls to Maud Lenard at the phone number Cass had given her kept ringing out. By the afternoon she began to wonder if she had the right number, so she phoned the retirement village office to check. A friendly office girl told her that Maud was in hospital, and a call there gave her the ward and bed number.

During the drive to the hospital she practised several ways of explaining her visit, but knew that all of them might prove useless if Maud couldn't comprehend what she was going to tell her. After all, the office girl had said the old woman had had a stroke. Perhaps her mental faculties had been affected along with her physical abilities.

Ellie mentally crossed her fingers that Maud would be able to tell her the painting's history. It still upset her that Cherilyn's murder had not been solved, but perhaps the mystery of Iris and *NL* could be revealed.

Geoffrey said goodbye to his mother and wandered out of the room and up the corridor. He wasn't sure how he felt about her news that the doctor had decided to send her home the next day on condition the Blue Care nurses would call in to help her and she got regular physiotherapy.

It wasn't that he didn't want his mother to leave hospital,

but he had become rather used to turning up at lunch time and having the ward attendants slip him a meal ordered for a patient who'd been discharged that morning. The fact that his visits extended long after he had eaten was something he chose not to think about.

Re-connecting with his mother at this stage in his life was something he would never have contemplated. Thinking of her with affection that could almost be classified as love would have been inconceivable only a few months ago. But somehow, without him being entirely conscious of it, her unswerving love for him had chipped away at the barrier he had erected between them, and her revelations of defying his father had re-ignited the admiration he had once felt for her quiet but determined spirit.

He reached the lifts and saw a small group of people waiting there had already pressed the Down button. Although he'd had a reasonable attempt at shaving, his reflection in the glass of a painting on the wall showed a middle-aged man with doleful eyes and baggy skin and the sallow gauntness of someone who preferred drinking to eating. Not the kind of person anyone would strike up a conversation with while waiting for a lift to arrive. He pretended to study the painting.

A ding heralded the arrival of the lift. He half-turned as the doors opened, then stopped, his attention caught by the reflection of one of the people exiting. A woman. Blonde. Thin. He recognised her immediately and turned away, heart pounding, mouth dry.

What the hell was she doing here? He fought the crazy

urge to turn around and yell the words at her. Her shoes clicked across the floor, and he sneaked a glance. She was walking up the corridor. She was probably just visiting a sick relative or friend, he told himself. It was pure coincidence she was here. A coldness prickled his neck. Or was it?

He watched her. She turned towards his mother's ward. Instinct for self-preservation kicked in. He followed her.

When he saw her enter his mother's room, something dark clawed at his guts. It would be too much of a coincidence if she was simply visiting a patient in his mother's room, and he didn't believe in coincidence. He waited a while, and when she didn't come out of the room, he ventured close enough to glance around the doorway.

Ellie checked the name labels above the beds as she moved through the room until she found the one that identified the fragile-looking woman lying there, seemingly asleep, as Maud Lenard. She hesitated, unsure if she should wake her.

A child ran into the room, calling out for his grandmother, and raced up to the patient in the bed next to Maud's. Maud's eyes opened. For a moment she seemed disoriented, then she saw Ellie and smiled. The smile was so kind, so gentle, Ellie found herself smiling in response. 'Mrs Lenard? My name's Ellie Cummins. I'd like to talk to you about your sister, Iris, if that's okay?'

'Come and sit down, my dear. I've been talking about Iris a lot lately.'

CHAPTER THIRTY-THREE

She was talking to his mother! Geoffrey pushed down the urge to panic and walked back up the corridor to give himself time to think. When he'd seen the woman in the units after she'd fallen down the stairs, he'd told himself she must have had something to do with the builder carrying out the renovations. Why else would she have been prowling around there at night? Now he really started to worry. Was she a cop? Had she seen him before she tripped on the stairs? Had she found evidence linking him to that girl's death? Had she come here to see his mother to find out where he was living?

The questions whirled through his mind. He couldn't afford to go back to prison, especially not until he'd got the painting and sold it and repaid his boss. Without that happening, he really was a dead man walking. He hurried to the small lounge room set aside for patients and visitors when they needed some privacy. It was empty, and he flopped into a chair that gave him a view of the corridor, picked up a magazine and pretended to read. His sprained wrist ached, and so did his head. He hoped the woman wasn't going to be too long with his mother. He had to find out what she wanted - one way or another.

'You found the painting?' Maud looked so shocked Ellie was worried the old woman might have another stroke. 'Iris told me she'd got rid of it.'

'Why would she do that?' Ellie asked. 'If Norman Lindsay was the artist, and the initials *NL* would indicate that he was, then it would be worth a small fortune.'

Maud propped herself up a bit higher in the bed. 'Oh, it was Norman Lindsay all right. Iris posed for him quite a few times, but that one was special. He gave it to her when she told him she was giving up painting and posing.'

Ellie listened with growing interest as Maud described how Iris had lived in an artist's commune in Brisbane and how she used to travel to Norman Lindsay's house in the Blue Mountains to pose for him from time to time.

'She was always a bit wild,' Maud said. 'Our parents couldn't understand her, and our sister refused to talk to her when it became known that she posed for Norman Lindsay. But Iris told me that he was most circumspect and not at all like people were saying.'

'Why did he give her the painting?'

'It was a farewell gift. He couldn't understand that she would give up what she loved for me.' Maud leaned forward as she explained why Iris had sacrificed her dreams for her sister's happiness. Ellie felt sorry for Iris, but understood how society's constrictions in those days would have influenced Maud's husband, especially as a member of the clergy.

'Iris showed me the painting just after I was married,' Maud continued. 'Unfortunately my husband walked into the room and saw it. He got so angry. There was a dreadful scene. In the end Iris promised she would get rid of it. I thought she meant she would destroy it.'

'It would have been hard for her to part with it. It probably meant a lot to her.' What we do for love, Ellie thought.

'I understood that later, but not at the time.' Maud's eyes misted with tears. 'I should like to see it, if that's all right. I was horrified at the time, seeing her nude like that, even in a painting, but I remember how beautiful she was, and how well Norman Lindsay had captured that, especially that little dimple that appeared in her cheek when she smiled in a certain way.'

'It's your painting, now, Mrs Lenard, you can do what you like with it.'

'I can, can't I,' Maud replied as though surprised at the idea. 'Could I sell it, do you think? You said it would be worth a lot of money.'

'Of course you can. I don't know how much you'd get, but a Norman Lindsay painting sold a few years ago for just over $300,000.'

'That much?' Surprise lit Maud's lined face. 'That would be wonderful. I have a son who's fallen on hard times,' she confided, her pale thin hand raised as though asking for understanding, 'and that would make such a difference to his life.'

'Would you like me to make enquiries for you about where to sell it?'

'Oh, would you, dear? That would be wonderful. And, I know I'm asking a big favour, but could you bring the painting to me at the village? They're letting me go home tomorrow morning.'

Ellie thought quickly. She was getting her stitches out tomorrow, but that still left plenty of time to go to the unit and get the painting and take it to Maud in the afternoon. She'd be back at work the following day so tomorrow it would have to be.

She assured Maud she would get the painting to her.

Geoffrey kept watching the corridor. What was taking the woman so long? She'd been with his mother at least twenty minutes. He swore silently. He needed to go to the toilet, but was afraid she might catch sight of him if he did so.

Five minutes of finger-tapping and leg-crossing later, he saw her walk past.

Following her was out of the question now. He waited another minute, then dashed to the toilet. Afterwards, relieved only in one area, he made his way to his mother's bedside.

Surprise and concern wrinkled her forehead as she looked at him. 'Geoffrey? Why are you back?'

The question startled him. He'd been so focused on the mysterious woman that he hadn't thought of any excuse for returning to soon. 'I ... I ... forgot to ask if you needed any help getting home tomorrow.'

'Bless you, dear,' she smiled, 'but I'll be fine. The nurse will call a taxi for me. But I have some wonderful news to tell you.'

It was like winning Lotto. Geoffrey couldn't believe his luck. He pushed the Down button on the lift and smiled at his reflection in the shiny doors. Only another day and he would get his hands on the painting, flog it to his contact, give the money to his ex-boss and feel free at last. He might have been out of a physical prison since his release, but the emotional one had been harder to cope with. His doubts about the boss being content with an amount that was far short of what the shipment had been worth niggled at him, but he ignored them.

He only hoped the painting was as good as he remembered it. He'd only seen it once. Iris had given him a bed when he'd come out of his first stay in jail and had nowhere to live. He could have accepted parole and been out months earlier, but he'd hated the idea of having to report to a parole officer every week and not be able to have a drink with his former associates. His father had disowned him, his mother had bowed to his father's command to not see him, but Iris had offered a refuge. Barely into his twenties, with an arrogance that had grown when he'd fallen in with one of the prison "gangs", he'd reluctantly accepted.

At first he'd despised her artistic friends with their talk about art and their embrace of the hippie movement, but it didn't take him long to realise that he had the contacts that could fill the needs some of them had in the growing drug culture. He wasn't sure if Iris ever found out what he was doing, but he'd soon had enough money to get a place of his own. But not before he'd seen the painting.

Iris had had an old friend to dinner, and Geoffrey had woken about midnight, thirsty. On his way to the kitchen, he'd seen the friend holding up the painting and admiring it while he and Iris talked about her meetings with Norman

Lindsay. Geoffrey had been so surprised at seeing his aunt naked in the painting that he'd slipped back to his bedroom. Within a week he'd left, and his memory of the painting had lain dormant until talking with the art thief in prison.

Now the painting was not only going to save his life, but hopefully give him enough money to move out of the rat hole in which he was living. He'd persuaded his mother to let him sell the painting, knowing that the art thief had contacts who would pay more than market value to have something that they thought no-one even knew existed.

The lift glided gently to a stop. The doors opened and he walked out into the subdued bustle of the hospital foyer. There was a lightness in his heart he hadn't felt in a long, long time. Yes, his luck had certainly changed.

Ellie hadn't quite mastered conference calling, so she breathed a sigh of relief that evening when she managed to get Cass and Kandy on the phone at the same time. She told them about Maud Lenard, then asked Cass to tell Joe she'd be there the next day to borrow his ladder again.

'Would you be able to meet me at the unit, Kandy?' she asked. 'I'll phone you when I know what time.'

'I'll be in and out of the office tomorrow, so just call my mobile.'

'How are things at home?' Cass asked.

'A bit strained to say the least. Phillip's so nervous I almost feel sorry for him. At least I know where I stand, even if it is out in the cold - and I'm not talking about the bloody weather - but I think Phillip's worried that the age difference with Nathan will be more obvious now that he's in his sixties.'

'It's *you* we're worried about,' Ellie chipped in, 'and how *you're* coping.' She refrained from adding that she thought Phillip deserved any grey hair and wrinkles he was getting.

'Well, I wouldn't say that I'm the happiest kitten in the litter, but I figure if I concentrate on expanding my catering business it will help me take my mind off everything.'

'Isn't that a little difficult? I mean, what with still living in the same house with Phillip?'

'It's a bit awkward, but I still have dinner with Phillip every night. In one way it's not like much has changed.'

Except your husband's in love with another man, Ellie thought, but left the words unsaid. She knew they were all thinking the same thing.

'And it's made me realise,' Kandy added, 'that maybe I've been deluding myself about our relationship for a long time. I think I wanted Phillip to be the love of my life, but he's actually been a mix of father figure and best friend.'

Ellie wondered if Kandy might be better off severing ties completely with Phillip, but if having him as a friend was still possible, then at least that was some comfort for her.

'How are you going with your favourite cop?' Kandy asked. 'Made any decisions yet?'

'Not yet.'

'Are you even seeing him again?'

'I ... I asked him to call me.' Ellie knew the words sounded pathetic, and she was beginning to worry that if she took too long to make up her mind, he might decide she wasn't worth waiting for. After all, she wouldn't want to lose her heart to someone who wouldn't commit to a relationship.

The doubt gnawed at her as she said goodbye to Cass and Kandy. It lingered as she cooked dinner and waited for Miranda to come home. It was still there after she'd listened to Miranda's tired but happy recount of her first day in her new job, and after she'd shared the details of her meeting with Maud Lenard, and irritated like an unscratchable itch as she lay in bed and tried to sleep.

The insistent ringing of the phone woke Ellie at 7am the next morning. She opened one reluctant eye, looked at her bedside clock, and waited for Miranda to answer it. A moment passed before she realised the other sound she could hear was the shower running. She tossed off the doona, scrambled into her dressing gown and slippers, ran up the hallway and grabbed the phone.

'Hello?'

The voice that croaked back at her was barely recognisable as Richard, and it took a while before she worked out that he was asking her to go into work today because two of the other staff members were sick with the flu and he had now succumbed as well. She quickly agreed, told him to look after himself, and hung up.

'Mum?' Miranda, body swathed in a large towel and hair covered by a shower cap, emerged from the bathroom. 'I thought I heard the phone. Was it for me?'

'No. It was Richard. He's sick, and I have to go into work.'

'But you're getting your stitches out today, and getting the painting.'

'I'll just have to go to the doctor's in my lunch break. And the painting will have to wait until the weekend.' She frowned, thinking of how excited Maud had been at the thought of seeing her sister's painting again. 'I'll have to let Maud know. She'll be disappointed.' She hesitated, remembering the old woman's frailty. A couple of days could be a long time at her age. 'Maybe I could get it after work today.'

Miranda raised an eyebrow. 'Not on your own, you won't. Not after last time. But if you really want to do it, I'll meet you there.' She pulled off the shower cap and shook out her hair. 'I wouldn't mind seeing this mysterious painting myself.'

'Okay. I'd better phone Kandy and let her know the change of plans.'

It was only as she sat in the doctor's waiting room at lunch time that Ellie remembered to phone Joe. He agreed to leave the ladder in Unit One and told her it was a good thing she wasn't leaving it until the weekend because they would be ripping down the false ceiling on Thursday. He assured her that Bruce knew nothing about the painting, but had apparently decided that high ceilings were more authentic.

She was just about to phone Maud and say she would be late getting around with the painting when the doctor called her name. She switched off her mobile and hurried into the surgery.

Although he knew his mother probably expected him to call in to see her once she was home, Geoffrey found he was reluctant to do so. It had been easy to visit her at the hospital. There was a certain anonymity in being one of the many visitors streaming through the foyer and into the wards. The other residents at her retirement village probably knew of his prison convictions, and although in the past he had always pretended it didn't matter to him who knew, he was strangely depressed at the thought of his mother seeing disgust on her friends' faces when they looked at him.

He was also afraid that if he visited his mother this afternoon, he might run into the woman who was bringing her the painting. He couldn't be sure she hadn't seen his face well enough that night in the darkened building to be able to recognise him, but it was a risk he wasn't going to take.

The five o'clock news had almost ended when his door shook under a determined knock. He didn't wonder who it could be - the landlord was the only person who bothered him, and that was only because he wanted the rent.

The knocking came again.

Geoffrey hauled himself to his feet and grumbled the short distance to the door and opened it.

And almost pissed himself in fright.

CHAPTER THIRTY-FOUR

It wasn't the size of the gun pointed at his heart that sent paroxysms of fear through Geoffrey's chest, but the silencer on the end of the barrel that signified the man holding it meant business.

His partner, taller and heavily built, gave the same impression, and he wasn't even holding a gun. Though the way his right hand was bunched inside his jacket pocket indicated there was more there than a handkerchief.

Dressed in worn jeans and padded jackets that kept out the wind and allowed easy concealment of weapons and other necessities of their trade, the two men blended easily into the working-class suburb where Geoffrey lived. They pushed him back into the room, lips smiling, eyes gleaming, and his knees trembled. He'd seen their kind before: prisoners who relished enforcing their "rules" on fellow prisoners. Although he'd never been on the receiving end, he'd witnessed the results of their "persuasion" techniques.

'You've been a great disappointment to your boss, Geoffrey,' the first man smiled and tapped the gun against Geoffrey's chin. 'Excuses, excuses, excuses. And no results. So he decided to send Rocco and me to give you one last chance.'

'The boss thinks you've been lying about that painting,'

Rocco chipped in. 'He reckons it doesn't exist.'

'It does! It does!' Spittle flew from Geoffrey's mouth with the words, and the man with the gun smashed it against his cheek.

A tooth splintered, cutting the inside of Geoffrey's cheek. He staggered to the side, howling with pain, and brought his hand to his cheek. Then screamed in agony as Rocco grabbed his sprained wrist and forced it behind his back.

'So where is it?'

'I haven't got it.' Geoffrey tried to spit blood onto the floor, only to have it dribble down his chin. 'But,' he spluttered as the gun was raised again, 'I know where it is.' He explained about the woman who was bringing the painting to his mother and how his mother was going to give it to him to sell.

The shorter man laughed. 'You don't seriously expect me to believe that someone who's got their hands on a painting worth that much is going to just turn it over to a little old lady who's close to kicking the bucket?'

'It's true,' Geoffrey whined. 'She said it's in the false ceiling. She's going to get it and give it to my mother. She's probably already done so.'

'Why don't we check out his old lady, Frank?' Rocco asked. 'We can go in with dipshit here and say we're the buyers.'

'But what if the woman who found it hasn't given it to her yet?' Geoffrey had a horrible image of what these two goons might do to his mother if that was the scenario.

'She better have it,' Frank snarled. 'Or you'll both regret it. Now let's get moving.'

'Let me get my coat.' Geoffrey went to walk to the wardrobe, but Rocco pushed him towards the table, 'It's on the chair, dipshit.'

Geoffrey looked down at his old jacket that was draped over the back of the kitchen chair. The gun Gazza had given him! It was still in the pocket. Shit! If Rocco saw it ... But maybe it might come in handy - a bit of insurance, so to speak. No matter what Frank said, Geoffrey couldn't be sure that he didn't have something else in mind. He couldn't see the boss paying two men just to get the painting.

By the time Ellie pulled up in front of the unit block she'd wished she'd left it another day to get the painting. She was tired and hungry, the sandwich she'd hastily scoffed on her way back from the doctor's surgery merely a memory in her stomach.

The traffic had been horrendous. It seemed everyone was impatient to get home. She couldn't blame them - it was already dark, the wind was icy, and the grey clouds that had delivered a bleak day now covered the stars.

She phoned Maud Lenard and apologised for not getting there yet with the painting.

'I understand, dear,' the old lady replied, but Ellie could hear the disappointment in her voice. 'And please don't worry about finding a buyer for me. I told my son about the painting, and he's coming tomorrow morning to get it. He said he knows someone who will pay more than he'd get on the open market.'

A little alarm bell rang in Ellie's mind. She'd wondered about this son who was "down on his luck". From the way

Maud had glossed over her son's life, it sounded as though she was desperately trying to create a good impression for someone who probably didn't deserve it.

Ellie's stomach growled so loudly she was sure Maud could hear it, and the thought of driving to the old woman's place before going home and eating became too much. 'Maud, I'm so sorry, but would you mind if I bring the painting to you tomorrow evening? I'm really tired and I have to work again tomorrow.'

'Oh. I can't let Geoffrey know. He doesn't have a phone. But,' her voice brightened, 'I suppose it doesn't matter, he can still come for a visit. It's so nice to have him back again. And he's changed so much. He needs to have another chance, Ellie. I couldn't bear it if they sent him back to prison, not now that he's turned over a new leaf. If he can get enough money from the painting he won't need to go back to his old ways.'

Ellie listened patiently as Maud talked. There was a touch of desperation in the old lady's voice, as though she still hoped her son would become the person she'd always wanted him to be. When she finally said goodbye, Ellie rubbed her eyes and slumped into the seat.

'Come on, Miranda. Come on Kandy,' she muttered.

The car's heater had created a warm cocoon, but that wouldn't last. She put her torch in her coat pocket and waited, trying to keep her mind from thoughts of Chris. He hadn't phoned since they'd said goodbye on Sunday, and although she kept telling herself it was only Tuesday night, and she really wasn't sure if she wanted to hear from him so soon, the need to feel his arms around her was increasing with each hour that passed. And her uncertainty about her ability to cope with having a relationship with someone in a high-danger occupation increased in equal measure.

Kandy looked at the blank screen on her mobile and shook her head in disbelief.

She'd left the mobile in her handbag in her office, but had spent most of the day in with her manager, and hadn't heard the beeps that signalled the battery going flat. Now it was as useless as her Porsche. She'd hardly driven a kilometre after leaving work when the engine had stopped. Just like that. Stopped. Without a groan or a whine or a bang or anything to indicate the engine had a right to simply cease operating.

Luckily she'd been able to pull over to the gutter and not be left sitting in the middle of the road holding up traffic and becoming a target for a driver with a road rage mentality.

Her day had been as lousy as the weather. Her manager's opinion of her ideas for diversifying hadn't coincided with her view of them as being "innovative". She didn't think "crazy" was a particularly kind way to describe them, but after he'd backed up his opinion with facts and figures she'd had to concede he was right. Then she'd had a chef misjudge when chopping meat, resulting in a trip to the doctor and an order being late.

Now she looked at the mobile screen that was as blank as her dashboard and fought back tears of frustration. Ellie would be waiting for her. Hopefully, she wouldn't go into the unit building alone, but Kandy couldn't rely on that.

Ellie could be stubborn when she chose to be.

Kandy stuffed the mobile into her handbag, got out of the car, and locked the door.

And swore like a wharfie as the cold wind knifed through her. Her light-weight coat was adequate for the car or the office, but couldn't stop wind that seemed to travel from the Antarctic.

Her eyes filled with tears, but she brushed them away and told herself it was just the wind. It was dark now, and the traffic looked like a slowly-moving snake of headlights in both directions. A higher set of lights caught her attention. A bus. She looked up the road, searching for, then spotting, a bus stop. If she ran, she'd make it before the bus did. Then she could get to a phone booth and call Cass to ask her to let Ellie know what had happened. Remembering Cass's home phone number was one thing, but Ellie's mobile was beyond her memory capacity at the moment.

Grateful she'd worn pants and low-heeled boots, she started to run.

Panic had almost immobilised Geoffrey. He sat in the passenger seat of Rocco's grey Toyota sedan and tried to think of a way to convince his captors that he was telling the truth and they only had to wait a day or two and he could prove it.

He'd told them where his mother lived, but the peak hour traffic had brought them to a crawl, and it was going to take a while to get there.

He twisted around to look in the back seat where Frank sat, gun held on his lap, street and traffic lights illuminating the annoyance on his face. 'Couldn't we go to the unit and take a look there first? It'll be quicker.'

With an impatient flick of the gun, Frank snarled, 'Do it, Rocco. If it *is* there it will save us some time.'

There was something in the way he said the words that sent a shiver up Geoffrey's already trembling spine.

Ellie was just about to phone Miranda and find out how much longer she'd be when Miranda's car pulled up on the other side of the road. Ellie quickly got out, locked her car and waited on the footpath.

'Sorry, Mum,' Miranda pulled her coat collar higher against the wind as she walked across to Ellie, 'it was a busy day and I wanted to go through some of the procedures with my boss so I wouldn't have to keep asking her tomorrow. I didn't realise the traffic would be so bad. Is Kandy still coming?'

'I don't know. I left a message for her. I hope she got it.' Ellie hitched her shoulder bag higher and flicked out her mobile as they walked up the front path. 'I'll try her again.' A recorded voice told her Kandy's mobile was switched off so she left another message, then she unlocked the door and they hurried inside.

Ellie found herself glancing nervously around the gloomy interior. Cherilyn's murder still weighed on her mind, and she felt that more should have been done to find her killer.

'Come on, Mum,' Miranda tugged at her coat sleeve, 'show me where the manhole is.'

'You didn't have to come and get me, Cass,' Kandy said as

she hopped into Cass's car and closed the door. 'I could have caught a taxi.'

Cass looked at her friend, saw the dark shadows that makeup hadn't concealed and eyes that had lost their sparkle. 'I know,' she smiled. 'But that's what friends are for.' She reached over and turned up the heater.

'Thanks, Cass,' Kandy said, and Cass knew she was talking about more than the blast of hot air now easing her goosebumps.

'I brought my old camping light,' Miranda said as they entered the unit. 'We don't want you having another accident.'

Ellie watched her take a fluorescent light from her overly-large handbag, turn it on and place it on the floor.

'And *I'm* getting up on the ladder, Mum.' Miranda looked at Ellie as though daring her to argue.

'Okay,' Ellie pointed the torch at the manhole, 'but be careful when you reach inside. The painting's old, we don't want to risk damaging it.'

Miranda's tiny harrumphing sound made Ellie sigh. *Note to self - don't tell grown-up daughter to be careful. Remember she is an adult.* She held the ladder and watched as Miranda moved the manhole aside and reached into the ceiling cavity.

'That's the building,' Geoffrey pointed, 'but it's locked at night. We'll have to go around the back and break in that way.'

Rocco snorted. 'Amateur.'

'There's a car parked out the front,' Frank observed. 'Perhaps your mother's friend is there now. Pull in behind,' he ordered Rocco.

The car glided gently to a halt. They sat for a minute, watching the building, noting the flashes of a torch beam inside one of the bottom units and then a steady but subdued glow partially lighting the room. After a while Frank shoved his gun inside his jacket and said to Geoffrey, 'We'll go in and see if she's got it. We'll play it nice and cool, and you'll tell her your mother's sent you to get the painting. And wipe your mouth, you look disgusting.'

'I can't find the painting,' Miranda called out. 'Can you pass me the torch.'

Ellie handed it to her and watched as she shined it into the cavity.

A scuttling sound had Miranda jerking back, and Ellie grabbed the ladder tightly to keep it steady. 'Yuk,' Miranda shuddered. 'There was a rat up here.' She reached out again. 'Got the painting.' She handed it and the torch to Ellie, then pulled the manhole cover back into place and climbed down.

Ellie turned as she heard the front door open. 'Is that you, Kandy?' she called. 'We're in the front unit on the right hand side.' She flicked the torch beam across the doorway.

Her mouth opened in shock as three men walked into the room.

CHAPTER THIRTY-FIVE

'She's got the painting!' Geoffrey tried to rush forward, but Rocco yanked him back by the collar.

'You've scared the ladies, Geoffrey.' Frank's voice held the kind of patience that Geoffrey knew was only two beats ahead of a back-hander. 'I think you'd better explain why we're here.'

Geoffrey could see the apprehension in the faces of the two women. His gut echoed the feeling. For the past couple of days he'd drifted in some kind of a drugged cocoon, almost oblivious to the threat that had now become shockingly real. His stomach kept clenching as though fighting the need to throw up, his fingers twitched, his legs trembled with the effort it was taking not to snatch the painting and run. 'I'm Geoffrey Lenard,' he almost stuttered. 'My mother, Maud, asked me to come and get the painting. She thought it would save you the drive to her place.'

He saw the puzzled frown on the woman his mother had called Ellie. 'How did she let you know I was here?' she asked.

'She phoned me.'

The frown deepened. 'But she told me you don't have a phone.'

Frank stepped forward, smiling, and took out his mobile. 'She let me know. I'm Frank, a friend of Geoffrey's.' He pocketed the mobile then shoved his hand into the front of his jacket.

Geoffrey almost stopped breathing. He knew Frank's fingers would now be wrapped around the butt of his pistol.

Ellie took a step back. Frank's mouth might have been smiling but his eyes weren't. And the man who said he was Maud Lenard's son looked like he was on the verge of a breakdown. His longish hair had been messed by the wind, and one cheek was red and swollen. But it was his eyes that scared her. Red-rimmed and bloodshot, they flickered constantly, as though trying to keep watch on her and Miranda and his two companions at the same time. His whole body seemed to thrum with impatience. Or fear. Or ... something. She looked at the third man and thought that he'd look more comfortable with numbers across his chest as he glared at a camera.

'Can you hand over the painting, please?' Frank asked, though it was more of a command than a request.

It wasn't her painting, and Geoffrey Lenard's reason for turning up here could be valid, but something about the whole situation didn't feel right to Ellie. Too little time had elapsed since her phone call to Maud - it didn't seem possible that the friend of the man purporting to be her son could have got a call from Maud and driven to the units in such a short time. And Maud hadn't mentioned anything about phoning Geoffrey's friend.

'I'm sorry,' she drew in a deep breath, 'but I promised Maud that I would take it to her. She was very anxious to see it again. Her sister meant a lot to her.' She picked up her bag, took a step forward, and reached back to grab Miranda's arm. 'We'll drive straight out to Maud's place now. You can follow if you like.' She went to walk past Frank but he moved quickly and blocked her way.

'How do we know that's the right painting?'

'What?' Ellie couldn't help the irritation in her voice. 'Do you think the whole damn ceiling is full of paintings?'

Geoffrey could see that Frank went quite still, and for one sickening moment he thought he would hear the phht of a bullet passing through the silencer. 'Why don't you just show it to me?' he said quickly. 'I remember what it's like.'

'Just do it, Mum,' Miranda muttered, 'and then we can get going.'

Reluctantly, Ellie took the painting from the bag, unwrapped it and held it up.

Geoffrey breathed a sigh of relief. It was just like he remembered. 'This is it.'

Ellie re-wrapped the painting and put it back into the bag. 'Now I'm going to take it to Maud.' She looked at Geoffrey, then Frank. 'She legally owns it.'

Frank stood perfectly still for several seconds, then motioned for Rocco and Geoffrey to move to the door. 'We'll *all* go.'

Geoffrey followed Rocco into the dark foyer. Frank waved Ellie and Miranda ahead of him. Miranda grabbed her camping light and followed Ellie.

As Ellie walked through the doorway, she saw Geoffrey silhouetted against the glass panel next to the front door. And gasped as memory rushed back. His face! And the jacket - the way the collar sat at an odd angle.

'You were there! That night!' she cried.

Geoffrey spun to face her, eyes widening in horror. 'What - what are you talking about?'

'The night I fell down the stairs.' Ellie looked at Miranda. 'He was here. That's why I tripped.' She turned back to Geoffrey. 'I'd locked the door.'

'If he broke in *that* night ...' Miranda frowned.

Her words and their implication hung in the air.

Geoffrey suddenly reached into his pocket and pulled out a gun.

Rocco was faster, grabbing and firing his before Geoffrey could pull the trigger.

Ellie gasped, staggering against Miranda in shock as Geoffrey cried out and collapsed against the wall.

Frank swore, low, slow, and with a meanness that was almost as shocking as what had just happened.

Heart hammering wildly, Ellie looked at him, then at Geoffrey as he moaned in pain and clutched his side. She looked at Geoffrey's gun where it lay on the floor, then up to the one in Rocco's large hand. Her brain somehow registered that the thick cylinder on the end of the barrel was a silencer. She heard Miranda's quick breathing and glanced at her long enough to note her ashen face and horror-filled eyes before turning to Frank. He too, now held a silenced gun.

'The painting.' He held out his left hand.

'The painting?' Ellie echoed in surprise. 'You'd shoot somebody for the painting?' she asked, but lifted it and placed it on his palm. As she did so, she moved her other hand and the torch shone on his face. He lashed out with the gun, smashing it against her hand. The torch spun to the floor, its beam throwing erratic slashes across the foyer.

Miranda sprang forward, but stopped as Frank aimed the gun at her head.

'Don't, Mirie,' Ellie cried. She held her injured hand by the wrist and fought back tears of pain. 'He just wants the painting.' Even to her own ears, the words sounded desperate, but she hoped they held some truth. She turned to Frank. 'Please, just take it and go.'

'There's a slight problem.' Frank drew out the words as though contemplating how best to explain that *slight problem*.

'We've been contracted to do a job,' Rocco smiled, 'and we can't have any witnesses.'

Ellie dropped her injured hand and clutched Miranda's arm. From the shock and horror on the face of the man who claimed to be Maud's son, it was obvious he realised that *he* was 'that job'.

Which meant that she and Miranda would be as well.

She looked at Miranda's face, saw her own terror reflected, and struggled to control the panic that welled up.

'Is that your Magna parked out front?' Frank asked her.

Ellie willed her mouth to move. 'Yes.'

Frank gestured at Geoffrey but spoke to Rocco. 'Get that piece of shit on his feet and make sure there's no blood on the floor. And pick up his gun.' He turned to Ellie and Miranda. 'Pick up that torch and turn it off, then get outside. Move!' He put the gun in his jacket pocket but didn't let go of it.

Ellie's mind raced, searching for a way to escape. Nothing presented itself.

'I said *move*.'

Heart beating madly, Ellie shoved the torch in her bag, watched Miranda put the camping light in hers, and hurried to the front door. She glanced back, hoping she might be able to pull the door closed and run before he got there, but he was only a pace behind them.

When they reached Ellie's Magna they stopped. 'Rocco, you take that one,' Frank nodded towards Miranda, 'and follow us. You,' he looked at Ellie, 'will drive your car, and Geoffrey will sit in the back with me. Just remember, if you try anything, Rocco and I will have no qualms about shooting you all before we get where we're going.'

'Why don't we just kill them inside?' Rocco asked. 'We can make it look like dipshit here did it and then disappeared.'

'Because we don't know if any of the neighbours have seen us. If we take them and her car there's nothing to link us to this place.'

The street light illuminated his face, and Ellie trembled at the utter lack of compassion she saw there.

Cass turned a corner and saw several cars parked in front of the unit building. 'There's Ellie, and Miranda, but who are those men with them?'

She slowed down and they watched as a big man pushed the man he was supporting into the back seat of Ellie's car, then grabbed Miranda, marched her to a grey Toyota sedan and pushed her into the driver's seat before getting into the seat behind her. The third man shoved Ellie into the driver's seat of her car then got into the seat behind her.

Cass started to brake so she could pull up behind the Toyota but Kandy yelled, 'Keep going!'

'But -'

'Something's wrong.' Kandy peered through the car window at the Toyota and Ellie's Magna as Cass drove past. Miranda appeared to be crying, and Ellie's face was ghost-like.

She could only see one man in the back seat, and wondered if the other man was crouching down. Though by the way the big man had half-carried him, it seemed more likely that he was ill or injured. If Ellie and Miranda were just helping take someone to the hospital, why would they make Miranda drive their car? She didn't look too happy about doing it, either. No, the body language was all wrong. Kandy's background and her years surviving on the streets had sharpened her instincts, and right now they were telling her that Ellie and Miranda were in trouble. 'We'll have to follow them and call the cops. Give me your mobile.'

Cass tossed the phone to Kandy. She tried not to panic as her rear-view mirror reflected the other cars' headlights coming on.

'Pull into that driveway up there,' Kandy ordered, 'the one without a gate.'

'Why? I thought we were going to follow them?'

'We can't follow them if we're in front. We'll just pretend that we live there and wait for them to go past, *then* we'll follow them.'

Surely that couldn't have been Cass's car? Ellie tried not to let herself hope too much. But it did look like Kandy in the passenger seat, and Cass's car had that same silly bumper sticker her grand-daughter had given her. But so did a lot of cars, she mentally argued.

Then the car turned into a driveway ahead and disappointment hit her so hard she felt like crying.

She was glad she was driving, even if it hurt her injured hand more - it gave her something to concentrate on, something to break the terrible inertia fear had created. She tried to recall similar scenarios she'd seen in movies where people had to get away from the bad guys. Crashing her car wasn't an option, not with Miranda in the other car and liable to be shot by the other moron.

Nothing she thought of was even close to possibly succeeding.

Her gut clenched with fear for Miranda, alone with the hulking Rocco, and she said a swift prayer that he would keep his hands off her.

Geoffrey had whimpered like a kicked dog when he'd been dragged to the car, but now he began moaning. She wondered how badly he'd been hurt, then almost laughed hysterically at her concern. Unless she could think of a way to get them out of this mess, it wasn't going to make any difference.

The pain in his side was so bad Geoffrey thought he'd throw up. He cursed himself for panicking and pulling out Gazza's gun. He should have waited. Should have told the stupid bitch he didn't know what she was talking about. Should have listened to his instincts and realised the boss wouldn't be happy with just a few hundred thousand to make up for a shipment that was worth half a mill.

Should have done what his mother wanted him to do years ago and got a real job.

The car turned a corner and he rolled further onto his side and the pain obliterated all thought.

'What did the police say? Are they coming?' Cass watched Ellie's car and the Toyota drive past and continue along the street.

Kandy put her hand over the mobile and whispered, 'They were a bit sceptical until I told them this was the same building where that girl was murdered. I gave them the rego numbers of the cars and told them I'd stay on the phone and let them know where they're going. There's a patrol car not too far away.'

'Thank God.' Cass watched Ellie's Magna disappear around a corner. The Toyota followed. She backed out of the driveway, sped up the street, and followed.

'Don't get so close,' Kandy warned. 'We don't want them to realise we're following them.' The two cars turned down the next street and Kandy tried to read the street sign as Cass followed, but a huge overhanging tree cast a deep shadow and made it impossible. She told the police the direction they had turned. After a couple of minutes she said to Cass, 'We're headed towards New Farm Park.'

Just as she was about to tell the police that, a familiar voice came through the mobile. 'Kandy, it's Chris Ryan. I've been patched through to you. I'm in a patrol car headed your way. We've just had it confirmed that the Toyota was stolen from a home where the owners are away on holidays. Don't get too close to it. Just keep me informed of where they're headed, but don't let them see they're being followed.'

'Right.' Kandy wished she felt as calm about it as he sounded, but she guessed he must have had a lot of practice at keeping his feelings under control.

As the two cars turned down Lamington Street, Kandy realised where they must be headed. The Powerhouse. The once-derelict power station that had been turned into a theatre, dining and conference centre on the banks of the Brisbane River in New Farm Park.

Seconds later the two cars reached a roundabout and drove straight ahead towards the Powerhouse.

'Don't follow them,' Kandy said. 'It'll be too obvious. That's the only way in and out. Quick, drive into the parking area over there,' she indicated an exit to the right, 'and stop as soon as we're off the roundabout.'

'But we'll lose them.'

'Not if we run fast enough.'

As Cass spun her vehicle into the park and slammed on the brakes Kandy opened her door and jumped out. She threw the mobile to Cass. 'I can run faster than you. Tell Chris what's happening.' She ran off before Cass could put the mobile to her ear.

Huge overhanging trees cast deep shadows over the car. Ellie shivered and eased off the accelerator.

'Keep going.' Frank didn't hiss, but the menace in his

tone increased Ellie's shivering to the extent her hands were drumming the steering wheel. 'Go to your left,' he ordered. 'Drive as far as you can and pull up.'

The river. The parkland on the left led down to the river. Oh, God! No time left now to speed off, crash the car or anything else. She glanced to her right, to where the Powerhouse loomed, its incongruous glass foyer tacked onto its old rust-red brick wall. At the end of the week or on a weekend there would be a steady stream of patrons to eat at the restaurants and see the shows, but tonight only the cold wind swirled beneath the lights illuminating the courtyard.

The roadway ended. She braked but didn't switch off the ignition. The heater poured warmth into the car, but her fingers were icy, her toes frozen, her stomach a solid lump of fear. She barely registered that the Toyota had stopped behind them, its headlights fading.

Geoffrey moaned, and she saw him slowly pull himself upright. 'Rocco's ... bastard. I wasn't ... gunna shoot him.'

'Out!'

Ellie jumped at Frank's growl so close to her ear. She turned off the ignition, then the headlights, and opened the door. Cold air knifed into her lungs. She shook her head, trying to focus. If the chance presented itself, she would get Miranda away, no matter what the cost.

The faint sound of laughter had her looking towards the Powerhouse entrance. A man and woman had come out and were sheltering from the wind, lighting up cigarettes.

'Grab your handbag,' Frank ordered. 'Act natural. We're just a few friends going for a walk.' He tapped his gun against her head as though reminding her of it. She shivered. As if she could forget.

Kandy tried to use the cover of the trees to avoid being seen by the man who appeared to be holding a gun on Ellie and Miranda and his cohort who'd dragged the injured man from Ellie's car and was now hauling him to his feet.

She ran to the last tree and leaned against the trunk, panting. And realised that what she'd thought was a large tree root was the leg of a person lying on the other side.

'Go away!' The voice was aggrieved. 'You upset the kitty.'

Kandy stepped over the leg and stared at the bundle of clothing disguising a skinny body. 'Mouse?'

'Who are you?'

'I'm Kandy,' she whispered. 'Miranda's friend.' She uttered a quick prayer to a god she wasn't sure she believed in. 'I need your help. Miranda's in trouble.'

She blinked in surprise at how swiftly Mouse put the kitten aside and got to his feet. 'Where?'

She pointed to the five people moving onto the path, Ellie and Miranda in front. 'Those men are going to hurt Miranda and Ellie. I need your help to -'

Before she could stop him, Mouse started running towards the group.

'Oh, shit!' she cried, hesitated a second, then ran after him, muttering, 'Stupid kid will get himself killed.'

Maybe if she made out he wasn't running towards them, but away from her ... 'Stop! Thief!' she called out.

Mouse didn't falter, just kept charging towards the group.

Frank cursed, slipped his gun under his other arm and glared at Ellie and Miranda. 'Don't say anything, just wait until these idiots go past.'

Ellie watched the man running towards them and the woman chasing him. There was something familiar about them both. Before she could work it out, Miranda dug her in the ribs and whispered, 'Mouse.'

Mouse? What the hell was he doing? She looked at Rocco, his right hand inside his jacket, but still holding his gun, one arm supporting Geoffrey who was half bent over.

She heard a squeal of tyres as a car sped through the roundabout. Mouse was only a few metres away when Frank realised he wasn't going to stop and brought his gun around.

Ellie yelled, reacted without thinking, swinging her handbag so it hit Frank on the side of his head, pitching him off balance. Miranda whirled her handbag in an arc. The sound of her camping light shattering almost eclipsed that of Rocco's nose breaking.

Mouse ploughed into Frank like a front row forward, sending them both rolling on the ground.

Frank's gun went off.

Mouse shrieked.

Geoffrey clawed at Rocco's gun hand.

Blood pouring from his nose, Rocco pulled his arm away and shot him in the chest.

A police car raced across the grass and screeched to a halt in front of them, headlights on high beam, blinding them.

CHAPTER THIRTY-SIX

Siren wailing, the ambulance sped away from the Powerhouse, Cass's car following sedately in its wake.

'Do you think Mouse will be all right?' Ellie asked Chris as he put his arm around her and led her to her car. She had found she couldn't stop shivering, and Chris had procured a blanket and wrapped it around her shoulders. She huddled into it now, grateful for the warmth, and the security of Chris's body against hers.

'He should be,' Chris replied. 'He was lucky the bullet went in at the angle it did. If it had gone straight in I wouldn't like his chances.'

'Thanks for letting Miranda go in the ambulance with him. I know your boss wasn't too keen.'

'He just wanted to question her a bit more while things were fresh in her mind. But I figured Mouse deserved to have a friend to hold his hand.'

'He certainly does. And a lot more than that.' Ellie looked around at what appeared to be organised chaos. The area had been cordoned off with police tape and lighting set up. Geoffrey's body had been photographed from every angle and then covered with a plastic sheet while they waited for another ambulance. Frank and Rocco had been taken into custody and scene-of-crime officers in their overalls still looked for evidence to corroborate Ellie's and Miranda's version of Geoffrey's murder. Police officers were keeping the media circus and onlookers at bay.

They reached Ellie's car and he opened the front passenger door. 'Get in. I'm driving you to the station to make your statement and then taking you home.'

'But what about Miranda?'

'Cass and Kandy are going to the hospital to be with her. They'll make sure she gets home safely. She can make her statement tomorrow.'

Minutes later, as they drove close to the street where the units were, Ellie cried, 'What will I tell Maud?'

'You don't have to. Someone's already been despatched to let her know.'

'Her only child is dead. She has no-one left.' Ellie started to shake, tears streaming down her face. 'It's my fault. If I hadn't found that painting he'd still be alive.'

Chris pulled to the kerb and stopped the car. He unclipped his seatbelt and hers and pulled her into his arms as far as the centre console would allow. He let her cry for a few minutes, then moved away a little and soothed her hair back from her face. 'From what you and Miranda told me tonight,' he said, 'I think Geoffrey Lenard must have been searching for that painting for some time. We might never know the truth, but it's probable he was responsible for Cherilyn's murder. And those two hit men weren't taking him to the river tonight for a friendly chat. Some years ago he was caught with half a million dollars worth of drugs and had only recently been released from jail. He was probably hoping the painting would get him out of the shit with the drug syndicate, but it wouldn't have made much difference if they'd already decided he was a liability.'

'Poor Maud. She was hoping he would turn his life around.'

Chris nodded, but said nothing, perhaps only too aware of the futility of that hope.

'Will she have to be told why Geoffrey wanted the painting?'

'The media will probably find out and they'll be pestering her to see it.'

Fresh tears threatened to spill, but Ellie brushed them away and sat back in the seat. 'We'll have to hide her away for a while. She doesn't need to cope with all that.' Just then her stomach growled, and she realised that the pain she was feeling was as much hunger as tension. She looked at Chris, saw him raise one eyebrow. 'Could we grab a hamburger?'

He smiled, but she noticed the strained lines around his eyes didn't lessen. She hoped that Miranda would get something to eat, but thought that with Cass there that would definitely happen. If there was one thing Cass excelled at, it was feeding people.

Several hours later Chris drove the Magna into Ellie's driveway. Ellie didn't get out immediately, and he looked at her, frowning. 'Are you all right?' he asked.

'Yes,' she half-smiled. 'Just thinking.'

'Good thoughts?'

'In a way. I was so scared tonight. Not just for myself, but for Miranda. I couldn't see any way we could escape. I was afraid I would do what I normally do in a bad situation

— nothing. Just freeze. Just look to everyone else to fix it for me. But I surprised myself.'

'You surprised Frank too. If you hadn't clobbered him with your handbag he would have killed Mouse.'

Ellie laughed. 'I really don't know why I did it. I couldn't let him hurt Mouse. I just got so angry.'

'Perhaps you were angry that someone else was taking control of your life again.'

'Possibly,' she acknowledged and opened the car door.

He walked her to the front door. She unlocked it, shivered a little at the blackness inside, then sighed with gratitude as he walked in and switched on the porch light. 'I think you should get a security light out there,' he said.

'I'll ring an electrician first thing tomorrow.' She closed the door and turned on the fan heater. She'd had hot coffee at the police station, but nothing seemed to dispel the cold that had gripped her from the moment Rocco had first shot Geoffrey.

Chris looked at her, his calm facade crumbling. 'You scared the daylights out of me tonight. When I was told your rego number and what was happening I ...' Pain stark on his face, he pulled her into his arms and crushed her to him. 'Damnit, Ellie, it was so close. If I'd used the siren he probably would have shot you before we could reach you.'

'Why didn't you use the siren?' Her words were muffled against his chest, but she didn't pull away. She needed his arms around her.

'It was a judgement call. Without the siren and lights we had the element of surprise.'

'It worked, thank heavens.'

They stood there a while longer, savouring the closeness, the surety of each other's presence, then eased apart as a car pulled up outside.

Cass and Kandy bundled Miranda inside, and hugged Ellie as if they'd been apart for years. Cass then went into Cass-mode, making cups of tea and coffee and a plate of hot buttered raisin toast. With the five of them sitting together, eating, drinking, and discussing the night's events, the tight core of ice in Ellie's stomach began to dissolve. Mayhem emerged, yawning, from Miranda's bedroom and wove tail caresses around their legs.

Some time later Cass and Kandy went to leave. Cass stopped at the door and turned to Chris. 'Would you like a lift? Or are you still on duty?'

Ellie watched him hesitate, heard the unspoken message in his voice as he said, 'My shift ended after I took Ellie to the station.' She glanced quickly at Miranda, then back to Chris. 'You could stay here tonight and I'll drive you home in the morning.'

Before he could reply Miranda said, 'I'd feel a lot safer with a cop in the house tonight.'

'That's settled then.' Kandy took Cass's arm, waved goodbye and walked her out the door.

'I'm off to bed.' Miranda yawned. 'I have work in the morning.'

'Are you sure?' Ellie couldn't hide her surprise. 'After tonight ...'

'Mum, I've waited years for this job, I'm not going to jeopardise it now.' She kissed Ellie on the cheek and hugged her. 'Thanks for what you did tonight. You were so brave to hit that bastard. I'm proud of you.'

Something wonderful swelled in Ellie's chest at Miranda's words. She didn't feel brave, but for the first time in her life she felt as though she might have a core of courage that she was only beginning to tap into.

'I can sleep on the lounge if you'd prefer,' Chris said as Miranda closed her bedroom door.

Ellie heard the lack of conviction in his voice and smiled.

A hot shower later they lay in bed, Ellie snuggling against him and savouring the warmth of his chest under her fingertips. She was tired, so tired, but her mind wouldn't turn off and let her sleep. Images kept flicking through her mind like a dream sequence. Geoffrey's face when Rocco had shot him in the foyer. The horror in Miranda's eyes. Frank's cold, controlled cursing. Mouse shrieking in pain. Geoffrey's blank, staring eyes as he died.

And the pain in her hand was a reminder that it had all been real.

Her hands started to close into fists, her muscles tightening.

Chris kissed her gently, his hands softly caressing, soothing, easing the tension from her body. Her fists uncurled, fingers spreading, seeking. She moved closer into his embrace, and his gentleness changed to passion, heat, possession, as though all his pent-up worry was flooding out in a desperate need to assure himself that she was still alive, still needing him, still wanting him.

She responded with a fervour that surprised her with its intensity, meeting his need with one just as strong. The feel of him deep inside her was almost not enough, but the thrust that took her over the edge wiped out the images from her mind so that all that remained was the slow slide into sleep.

When she woke early the next morning he was gone and a note beside her bed said he had an early shift and that he would call her.

He'd signed it, "Love, Chris".

CHAPTER THIRTY-SEVEN

The aroma of spicy chicken wings wafted in the warm winter sunshine as Ellie carried a tray to a large gazebo where Miranda sat talking with Joe and Phillip and Maud and Damien's father, Bert. She found it hard to believe it was only five days since Maud's son's death. It felt like a lifetime had passed. In the peaceful Japanese-inspired garden in the grounds of Phillip's property it was almost possible to believe that the violence and death had never occurred.

She'd been touched by Kandy's lunch invitation, more so when Kandy told her who else she'd invited. Phillip had seemed a little stiff when the guests had first arrived, but had gradually relaxed. Ellie suspected he hadn't been too sure how everyone would react to his newly-exposed sexuality. She was pleased to see that he and Kandy were still friendly with each other, but wondered how that relationship would be affected when Nathan moved in.

'Mum, do you need a hand in the kitchen?' Miranda rose to take the tray.

'We're fine. Kandy has it all under control. These are just nibbles - we'll have lunch when Chris arrives. When he gets off his shift he has to go home and change and pick Danny up, but he should be here soon.' She smiled at the others and walked back into the house.

When she reached the kitchen door she stopped. Kandy and Cass were engaged in a spirited discussion about different brand marinades and their effectiveness. It was so wonderfully normal that just listening to it was like soothing balm on her nerves. For the past few days nothing had seemed "normal". In spite of police efforts to protect her and Miranda's identities, the news media had tracked them down and had hounded them for an interview until an environmental disaster off the coast had turned them into "old news" and they'd slid back into anonymity.

Bruce had informed her that the publicity about the Norman Lindsay painting being found in one of the units had prompted several enquiries from prospective purchasers. Everything was now "all systems go" and she'd "better start putting in orders for the furnishings". Apparently people were rapt in her idea of individually-themed units and were eager to see her drawings.

Kandy looked up and caught her staring. 'How's Maud doing?' she asked.

Ellie walked into the room and picked up her glass of wine. 'She'll be okay. I think deep down she knew that Geoffrey wasn't going to change. All the residents at the retirement village have formed rosters to make sure she isn't alone at any time and they're keeping the reporters from getting to her. They're screening her phone calls and all her visitors. They're very protective.'

'Good!' Cass poured some of the disputed marinade over some steak. 'Poor old dear can't be blamed for what her son did. Has she decided what she's doing with the painting?'

'Yes. She's decided to sell it and give the proceeds to a prisoner rehabilitation facility.'

'But I thought she wanted to keep it to remind her of her sister?'

Ellie smiled. 'I took a photo of it - just the face - and had it enlarged for her. She's happy with that.'

Kandy chuckled. 'I'll bet some of the old boys in the retirement village would have been happier to see the original.'

'Before all this happened,' Cass said, 'I was starting to wonder if there might be something missing from my life.' The other two looked at her in astonishment, but she held up a warning finger and continued. 'Maud might have married a man of the cloth but I'd married a man of the sloth,' she glared mock-warningly as Ellie and Kandy started to laugh, 'and my mother was driving me nuts. Still is,' she muttered. 'But after the other night I've realised that I'm okay with that. I don't need too much excitement in my life. Having my family and my friends safe and well is good enough.'

'Speaking of family,' Kandy said, 'Vanessa phoned me a couple of days ago.'

'Phillip's daughter?' Cass looked surprised.

'Yes. She wanted me to know that she's coming to visit Phillip after Nathan moves in. She thanked me for not standing in their way.' She picked up her wine glass and drained it. 'Apparently,' her face lit with pleasure, 'she likes me and hopes we can be friends.'

'So are you going to stay here?' Ellie asked.

Kandy shrugged. 'For the time being. It's my home too. And Phillip and I still get along really well. Once Nathan arrives I'll re-evaluate the situation.' She went to the fridge and took out a bottle of wine, filled her and Cass's glasses and topped up Ellie's. 'To friends,' she said, and raised her glass and grinned.

'To the friends who saved Miranda's life, and mine,' Ellie toasted, eyes misting with emotion. 'To you both.' She took a long sip. 'It's a shame Mouse isn't well enough to be here. But I think he's enjoying all the attention he's getting in hospital. He just worries about his cats.'

'Speaking of which,' Cass rolled her eyes, 'that one you foisted onto me has an attitude that would make any teenager proud. Demands to be fed, eats like a pig, then stalks off and leaves a mess.'

The laughter that followed almost drowned out the sound of the doorbell.

'Granddad's having a good day,' Miranda said as she helped Ellie carry plates into the kitchen. 'He hasn't once called me Ellie.'

'What about you, Mirie? Are you having a good day?'

'Actually, I'm enjoying myself more than I thought I would.' She placed the plates on the bench. 'Danny's amazing with what he knows about computers. He's promised to do some upgrades on mine. It wouldn't hurt to have a computer geek in the family,' she winked as she saw Chris approaching, and walked outside.

Between work and fending off the media horde, Ellie had had little time to herself the past few days, and Chris's shifts had relegated their communication to a few brief phone calls.

'We haven't had much of a chance to talk,' he said as he walked up to her. He put his glass on the bench. 'How are you and Miranda coping?'

She saw the concern in his eyes, the uncertainty that was as much for her welfare as for the situation between them. 'It's funny,' she said, 'but we both feel it's like a dream - or a nightmare. I guess we were so terrified that it didn't seem real, like it was the kind of thing that happens to other people like druggies and criminals, not ordinary people like us. But you won't find either of us going into a room without lights on any more. And we do tend to jump if there's an unexpected noise.

'Last night I started thinking about it again and didn't realise I'd dialled Miranda's mobile number into the microwave oven.' She smiled wryly. 'I blew up the coffee mug.'

His answering smile sent a shiver through her that had nothing to do with shattered china. She wondered if he knew how extraordinarily sexy she found him.

'Have you thought any more about ... us?' he asked.

'Actually, I've been giving that a lot of thought lately. These past few months have been a big learning curve for me. I'd been trapped for years in a situation that I couldn't get out of because I thought it was up to me to save my marriage and because I'd never really allowed myself to become my own person. I think I'm finally finding the courage to become that person. It could be a long journey, and I've only just begun.'

'I see.' Chris looked away, but not before she'd seen the pained acceptance in his eyes.

She took his hand, smoothed her fingers along his, felt the roughness of his skin, the solidity of bone and flesh, and ached with the love she felt for him. 'But there's no reason I can't have a friend come along on that journey,' she said, and smiled as he turned to look at her again, fledgling hope making the blue of his eyes more brilliant. 'Especially one who is so good at cooking with avocado oil.'

Her heart raced at the expression on his face, and she smiled as he took her in his arms.

'Lady,' he said, 'you haven't seen *half* the recipes in my cook book yet.'

If what she read in his eyes was any indication, she was going to have a lot of fun finding out.

###

Excerpt from

PASSION, PENGUINS AND PREGNANT PAUSES

'Jab!'

Kandy Breckham clenched her fist and punched out, wishing she was connecting with Phillip's jaw instead of air. *Right fist; left fist; focus on controlling the movements.*

'Uppercut!'

Anger fuelled the swing that would have done satisfying damage if it had connected. Kandy let it flow through her, hating herself for feeling the emotion when she'd always considered herself tolerant and able to forgive. Okay, she wasn't really a woman scorned, and she knew Philip loved her, though not in the way she wanted, but his betrayal still stung. Even after three months she found it hard to come to terms with how her life had changed.

'Hook!' the instructor called out, and Kandy automatically changed her movement, keeping to the rhythm of music that had been popular when she was a teen. She glanced across to Cass Brighton and tried to hide a grin at the sweat pouring off her friend's plump face. Cass wasn't exactly a poster girl for gym membership, but that had been one of the reasons for the three friends joining this after-work exercise class for women two months ago. When

Ellie's life had been in danger, Kandy had sprinted to try to help her, and Cass had felt terrible that she wasn't fit enough and would only have slowed Kandy down if she'd gone with her.

It wasn't a modern gym, but an old suburban timber hall that had taken on another life, and the exercise class was confined to a carpeted section in one corner, barely a body width from the rows of weight benches, treadmills, and other machines that occupied the rest of the floor. But it was the closest to their workplaces and had convenient parking.

'I saw that expression,' Ellie Cummins smiled. She took a step sideways and punched Kandy playfully on the arm. 'Couldn't you just pretend to be breathing hard so the rest of us don't feel so out of condition?'

'You're doing okay. Must be all that night-time exercise you're getting these days.' She easily avoided the fist that tried to connect with her shoulder and laughed. Ellie had finally started putting some curves on her too-slim frame, and Kandy knew it had more to do with one rugged, lanky police officer bringing some joy into her friend's life than any gym work or increased calorie intake.

As they gradually wound down to stretching and relaxing, Kandy glanced around at the other women in the class. All of them were, like her and Ellie and Cass, in their forties or early fifties, working women whose lifestyle had meant exercise had slipped to low priority and they were now trying to reverse that. All of them friendly and happy to exchange names and the social details that allowed them to assess the parameters of possible future friendships. All except for Sarah, a quiet, slightly-built brunette in her mid-twenties who always arrived on time, left as soon as the class finished, and while not being rude, barely returned a smile or greeting. Her responses to Kandy's attempts to engage her in conversation had always been polite, but apart from finding out that she worked in admin and didn't have a boyfriend, they knew nothing about her.

The young woman intrigued Kandy. There was something lost about her, lost and lonely, and Kandy had experienced enough of that to want to reach out and ease some of the emptiness she sensed Sarah was feeling. Even now, as they all gathered their belongings and farewells and laughter echoed in the room, Sarah patted her face with her towel, stuffed it into her bag and hurried towards the exit.

'Hey, Sarah,' Kandy called out, surprising herself as much as the young woman whose head jerked around as though she'd been shot at. Thinking quickly, Kandy continued, 'Would you like to go for a drink? Ellie and Cass and I are going to the hotel up the road for one and maybe a counter meal.' She felt the 'Huh?' waves coming from her friends but was grateful they didn't protest that this was news to them.

Sarah's mouth literally dropped open. Kandy doubted that a kangaroo hit by a Mack truck could have looked more stunned. For a second Kandy thought she was going to agree, but she shook her head. 'Sorry, I can't. But ...' gratitude tinged with real regret flickered through hazel eyes, 'thanks for asking.'

As Sarah walked away, Cass threw her bag over her shoulder and asked, 'What was that all about?'

Kandy shrugged. 'Don't you ever get the feeling that

someone needs a friend?'

'Yes,' Ellie agreed, 'Sarah reminds me of the dog we got when our girls were young - all skittish and afraid of everything that moved. We got it from the RSPCA and they warned us it had been mistreated by its former owner.'

'You think she's in an abusive relationship?' Cass's voice held genuine concern.

'No,' Kandy shook her head, though she didn't feel too certain, 'but she seems like she's scared of something.'

They walked after Sarah, watched as she scurried down the four stairs to ground level and pushed open the heavy timber and glass door. Kandy was about to call after her to wait, that she wanted to talk to her, but thought it was probably better not to put too much pressure on the young woman. She'd have to take it slowly if she wanted to gain her trust.

Spring had burst upon Brisbane a week earlier, budding green onto winter-bare trees and turning cold winds into balmy breezes that caressed them as they walked out onto the well-lit street with its mix of fifties-era houses and modern apartments. Sarah was further ahead of them now, almost to the next block where the blackboards outside several small shops advertised takeaways from kebabs to pizzas.

'Anyone for fish and chips?' Cass asked.

Kandy laughed, knowing her friend's love of food would always have her battling her weight demons. She turned to answer, but stopped at the sight of a man standing on the opposite side of the road.

Angular face, black hair, body stiff, almost at attention,

he was staring at Sarah's retreating figure, and the intensity of his gaze sent shivers down Kandy's spine.

'Kandy?' Ellie turned to see what had caught Kandy's attention. She saw a man who appeared to be in his mid-forties start to walk down the footpath before crossing the street and heading towards the shops.

'I think he's following Sarah,' Kandy frowned.

'What?' Ellie's breath caught in her chest as she remembered her terror at being held at gunpoint only three months ago. She slowly forced herself to relax. The criminals were currently behind bars and the court had refused them bail. She had nothing to fear. Besides, she reminded herself, they hadn't really been after her, she and Miranda had simply been in the wrong place at the wrong time. But the taste of fear lingered in her mouth. 'Don't be paranoid,' she told Kandy, but knew she meant the words more for herself.

'When we came out, he was standing there, watching Sarah, and now he's heading in the same direction.'

'It's a free world, Kandy,' Cass said, 'perhaps he's just going to the shops as well.'

'Perhaps,' Kandy agreed, but Ellie could hear the reluctance in her tone.

The muffled tones of a mobile phone ringing came from the depths of Ellie's bag. She dug it out and answered it. Her eldest daughter's voice, normally controlled and more than a little authoritative, if not slightly patronising, quavered as she informed Ellie that she was boarding a flight from Sydney in a few minutes and could Ellie please pick her up at Brisbane airport. Ellie only had time to ask what time the plane would arrive and listen to the brief response before the connection was severed.

'That was Pru,' Ellie closed the mobile and looked at Cass and Kandy. 'She wants me to pick her up at the airport. Tonight.'

'Pru?' Cass couldn't keep the incredulity out of the word. 'Pru is doing something that hasn't been planned for at least two weeks and worked out to the last detail?'

Ellie nodded. With her unbending attitude and rigid control, Pru was the antithesis of her younger sister Miranda. For Miranda, being organised meant remembering to grab something out of the freezer for that night's dinner before she ran out the front door in the morning. Pru planned meals a month in advance and put the ingredients on a tick list on the pantry door.

'She sounded ... odd. Very un-Pru like.' Ellie's stomach sank. Pru made her feel inadequate, like she was a naughty child whose behaviour was only just tolerated. Six months ago Ellie's marriage to Damien had finally disintegrated, Damien had relocated to Sydney for a new job after going bankrupt and losing everything they owned, and Ellie had discovered he'd also relocated to a lover who'd obviously been waiting for him. And Pru's sympathies had, as always, remained with Damien. Miranda, bless her perceptive little heart, had told Ellie to stop being a door mat and encouraged her to take control of her life.

'When does her plane arrive?'

Ellie looked at her watch. 'Oh, hell. In about an hour and a half. I'll have to race home, shower and change and get out there.'

'Why don't you just duck back into the gym and change back into your work clothes in the toilet?' Kandy asked. 'It'll save you time.'

For a second, but only a second, Ellie considered that option, but quickly discarded it. She'd feel much better meeting Pru looking and feeling refreshed, and pretending to be relaxed, than hoping her deodorant hadn't failed on the drive to the airport. 'Besides,' she murmured, as much to herself and to Cass and Kandy, 'I'll have to let Miranda know and get her to do a quick tidy up. If I phone and tell her she might decide to run away.' She rummaged in her bag and found her car keys. 'Wish me luck.'

As she hopped in her car and drove away, she hoped luck wasn't all she was going to need.

'Pru is coming here? Tonight?' Miranda scrunched her fingers in her long blonde hair and pulled it away from her head as though to ease the pressure of thinking about her bossy older sister. 'Why?'

'I don't know.' Ellie tried to stay calm. Her life had finally entered a phase where things actually seemed to be going well and she didn't need the stress she knew having Pru and Miranda under the same roof would bring.

'And where's she going to stay? We only have two bedrooms, remember?'

That problem had gnawed at Ellie on the drive back to the house she now shared with Miranda, a small post-World War Two weatherboard house that belonged to Damien's father, Bert. After Damien's mother had died, Bert's

Alzheimers had worsened, and he was now in a nursing home. 'She can sleep on the lounge.'

Miranda looked only half-convinced. 'She's lucky you got rid of that old horse-hair monstrosity and bought a new one.'

Ellie glanced at the tapestry lounge with its delicate, muted shades of apple green and rose pink. As she could afford it, she was gradually replacing the furniture that had been there since Damien's childhood. Curtains in a matching green now covered the window, and a corner china cabinet and rosewood coffee table complemented the curving lines of the lounge. Even Bert's antiquated television had been usurped by a LCD model with a screen bigger than the previous set and cabinet combined.

'And what about Mayhem?' Miranda asked as a small tortoiseshell cat uncurled itself from a corner of the lounge and yawned. 'You know Pru doesn't like cats.'

Ellie sighed. 'I'm going to have a quick shower. Can you please check and see if we need to buy any groceries? I don't know how long she'll be staying. And can you please tidy up the kitchen? You know what she's like.'

Miranda's snort conveyed her thoughts on that, but she shrugged and walked to the kitchen.

As she showered and dressed, Ellie worried about what could have happened to make Pru do something so totally unexpected. And so contrary to her well-regulated life. Perhaps she'd broken up with her husband Rodney? No. Unthinkable. They were so alike they could have been cloned from the same nitpicker.

'Mum, are you having some quiche before you go?'

Miranda said as she came out from the kitchen. 'It's what I made for dinner tonight.'

Ellie tossed up whether to take the risk of having her stomach rumble all the way home from the airport through hunger or having it churn the quiche into a hard ball before she drove two suburbs. She opted for rumble, apologised to Miranda, and headed for the door.

'Mum!' She jumped at Miranda's stern tone and turned to face her. Miranda walked over and gave her a hug. 'Don't look so worried, Mum. I promise I won't fight with Pru. Would you like me to go with you?'

The offer was tempting, but Ellie had promised herself several months ago that she would no longer be an emotional coward. She shook her head. 'Thanks, Mirie, but it'll be all right. Maybe Pru just had an urge to visit.'

'Just like pigs have urges to fly,' Miranda offered, but Ellie could tell her heart wasn't behind the sentiment.

Kandy couldn't stop the wave of self-pity that swept over her as she drove home. Ellie might have trouble getting on with Pru, but she had a great relationship with Miranda, and Kandy would give anything to have a child, even one she had to work hard to get along with.

Damn Phillip! She punched the steering wheel. She must have been blind not to see it. When she'd begun to suspect him of having an affair, she'd been devastated to think that he had fallen in love with someone else. That that "someone else" had turned out to be a man her age with whom Phillip had fallen in love years ago was almost as shocking as learning that Phillip had been married at the time and hadn't seen his daughter or son since his wife divorced him shortly after finding him in bed with his lover.

The magnitude of his deceit had hurt her more than she thought it would, and she'd questioned whether the kind, gentle man she'd married had been a facade.

As she swung her Porsche Boxster into the driveway of their Bridgeman Downs home with its marble portico and extensive gardens, she looked up to the first floor to see if the light was on in what had once been their bedroom. It was, and she wondered if Phillip and Nathan... No, don't even think about it. She forced herself to look away and not let her imagination cause her any more pain.

She drove around the side of the house and pressed the remote that opened the guest wing garage door. She'd moved there when she'd realised that fighting for Phillip's love would be futile. He'd been distressed at causing her pain, but he couldn't deny where his heart lay. Inviting his lover, Nathan, to meet with them had been her decision, and despite wanting to hate the man, she'd had to concede his love for Phillip was genuine.

Yes, it had been a noble gesture, moving aside and allowing the man she loved his happiness, but she hadn't felt noble. Some smashed mementoes and innumerable laps of their swimming pool had confirmed that.

Now Phillip had Nathan, and she had ... nobody.

If the plane was on time, Ellie thought as she drove into the airport, Pru would now be walking to the pick-up area or be there already. She drove into that lane with its slow-moving traffic and scanned the figures waiting with their varying amounts of luggage. No Pru. She coasted along, hoping Pru's portly figure hadn't been concealed by a car or van. She'd almost reached the end of the lane when she spotted her daughter, large suitcase in tow and carrying a hefty shoulder bag, struggling towards the pedestrian crossing. She waved frantically, hoping Pru would see her, then pulled into the last available park, dashed out, and yelled Pru's name.

She ran towards her, expecting to see the exasperated look that normally furrowed Pru's brow at her mother's lack of reliability and dignity. She barely had time to register the relief that washed over Pru's face before her daughter propped her suitcase and grabbed her in an embrace that had Ellie grateful she didn't have brittle bones.

'Mother, I'm so glad to see you.'

Ellie's shock took a second to wear off. She was used to the affectation in Pru's drawn-out "Mother", but she couldn't remember when Pru had ever said that she was glad to see her. She drew back. 'Let's get to the car before I get fined for staying longer than two minutes.'

Ellie decided not to ask Pru the reason for her sudden flight to Brisbane on the drive home. Pru sat in the front passenger seat, replying to Ellie's friendly queries about her job and the weather in Sydney in a too-calm voice while her fingers shredded her boarding pass into minute pieces. When they pulled into the driveway at the house, Pru looked down at the square confetti on her lap and burst into tears.

###

ABOUT THE AUTHOR

Sandy Curtis writes contemporary romance for Ormiston Press's Lavish Novels line, and is also the author of seven romantic thrillers published in Australia and Germany, two of which have been finalists in the Romantic Book of the Year Award.

Sandy has presented many writing workshops including 10 days teaching creative writing at the University of Southern Queensland McGregor Summer Schools, given library talks, and been a panellist at writers' festivals.

She is a member of many writing organisations, and has organised the Bundaberg writers festival, WriteFest, since its inception in 2005.

In 2010 she was awarded the Regional Arts Australia Volunteer Award for Sustained Contribution to the arts in regional Queensland, and in December 2012 she was selected by the Queensland Writers Centre to receive the Johnno Award for outstanding contributions to writing in Queensland.

A note from Ormiston Press:

Writers are like small businesses. They rely on word-of-mouth and good reviews to help grow their business. They need reader support to keep publishing their stories. So please, if you enjoyed this book, write a review on Amazon or Goodreads.

CPSIA information can be obtained at www.ICGtesting.com
Printed in the USA
LVOW09s1109140516

488170LV00017B/62/P